Transfiguring Headship

"*Transfiguring Headship* doesn't simply offer new answers to old questions. More generatively, it reframes old questions for the good, not just of the genders individually, but of the social units of the family and church. With Jost's academic work now available to a wider readership, it will test cherished assumptions, insisting that the Holy Scriptures define our reality. Like all good scholarship, the dogged pursuit of truth in these pages is sure to disturb, even as it instructs."

—JEN POLLOCK MICHEL, author of *In Good Time*

"This significant re-consideration of the concept of headship in both the Scriptures and Western culture is a cogent and refreshing reflection on what has become a heavily disputed subject."

—MICHAEL A. G. AZAD HAYKIN, Professor of Church History and Biblical Spirituality, The Southern Baptist Theological Seminary

"Jost's monograph is clear-eyed about both the intramural and extramural challenges that a rehabilitation of 'headship' invites. . . . Especially significant is his refusal to countenance sleights-of-hand that would smuggle the post-industrial, monadic, genderless subject into theological discourse as if it were identical with the gendered, embodied, radically relational subject of biblical anthropology."

—JENNIFER NEWSOME MARTIN, Director, de Nicola Center for Ethics and Culture, University of Notre Dame

"Christians wrangle about male headship in the home and the church without quite knowing or agreeing what they mean by 'head.' That's why we need Lyndon Jost's *Transfiguring Headship*. Through a comprehensive exploration of headship in Scripture, he concludes that a head is a 'soteriological representative' who takes responsibility for the body he represents, mediating blessings and curses. By setting that biblical figure in a rich historical and sociological context, Jost makes a singular contribution to the theology of the sexes."

—PETER LEITHART, President, Theopolis Institute, Birmingham, Alabama

"*Transfiguring Headship* addresses the intra-evangelical Protestant argument over 'male headship,' one of the cleavage points between evangelical and mainline Protestant churches. Jost seeks in part to relocate the debate over gender roles from a reliance on reading Scripture as thin prooftext alone to a fuller reading of Scripture as figure. Headship thus becomes the sacramental pointing to the headship of Jesus Christ over his bride, the church. Highly recommended for those interested in the evangelical framing of 'male headship' as well as their understanding of the nature of Scripture itself."

—Kathryn Greene-McCreight, author of *Feminist Reconstruction of Christian Doctrine: Narrative Analysis and Appraisal*

"The apostle Paul's claim that 'the man is head of the woman' is widely derided nowadays as being patriarchal, hierarchical, and oppressive toward women. Lyndon Jost's *Transforming Headship* addresses this difficult teaching head-on. Neither defending patriarchy nor dismissing the authority of Scripture, Jost helpfully reframes our view of gender relations in light of the gospel of Christ. This is a splendid book by a promising young theologian."

—Joseph Mangina, Professor of Systematic Theology, Wycliffe College, Toronto School of Theology

"What do you get when you bring together Ephraim Radner's figural reading of Scripture, Barth's Christological anthropology, Augustine's *totus Christus*, Ivan Illich's genealogy of modern gender and his account of gender's 'vernacular' character, Reformed federal theology, and a historically and semantically careful reading of biblical 'headship' texts? In *Transfiguring Headship*, Lyndon Jost delivers a genuinely significant advance in contemporary theological debates about gender. Jost offers a rigorously argued, gender-realist alternative to both essentialism and constructivism, situating sexual difference within a sacramental cosmology and a figural, soteriological account of representation. This is a bold and promising work, one that deserves a wide reading."

—James R. Wood, Associate Professor of Religion and Theology, Redeemer University

"*Transfiguring Headship* upends stale polarized positions in debates about gender roles, helpfully reframes the discussion, and makes a biblical case for seeing the head as the representative member responsible for the whole body, and the body as the glory of the head. Jost has produced a rich and rewarding study of the scriptural figures of head and body in their relation to Christ that challenges our culturally conditioned concepts of what it is to be male and female."

—Kevin J. Vanhoozer, Blanchard Professor of Theology, Litfin Divinity School, Wheaton College

Transfiguring Headship

A Figural Theology of Gender

LYNDON JOST
Foreword by Ephraim Radner

☙PICKWICK *Publications* · Eugene, Oregon

TRANSFIGURING HEADSHIP
A Figural Theology of Gender

Copyright © 2026 Lyndon Jost. All rights reserved. Except for brief quotations in critical publications or reviews, no part of this book may be reproduced in any manner without prior written permission from the publisher. Write: Permissions, Wipf and Stock Publishers, 199 W. 8th Ave., Suite 3, Eugene, OR 97401.

Pickwick Publications
An Imprint of Wipf and Stock Publishers
199 W. 8th Ave., Suite 3
Eugene, OR 97401

www.wipfandstock.com

PAPERBACK ISBN: 979-8-3852-5304-3
HARDCOVER ISBN: 979-8-3852-5305-0
EBOOK ISBN: 979-8-3852-5306-7

Cataloguing-in-Publication data:

Names: Jost, Lyndon [author]. | Radner, Ephraim [foreword writer]

Title: Transfiguring headship : a figural theology of gender / by Lyndon Jost.

Description: Eugene, OR: Pickwick Publications, 2026 | Includes bibliographical references.

Identifiers: ISBN 979-8-3852-5304-3 (paperback) | ISBN 979-8-3852-5305-0 (hardcover) | ISBN 979-8-3852-5306-7 (ebook)

Subjects: LCSH: Sex roles—Religious aspects—Christianity. | Sex roles—Biblical teaching. | Men (Christian theology). | Women—Religious aspects—Christianity. | Women—Biblical teaching.

Classification: BT704 J678 2026 (print) | BT704 (ebook)

Unless otherwise stated, Scripture quotations are from the ESV® Bible (The Holy Bible, English Standard Version®), copyright © 2001 by Crossway, a publishing ministry of Good News Publishers. Used by permission. All rights reserved. Emphasis added to Scripture quotations.

Scripture quotations from La Bible de Jerusalem are copyright © 1998 Les Éditions du Cerf. Used by permission. All rights reserved worldwide.

Scripture quotations from La Bible du Semur are copyright © 2015 Biblica, Inc. Used by permission. All rights reserved worldwide.

To my wife Lami and our children:
Naomi Olamide, Knox Ayomide, Micah Obamide,
and Jesse Aramide.
My wealth (*ọlá*), my joy (*ayọ̀*), my King (*ọba*),
my people (*ará*) have come.

Now, however, I wonder if we shouldn't have a look at ourselves, if we shouldn't think about [Christ's] body, because he is also us. After all, if we weren't him, this wouldn't be true:

When you did it for one of the least of mine, you did it for me [Matt 25:40].

If we weren't him, this wouldn't be true:
Saul, Saul, why are you persecuting me? [Acts 9:4].
So we too are him, because we are his organs,
because we are his body, because he is our head,
because the whole Christ is both head and body.

—Augustine of Hippo (*Sermons*, 133.8)

Contents

Foreword xi
Preface xv
Acknowledgments xvii
List of Abbreviations xix

Introduction: Transfiguring Headship:
A Response to the Evangelical Headship Controversy 1
    Methodology 8
    Outlines 10
    Concluding Remarks 13

Chapter 1: Problems with Male Headship:
Cultural Evolutions and the Matter of Sexual Difference 15
    Male Headship and Male Dominance: Mapping Cultural Evolutions 17
    Essentialism, Constructivism and Realism: Mapping Gender
        Difference 21
    Sexual Difference in a Theological Perspective 29
    Conclusion 30

Chapter 2: On the Etymology of Headship: Defining the Head 33
    Western Etymologies of Headship 34
    Hebrew Headship: A Near-Eastern Seed Planted in Western Soil 49
    Conclusion 56

Chapter 3: On the Genealogy of Heads: Headship in History 58
    Patriarchalizing Headship: On the Origins and Scope of Patriarchy 60
    Depatriarchalizing Headship: On the Myth of Male Dominance 72
    Conclusion 78

Chapter 4: Revisionist Heads: Headship in Modern Interpretation 79
    Modernizing Theology: Foundations for Feminist Hermeneutics 82

x CONTENTS

    Modernizing Work: The Industrial Revolution as a Sexual
        Revolution 90
    The Modernized Self and the Headship Debate: Beyond a Feminist
        Hermeneutic 99
    Conclusion 100

Chapter 5: Soteriological Heads: Headship in Canonical Perspective 102
    The Head as Soteriological Synecdoche 104
    Salvation History: A Tale of Heads 113
    Conclusion 132

Chapter 6: Figural Heads: Toward a Constructive Theology of Gender 135
    The Man as a Figure of Christ the Head 138
    The Woman as a Figure of Christ the Body 147
    Conclusion 154

Conclusion: Transfiguring Headship 156
    Headship in a Secular Age? 157
    Headship in a Sacramental Cosmos (Concluding Remarks) 166

Bibliography 171

Foreword

By Ephraim Radner

It is not surprising that the omni-politicized culture of contemporary North America should drastically obscure the actual breadth of human experience. Politics orders communal human decision-making; it does not constitute life. Politics versus life: limited procedural habits versus being. When politics becomes confused with being, human persons and their lives together are intrinsically degraded, often massively so.

One corollary of this dynamic is that the politicization of Scripture and its revelatory ordering of creation will result in deformative visions of human life that must inevitably obscure God and the very place of human life in relation to him. That Scripture is, in a primary way, politically oriented stands as one of the common assumptions of late modern Christian theology and preaching: Scripture not only tells us what to do, and maps our proper relational engagements, but actually stands as the touchstone of our social decision-making. With such an encompassing framework in place, entire realms of reality simply vanish from our view: agonies, stretchings, aporias, yearnings, disappointments, sighs, laughter, contentment, restlessness, adorations, abnegations, dependencies, incapacities, hopes. When Scripture is understood as intrinsically political, everything a creature must experience and everything by which creaturehood is defined disappears into the stunted realm of debating, planning, reforming, strategizing, policing, imposing. There is no practical room—for practice is all there is—for the traditional virtues of the Christian life of humility, mercy, gentleness, generosity, meekness. And with these occluded there disappear as well, behind the flurried dust of praxis, the vast realms of actual, real, human creaturely being that Scripture in fact enfolds and unravels. We might rightly wonder: What light and wealth simply lie lost to our eyes and hearts in such a day as this?

There is no simple repair that might remove the veil—not when the very organs of Christian understanding are themselves caught in the obscuring forces of a now ingrained set of political habits that define the now assumed shape of Christian understanding in our day. Instead, and besides the dreaded catastrophes that do in fact reorder human (and Christian) sensibilities tout court at times, we must rely on the slow therapies of reconsideration, wherein habits are tentatively reexamined, dug around, replaced bit by bit. Or perhaps catastrophes and therapies go hand in hand, as in the eighth and sixteenth centuries. Hence, the emerging catastrophes in our era of familial disintegration and demographic collapse may well be giving rise to new, if cautious and careful, reexaminations of the Scriptures that lie behind, and often are obscured by, today's political obsessions.

Lyndon Jost's remarkable work here, I dare say, does in fact fall within the promise of such new therapies of scriptural vision. Aiming his investigation directly at the highly and passionately politicized biblical notion of "headship," Jost here attempts to massage, sometimes forcefully and perhaps even painfully, our calcified assumptions about "headship" in a way that loosens their grip, turns over their embedded soil, brushes off their encrusted accretions. The result is not so much an epiphany as it is a significant recovery of capacity, in this case of hearing the Scriptures themselves on this topic and of beginning to make out the long and intricate lines of the topic's web of divine meaning.

The matter of "headship" in the Bible is one of intense political interest, and it has been especially so within more evangelical Protestant churches for some decades (though, as Jost shows us, some of the nuances coloring this interest echo back for centuries, if in quite different contexts of social life). In particular, headship has been at the center of sometimes fierce and certainly adversarially passionate debate among many Christians over how it relates to the question of women's leadership in the church, and women's roles within the family and larger civil society. In many ways, the lines of the debate chronologically precede the attempt to apply the biblical topic to settling the "place of women" in our common life. Indeed, "headship" as a scriptural category putatively aimed at organizing the practical (including ecclesiastically practical) roles of women in relation to men, is an only recently forged tool of exegetical argument. That is, the social and political concerns regarding the ecclesiastical and familial roles of women and men, and the lines of attitude about this, long predate an examination of the scriptural concept of headship, and have clearly invaded and occupied the exegetical consciousness long before headship emerged as a key biblical figure. Patriarchy versus emancipation, quietude versus franchise, subordination versus equality, oppression versus rights. It is true that our late modern dismantling of the notion of sexual differentiation in even a quasi-biological fashion, and with a specific aim to refashion (or in some cases eliminate) human procreative culture and its processes, is a mostly novel goal, tied up with a wider rejection of long-held commitments to promoting human life. This only demonstrates how omni-politics is not only voracious and obscuring, but may also have its own internal character that drives matters in a singular and humanly self-destructive direction. Yet the direction itself, however much regretted by many who hold diverse stances in the contemporary headship debate, at least alerts us to the possibility that the notion of biblical headship may be lodged in some deeper scriptural precinct than that to which struggles over gender politics would assign it.

So Jost proposes a theological and historical therapy for our scriptural thinking. His wide-ranging exploration of history, sociology, intellectual genealogy, interpretive tradition, and most especially biblical exegesis, is deeply important on several fronts. First, he clearly shows that "headship" is a scripturally *rich*, not socially narrow reality. Obviously, the brief (though not insignificant) use by Paul of the concept when addressing the relation of men and women in the church's life (even in its creationally rooted meanings) has proven the great nettle painfully seized by Christian antagonists in, for instance, the contemporary debate over women's ordination, and then in insistences on family organization. But Jost uncovers the deep and broad reach of headship within the *soteriologically* central landscape of scriptural discussion regarding God's redemption of humanity, indeed of his creation, as it moves from Genesis through Israel's life to the life of Israel's Messiah and his body, the church. The field of discovery laid out by Jost in this investigation is thus vast, not constricted to struggles over sex. In many cases what he finds is alluring, though in some also disturbing. And if Jost is not in a position to explore this terrain in detail, he lays out its promise.

This means, secondly, that we can hardly afford to avoid following through on our own excursions into this world of scriptural headship, however cautiously and certainly with whatever rigor is required. For all its fury, the debate over headship within some of our churches today is limited, not because its elements are unknown, but because, in their so purely political posture, most Christians are already set in their judgments on what is at stake—much as citizens might know what they think on taxes and immigration, and therefore never bother to study these matters in ways that reveal actual possibilities of nuances and ignorances. Jost persuades us that Christians cannot faithfully escape the divine concern with headship (however understood); they cannot, simply because it is tied up with the greatest of gifts that, at least as our Scripture would have it, God offers us, the gift of his own self in Christ Jesus.

One of the key elements in Jost's treatment of headship is that it comes to us, in biblical terms, as a "figure," not as a law, whether natural or legal. I will let Jost explain how he understands the figural character of headship, and of figuration more generally. It is enough to say here, however, that a scriptural figure is that divine form according to which human life is in fact lived within the history over which God's providence is exercised. With respect to the figure of headship, Scripture presents the world as shaped by "heads" in relation to their "bodies." That is because God himself "takes" a "form"—a figure—that itself embraces and orders the whole of creation. In so doing, the "head" that is the Son of God with respect to all that God creates gives each aspect of that creation its shape and character. While all of Scripture needs to be traced figurally, so that the shape of our own lives can be discerned, the figure of headship turns out to be a key condition for just such a promise. It is a promise, as I indicated, of enormous profusion and wondrous intricacy.

Profusion and intricacy are not political terms, however, let alone goods. To be sure, Jost's own discussions are in fact filled with politically tinged elements. He cannot escape these, given the historical, sociological, and contemporary interpretive contexts of his investigations. Yet if readers take these colorings as the core of his project, rather than as the inevitable registers of the otherwise multilayered material he engages, they will miss precisely the graciously therapeutic, the transformative value of his arguments, themselves richly set forth and precisely placed so as to unearth mislaid assumptions and to refocus on long-concealed truths. Jost will not shy away from indicating paths of consideration on the matter of headship, and of gender and sex. Any good teacher will venture such possibilities. But more than anything, this is a book of equipping rather than determining. It will rattle some political imaginations. But it also provides them new nourishments, ones that I hope will make them fitter to their limited tasks, and more open to the gifts of God. Not just a teacher, Jost is a truly Christian one.

Preface

The man is the head of the woman. (1 Cor 11:3)

THERE WAS A TIME when this claim was uncontroversial, taken as part of the fabric of the "good news" announced in Christ, and bound up with claims concerning the church's salvation in him (Eph 5:23–33). But this time has long passed. This project explains how it came to be that the language of the Scriptures concerning male and female generally, and the naming of the man as "head" specifically, has come to be heard not as good news but as a word of offense.

A significant part of this study traces, historically and sociologically, the genealogy of "headship" and its waning acceptance as a compelling theological and civil category. Constructively, I offer a theological account of sexual difference by developing a biblical theology of headship that is founded on a figural hermeneutics, of the kind explored among a range of theologians and literary critics such as Erich Auerbach and Hans Frei, and more recently Richard Hays and Ephraim Radner. This account explores how, in scriptural terms, the man is understood as a figure of Christ the head, and the woman as a figure of Christ the body. My discussion attempts to unpack centrally the interpretive claims of the apostle Paul (Eph 5:23–33) and the way in which Paul's outlook is developed in Augustine's *totus Christus* principle—namely, that the "whole Christ" (*totus Christus*) is both head and body. What we will discover is that the head is to be understood as the *representative member* of the body, and the body as the *glory* of the head (Gen 2:23; 1 Cor 11:3, 7); and these categories are determinative for what it means to be created "male and female," even in the image of God.

In presenting a *figural* theology of gender, I do not claim to present a *comprehensive* theology of gender. Rather, I propose that "headship," as a figure, offers one lens, one avenue—and not the only one—through which we might explore a larger theology of gender.

Acknowledgments

THIS BOOK IS THE reworking of my PhD dissertation, written under the supervision of Professor Ephraim Radner, whose teaching had already exercised a profound impact on me in advance of beginning my doctoral studies. Each chapter has been indelibly shaped by his constructive and critical feedback, though I take full responsibility for the ideas expressed herein.

For all who took time to read and provide feedback on chapters and drafts of this work, including each member of my examining committee—Joseph Mangina, Rebekah Smick, David Novak, and Jennifer Newsome Martin—along with friends and colleagues—early on from Jen Michel and Wendy Stringer, later on from Al Wolters and Dawn Berkelaar—thank you for your encouragement, along with incisive questions, criticisms, and sharpening feedback.

For the two churches—Grace Toronto and Christ Church Toronto—which afforded me the opportunity to pursue pastoral ministry simultaneously with PhD studies, I am most grateful to have been upheld within these worshiping communities, pressing me toward thinking, writing, and working ever for the peace and purity of the church.

For my wife, Lami, with patient endurance, wise counsel, and total commitment, to me and to our children, you have come to shape my intuitions about everything and rooted me in love. "The lines have fallen for me in pleasant places; indeed I have a beautiful inheritance" (Ps 16:6).

For my parents, Randy and Evelyn Jost, who together have been my foremost examples in the life of faith, hope, and love, I am most grateful for their demonstrating the good news of Christ and the church in their life together. Until my father's too-early passing in April 2021, Randy and Ev had enjoyed forty-one years of living the nuptial mystery together (Eph 5:31–32). For you both I will forever be grateful.

Abbreviations

ACCS	Ancient Christian Commentary on Scripture
ACW	Ancient Christian Writers
APA	American Psychiatric Association
AT	Author's translation
ATR	*Australasian Theological Review*
BDB	Brown, Francis, S. R. Driver, and Charles A. Briggs. *A Hebrew and English Lexicon of the Old Testament*
BECNT	Baker Exegetical Commentary on the New Testament
BibInt	*Biblical Interpretation*
BJS	Brown Judaic Studies
BSac	*Bibliotheca Sacra*
ca.	circa
CBQ	*Catholic Biblical Quarterly*
CD	*Church Dogmatics.* By Karl Barth. Edited by Geoffrey W. Bromiley and T. F. Torrance. 4 vols., in 13 parts. Edinburgh: T&T Clark, 1956–75
CCSL	Corpus Christianorum: Series Latina. Turnhout, Belg.: Brepols, 1953–
CD	*Church Dogmatics*
CH	*Church History*
Dial.	*Dialogus cum Tryphone (Dialogue with Trypho)*

DSM-5	*Diagnostic and Statistical Manual of Mental Disorders.* By American Psychiatric Association. 5th ed. Arlington, VA: American Psychiatric Association, 2013
EEBO	Early English Books Online
Ep.	*Epistula, epistulae*
ESV	English Standard Version
FC	Fathers of the Church
HTR	*Harvard Theological Review*
JAAR	*Journal of the American Academy of Religion*
JBL	*Journal of Biblical Literature*
JBQ	*Jewish Biblical Quarterly*
JETS	*Journal of the Evangelical Theological Society*
JRE	*Journal of Religious Ethics*
JSJ	*Journal for the Study of Judaism in the Persian, Hellenistic, and Roman Periods*
JTS	*Journal of Theological Studies*
LNTS	The Library of New Testament Studies
LXX	Septuagint
NIBCOT	New International Biblical Commentary on the Old Testament
NPNF[1]	*Nicene and Post-Nicene Fathers*, Series 1
NT	New Testament
NTS	*New Testament Studies*
OBT	Overtures to Biblical Theology
OED	*Oxford English Dictionary* (https://www.oed.com)
OT	Old Testament
OTL	Old Testament Library
PG	Patrologia Graeca. Edited by J.-P. Migne. 162 vols. Paris, 1857–86
PL	Patrologia Latina. Edited by J.-P. Migne. 217 vols. Paris, 1844–64

ProEccl	*Pro Ecclesia*
SHCT	Studies in the History of Christian Thought
SJT	*Scottish Journal of Theology*
SSN	Studia Semitica Neerlandica
STDJ	Studies on the Texts of the Desert of Judah
TDNT	*Theological Dictionary of the New Testament.* Edited by Gerhard Kittel and Gerhard Friedrich. Translated by Geoffrey W. Bromiley. 10 vols.
Them	*Themelios*
ThTo	*Theology Today*
TJ	*Trinity Journal*
TNTC	Tyndale New Testament Commentaries
TOTC	Tyndale Old Testament Commentaries
VT	*Vetus Testamentum*
VTSup	Supplements to Vetus Testamentum
WBC	Word Biblical Commentary
WCF	Westminster Confession of Faith
WSA	*The Works of Saint Augustine: A Translation for the 21st Century.* By Saint Augustine. Edited by John E. Rotelle. Hyde Park, NY: New City, 1990–

Introduction

Transfiguring Headship: A Response to the Evangelical Headship Controversy

OVER THE PAST HALF-CENTURY, the topic of women's ordination has become a fault line dividing Christian churches and entire denominations one from another. In the West, the division has cut between mainline Protestant Churches on the one hand and, on the other, Roman Catholic and Eastern Orthodox Churches, joined by a majority of evangelical and conservative Protestants.[1] Whereas the Roman and Eastern Churches have persisted in upholding a male-only priesthood for reasons that have

---

1. Within the North American context, women's ordination was a central issue in the division of the largest Presbyterian denominations in America, when what is now the Presbyterian Church in America broke away from the Presbyterian Church (USA) in 1973. It was likewise a central issue in the break-off movements of the "Continuing Anglican movement" from the Anglican Communion in 1976. Twenty years later, when the Christian Reformed Church in North America began ordaining women (in 1995), the United Reformed Churches in North America was formed in protest, with the former suspended from the North American Presbyterian and Reformed Council (NAPARC) two years later (in 1997). The Lutheran Church—Missouri Synod, the second largest Lutheran body in America, continues to affirm its position against women's ordination and has been fraught with inner pressures since the late 1980s on this matter. Baptist churches and denominations have had instances of women's ordination dating back to the 1700s, even if such instances were rare until the latter half of the nineteenth century. Still, America's largest Baptist fellowship, the Southern Baptist Convention, does not support women's ordination. While Roman Catholic and Orthodox Churches continue to formally affirm a male-only priesthood, there is presently much consternation within these churches, too, over the question of women's ordination. See I. Jones et al., *Women and Ordination*. For a more traditionalist reading of this history, see Kirk, *Without Precedent*. For a brief summary of twentieth-century denominational disputes and schisms over women's ordination in the American context, see Melton and Ward, "Survey of Women's Ordination."

centered on sacramental integrity (with the priest conceived as an icon of Christ), for Protestants questions of women's ordination have typically centered on matters of pastoral authority, often construed as a hermeneutical issue.[2] (E.g., did Paul insist on male-exclusive ordination in the early church? If so, did he really intend to bar women from ordination indefinitely, for millennia?)

From the 1970s onward, the intra-Protestant debate over women's ordination often centered on the interpretation and application of a few Pauline texts where the man is deemed "head" (viz. leader, authority) of the woman (e.g., 1 Cor 11:2–17; Eph 5:22–33), or where the woman is deemed to be under the authority of the man (e.g., 1 Cor 14:34–35; 1 Tim 2:11–15). Gaining traction among North American Evangelicals in particular, this debate subsequently became known as the "evangelical headship controversy."[3]

On one side of this evangelical debate are the "complementarians" for whom such passages, along with the rest of Scripture, uphold the permanent place of the man as "head" (leader, ruler) of the woman in household and church. On the other side are the "egalitarians" for whom male headship as such is no longer relevant or applicable in our day, whether for text-critical, historical-cultural, or other hermeneutical-theological reasons. Conceived as denoting a relation of authority and submission, male headship is thus either upheld as the enduring biblical paradigm for gender relations or thoroughly excised from contemporary faith and practice.

But what if Paul's "headship" teaching is less about defending a gendered relation of authority and submission and more about affirming the mutuality, love, and deference appropriate to a one-flesh union? Further, what if the chief purpose of Paul's exposition on headship is not simply to prescribe *what humans are to do* as it is to proclaim *what God has done in Christ*?[4] It is indeed my contention that "male headship" is not fundamentally about *rule* but about *representation*. Moreover, it is not simply a particular injunction to a particular culture (which we can take

---

2. See Witt, *Icons of Christ*. See also Raab, *When Women Become Priests*, introduction. For prominent exemplars of Roman and Eastern perspectives on women's ordination, respectively, see John Paul II, "Apostolic Letter"; and Kallistos Ware, "Man, Woman and the Priesthood of Christ," in Behr-Sigel and Ware, *Ordination of Women*.

3. See Lakey, *Image and Glory*, esp. 31–32.

4. So, Paul: "For the husband is the head of the wife . . .—but I am talking about Christ and the church" (Eph 5:23, 32; see also 2:16).

or leave), but is a theme deeply embedded in the fabric of the Christian story, and as such cannot be excised from the narrative in which we live as Christians.

It appears that the evangelical headship controversy has consistently missed and misconstrued the central meaning and purpose of headship, which is arguably the meaning and purpose of all of Scripture—namely, to point to and to proclaim the good news of Jesus Christ. My proposal is thus to enter into and broaden the discussion concerning male headship by exploring the theme of "headship" (to use the modern term) from a canonical and christological perspective. My hope is that, from such a perspective, the man's identity as "head" might be "transfigured" and received by the church anew as definitively good news in Christ, the true head, for the whole church, his body.

In order to illuminate the theological significance of the "head" we will concentrate much attention (particularly in the first four chapters) on the sociohistorical development of this term, and how these developments pose both problems and possibilities for a constructive theology of headship. This focus on social history may come as a surprise to readers, especially when such history is cast as part and parcel of a constructive theological program. It is my conviction, however, that theological terms in general (including "head" and "headship") cannot be adequately grasped apart from their social and historical expressions. As I will argue, theological concepts, if they are truly theological, lay claim to the way the world is, and as such cannot be treated merely as literary "intra-canonical" terms whose significance remains cordoned off from social histories or contemporary practices. Instead, there is a necessary relation between theological concepts and the world in which they take shape. Moreover, if this is the case, one would expect that social history will help to elucidate the meaning of theological concepts, and that theological concepts will in turn provide keys and clues for understanding social history. Such convictions and claims emerge from certain basic theological commitments, which I will explain further below.

Behind my detailed study of the "head" concept in theological and social terms lies my central conviction that informs the main conclusion of this book: *that the "head" in Scripture is a soteriological figure that everywhere figures Christ and his headship (with respect to his bride, the church)*. Christ's headship is indeed prefigured through all sorts of scriptural "heads"—from Adam through Israel in the OT—and this function of male headship persists in and for the church as an indispensable sign, or a *sacramentum* or "mystery" which proclaims the gospel of Christ, our true and final head (Eph 5:23–32).

And the head, scripturally speaking, is not without a body.

It is in these two figures—Christ the "head" and Christ the "body"—that we discover the basic contours of a theology of gender.[5]

To be clear, such a theology of gender will be limited in content and scope by the scriptural figures it engages. The Bible offers no easy or singular answer to the question "What is a man?" or "What is a woman?" Instead, it offers to us *this* man and *this* woman, narratively depicted. It presents Adam and Cain, Abraham and Isaac, David and Uriah; and, along with them, Eve and "Cain's wife," Sarah and Rebekah, Abigail and Bathsheba. It presents single, married, and widowed women, and men of like status. In their primordial form the male and female emerge in the scriptural narrative as individuated beings, from and for each other (Gen 2:21–25; 1 Cor 11:11–12), as whole individuals who discover a new kind of wholeness in nuptial union with the sexual other, together engaging the world as a unified yet different dual power, co-regents under God's sovereign rule.

Admittedly, what it means to be male and female, respectively, is no less varied or complex in the scriptural world than it is in our own. Ours is in fact a mirror of the scriptural world. In the end, then, we will find no fulsome list of specified male or female qualities or capacities but rather "figures" which provide us with lenses through which the male and female might be engaged within the scriptural landscape, and within our own. The scriptural world is one that assumes a gendered unity-through-difference and which, in its correspondence with our own world, sheds light on the unity-through-difference of the male-female union throughout history and into our own day. The Bible in this sense names us as we are—Adam and Eve, male and female, head and body—and calls us to live within its capacious contours as such.[6]

---

5. I use the phrase "Christ the body," referring to the church, in order to make explicit the notion that "the body of Christ," the church, is in fact *Christ*—a body united in his own flesh (Col 1:24; Eph 1:22–23). In this perspective, the body is not an inferior entity, separate from Christ, theologically speaking, but is one with Christ, identified with Christ. That the church is at times referred to as "Christ" in the NT is noted and developed by Augustine. See, e.g., WSA 3.16:37.6, 39.5.

6. There are, of course, exceptions that do not seem to fit within these scriptural figures of "male" and "female" as binary modes of being human—namely, experiences of gender dysphoria and intersex. In the medical literature, these phenomena have typically been described not as exceptions to the male-female binary but rather as identity and developmental disorders, respectively. It is important to note that this

It is important to note that these proposals are rooted in explicitly theological presuppositions, as I have already indicated, which differ radically from the basic assumptions that have dominated much of biblical scholarship since the Enlightenment era.[7] The present work conversely presupposes both (1) a sacramental ontology and (2) the necessity of what can be called "figural exegesis" of Scripture. I will describe each briefly, in turn.

Ours is a sacramental world, given as a gift of God as a means of knowledge and communion with him. Understood this way, all of material reality subsists in and points to its Creator in unrelenting proclamation. The world, made by God for God, is teeming with divine revelation, embedded everywhere in the fabric of creaturely life, to make God known and to draw creatures into his presence and into the knowledge of his glory (Hab 2:14).[8]

All of creation is, in this sense, given and taken up by God for his self-communicative purposes, every part indicating something of God's own nature and purposes in creation. And *heads*—whether anatomical, household, tribal, or fluvial—are by no means excluded from such sacramental significance.[9] Rather, in such a sacramentally profuse world, even *heads*, in their pluriformity, are necessarily given by God for a self-communicative purpose. In this world, the fact of the general human

---

terminology is changing, however. E.g., the *Diagnostic and Statistical Manual of Mental Disorders* has discontinued the use of the term "gender identity disorder," now using the term "gender dysphoria" in its place, defined as "the distress that may accompany the incongruence between one's experienced or expressed gender and one's assigned gender." This definition differs from the previous editions (up to and including DSM-4-TR), where the phenomenon was described as a "gender identity disorder," and was clearly distinguished from "disorders in sexual development" (referred to as DSD or "intersex") (DSM-5 451–59). According to Cynthia Kraus, this definitional change has done a disservice to clinicians and those experiencing GD, generally, increasing risk of stigma and misdiagnosis ("Classifying Intersex"). For a brief survey of the ethical and legal challenges in present discussions related to gender dysphoria and transsexuality, see Dickens, "Transsexuality"; Zucker, "Sex/Gender Research"; Zucker, "Epidemiology of Gender Dysphoria."

7. See chs. 1–3 in Frei, *Eclipse of Biblical Narrative*.

8. The term "sacramental ontology" is borrowed from Hans Boersma, *Heavenly Participation*. While I appreciate Boersma's desire to retrieve a premodern Platonic metaphysical framework in which the Scriptures find a more natural "fit"—compared to, say, the naturalistic materialism of the modern West—my aim is not to retrieve a Platonic worldview in which to fit the Scriptures, but to assert and reclaim a scriptural world which offers its own distinctive sacramental ontology (as will be explained).

9. So Kirschbaum: "All forms of worldly order can be but pointers to the divine order" (*Question of Woman*, 63).

social ordering under heads of families, tribes, and nations necessarily participates in and points to a reality beyond itself—namely, God's own headship over all things.

To be clear, none of this is to suggest that a male-headed "patriarchy" corresponds to "God's own headship," or that patriarchy is the divinely sanctioned form of life under God. To invoke a figural reading of the "head" in service of bolstering, or returning to, some traditional form of Western patriarchy would be a misuse and misapplication of the figure (see ch. 2). Rather, what must be affirmed is that creaturely forms of "headship"—whether identified with the male or female—are theologically related, by analogy, to God's "headship." Of course, this assumes a prior understanding of what heads are, what heads do, and what "headship" means—all of which will be explained in due course in service of a "re-sourced" understanding of the term.

Second, this proposal assumes a premodern interpretive approach to Christian Scripture—namely, a "figural approach"—whereby Scripture is received and understood as a living narrative which not only tells us something about the world in which we live and how we ought to live in it, but reveals the archetypal story according to which the world itself has been fashioned. The Scriptures, then, present us not with a "product of history" but with the Word of which history is itself a product—that Word which both orders our world and gives shape to our lives. Scripture, as the very word of God, is here recognized as the same divine power as that which was spoken to form the world "in the beginning."[10]

By recovering and employing figural exegesis, the world is envisioned and apprehended anew through the lens of these Scriptures. In the use of a figural perspective, we discover a world in the Scriptures—our own world—that has been authoritatively narrated for us. *This* (scriptural) story proclaims *our* story, and so presents to us the world as it really is, and interprets for us the meaning of our lives as creatures made by God, for God, in the image of God. Indeed, the significance of everything in all creation is given in its narratival depiction in the church's Scriptures.[11]

---

10. This is not to equate the word of God (Scripture) with the Second Person of the Trinity, but to indicate that the word of Scripture shares an analogous status with the Word made flesh, as a word fully human and fully divine. Such an understanding upends simple categorization of Scripture as a merely human text that only "testifies" to the divine Word. Instead, these human words (as with Christ's human flesh) assume a status within the divine life of the eternal God. This kind of expansive figural approach is expounded in Radner, *Time and the Word*.

11. The recovery of such a figural reading is argued for in, e.g., Frei, *Eclipse of*

In this way, a figural reading of Scripture opens up innumerable possibilities of correspondence, both within the textual world of Scripture, and between this textual world and our own, since the same God stands behind them both, speaking Word and world into existence, and ordering each in accordance with his divine plan (Eph 1:11).

Accordingly, the significance of the head (and of headship) is also figured in the Scriptures, its meaning revealed in the scriptural story—thus shedding light on the meaning of heads (and of headship) in our own contexts. More specifically, the meaning of headship is scripturally given in the archetypal Head, Christ, whose headship comes into view as the culmination of the scriptural story.[12] Here, Christ is indeed revealed as the true Head according to whom all other heads might be judged. In such a scripturally ordered world, Christ's headship necessarily sheds light on all other heads, even as all other heads, through Christ, discover their own meaning in God's redemptive purposes for the world.

Moreover, I contend that these theological presuppositions—a sacramental ontology and a figural approach to Scripture—are in fact necessary for making sense of Paul's gendered claims, especially in Eph 5:21–33, where the male and female, as a head and body union, are created to reflect the head and body (Christ and church) form of God's own life given for us.[13]

In accordance with my previously stated theological claims, and consonant with a "gender realist" framework (to be developed in the first chapter), the practical significance of a theology of headship consists most basically in the call of each person to live into his or her creaturely status as male or female, as (1) distinct and (2) complementary ways of being—a call that may or may not find expression in marriage.[14] This will

Biblical Narrative, 1–65. For examples of figural engagements with Scripture, see, e.g., Augustine, *On Genesis: Manichees*, 2.13.19; 2.24.37; 2.26.40; Augustine, *Literal Meaning of Genesis*; Hugh of Saint-Victor, "De Noe Arca Morali," 1.14; J. Edwards, *Typological Writings*. For examples of modern retrievals of figural exegesis, see Vanhoozer, "Ascending the Mountain"; Lubac, *Scripture in the Tradition*; O'Keefe and Reno, *Sanctified Vision*; Dawson, *Christian Figural Reading*; Hays, *Reading Backwards*; Leithart, *Deep Exegesis*.

12. Rom 5:12–21; 1 Cor 15:22–28; Eph 1:22–23; 3:4–11.

13. Barth develops a similar claim in *CD* 3/1.

14. The scriptural category of the "eunuch" is one instance of a distinct call that precludes marriage (see Matt 19:12). Still, eunuchs do not escape gendered existence, even if their vocation as sexual beings is reproductively constrained. Indeed, the church, throughout her history, has, in better and worse ways, upheld *two* unique spiritual vocations, in terms of sexual expression: that of singleness, which anticipates the eschaton,

involve, most basically, the man signifying in his being and actions Christ the head in relation to his body (the church), and the woman signifying in her being and actions Christ the body (the church) in relation to her head.[15]

None of this is to propose a form of "gender essentialism" which posits the existence of male and female "forms" according to which all culturally instantiated expressions of maleness and femaleness are to be judged. Rather, I will propose a "gender realism" which, admitting the contours of a basic *reproductive interdependence* between the sexes, acknowledges the culture-bound nature of gendered expression and leaves the specifics of a "gendered ordering" of male-female life to be negotiated by men and women within the bounds of the various social contexts in which they find themselves.[16] Of course, for Christians, the primary social context is the new civilization, the church. The only "essentials" of this gendered ordering, then, are that the male-female, head-body unitive duality of the sexes, specifically within familial and ecclesial households, reflect and participate in the head-body one-flesh duality of Christ and church.

METHODOLOGY

Methodologically, a figural approach involves close attention to the scriptural text, with the canon as the primary context for illuminating the sense that inheres in a given passage. This stands in contrast with a historical-critical approach that understands each text's historical context to be a primary factor in interpretation. On the contrary, figurally speaking, Scripture is not a story which finds its fit in another story (the "history behind the text"), but provides its own overarching narrative into which all of history is fit and found.

Figural exegesis also involves a christological reading, where Christ is the interpretive clue and center for the Scriptures as a whole and hence

---

when we will "be like the angels" (Matt 22:30); and that of marriage, which anticipates the final eschatological marriage between Christ and the church (Eph 5:23–33). See Grant, *Divine Sex*, 159; Radner, "Nuptial Figure."

15. In making these points, I closely follow Kirschbaum's Christocentric reading of the man as "head" in relation to woman. These dynamics will be further explored in chs. 5–6.

16. On this point I follow Ivan Illich, who insists that an "asymmetric gender complementarity" characterizes all of our existence as gendered beings—except for where such complementarity has been seriously attacked and/or suppressed (*Gender*).

for the entire human story.¹⁷ In this way it assumes a methodological binding to Christ—in his eternal deity and human life, death, resurrection, and ascension in time—as the key to understanding the whole of the Scriptures. In a Christian figural understanding, the Scriptures principally proclaim Christ: every story, psalm, proverb, and exemplar in the law, the prophets, and the writings, each in their own way points to, prepares for, and/or elucidates the nature and work of Christ (see Luke 24:25–45). Such canonical and christological approaches have governed the church's own interpretive practices from its inception, beginning with the NT authors themselves, their own approaches being consistent with previously developed Jewish approaches in terms of their intertextual, and finally messianic, figuralism. It is indeed Paul's own engagement with "the head" as a soteriologically rich scriptural figure (e.g., in Eph 5:22–33) that will serve to guide my own figural engagement with the same. In this sense, here I seek to do nothing methodologically new but to follow the lead of Paul, along with patristic, medieval, and Reformed theological interpreters.

Governed throughout by historic figural practices, this work will employ a number of methodological tools, including comparative analysis with respect to the metaphysics of gender, and with respect to hermeneutical approaches to gender; and a "genealogical" approach to the historical nature and development of gender relations, appropriating the views of philosopher, priest, and polemicist Ivan Illich.¹⁸ Still, all such

---

17. Such a christological reading involves the acknowledgment that all of the OT law and prophets testify to Christ (Luke 24; John 5); all of the NT apostolic writings testify to Christ; nature itself is bursting at the seams with testimony to Christ (Luke 19:40), as that which was made by him and for him (Col 1:16) and finds its healing and restoration in him and through him (Rom 8:22–24).

18. Michel Foucault outlines genealogy as a philosophical method ("Nietzsche, Genealogy, History," 76–77). Following Ivan Illich's genealogical method, I draw out a genealogy not of gender generally (as does Illich) but of the "head"/"headship" more specifically, with attention to changes in economic and political structures and the effects of such changes on linguistic and cultural understandings of "headship" as a gendered category. Like Foucault (and Nietzsche before him), I understand the shifts in the use of ethical terms/concepts largely in terms of power dynamics. E.g., in the present case, the term "head" is developed and used in ways to shift, limit, gain, or maintain power for one group over another (e.g., men over women, the church over the state or vice versa, the papal office over churches, etc.). Where I differ sharply from Foucault is in employing such a genealogical approach within an explicitly theological framework. The ultimate "transvaluation" of all values is revealed in the mystery of God incarnate, suffering with and for an estranged people. The meaning of the "head" cannot finally be defined in service of any particular ideological cause but by the one—Jesus Christ—who illuminates the true nature of "headship." See Nietzsche, *On Genealogy of Morals*.

comparative and genealogical work will ultimately be compared with and ruled by a figural (canonical, christological) interpretation of headship.

Admittedly, this project is methodologically atypical as a work of constructive theology, since much time will be spent engaging theological terms as they develop concretely in history before finally engaging directly in what might be understood more traditionally as theologically "constructive" work. Indeed, the first four chapters relate the "head" to philosophical, etymological and social histories. Only in chapters 5 and 6 do I develop at length the notion of the "head" as a canonical and christological figure.

Again, it is important to note that this methodological order arises from the conviction that theological concepts must be understood in their sociohistorical dimensions as they come to be used and understood in concrete cultural contexts. This being the case, the first four chapters are not simply a matter of "ground clearing" for the later constructive contributions (although they are that too), but they contribute in their own way to shaping the theological conclusions reached in those latter chapters.

OUTLINES

In the first chapter, "Problems with Male Headship: Cultural Evolutions and the Matter of Sexual Difference," I identify two of the most pressing objections to male headship as a contemporary ecclesial category: first, its apparent commendation of male dominance as a social norm; second, its apparent commendation of a gender essentialist framework which historically has undergirded culturally entrenched forms of male dominance. With regard to the first of these objections we will consider the forms in which male headship has persisted into the present, suggesting that male headship, particularly as it has been articulated in certain modern evangelical contexts, is in fact a theologically and socially problematic category. With regard to the second, I will set out and critically engage with two of the historically dominant approaches to gender—essentialism and constructivism—and offer as a "middle way" a "gender realist" position, following the Latin American philosopher Linda Alcoff. These "realist" claims will be clarified and briefly compared to a theological account of sexual difference, where I will propose that a gender

---

See also Foucault, "On Genealogy of Ethics."

realist approach corresponds to a biblical theology of headship and its "gendered ordering" of creaturely life under God.

In the second chapter, "On the Etymology of Headship: Defining the Head," I will argue that headship in modern contexts has come to carry with it a distinct set of connotations that create unique problems for contemporary use of the term, compared with ancient understandings. I will demonstrate that *in modern Western contexts headship has become unmoored from its antecedent usage in scriptural contexts.* More specifically, *male headship has come to denote male superiority.* This modern development will be contrasted with the meaning of headship in the ancient Hebrew context of the OT, later received into the NT, where the head, as a title, most fundamentally denotes *representation,* not rule, leadership, or authority. To demonstrate this, I will outline the etymological shifts which have led to the present-day notion of "headship" as it has developed in the West.

In the third chapter, "On the Genealogy of Heads: Headship in History," I trace the genealogy of headship as a social category, exploring the ways in which household and tribal heads functioned in a gendered pre-industrialized world, and how male headship largely lost its familial and societal place in a post-industrialized world. Through this genealogical account I will argue that preindustrial norms of male headship, carefully defined, did not necessarily indicate a relation of one-sided dominance, but rather was ingredient to a larger framework of reciprocity between the genders, at least in certain contexts.[19] Finally, I will argue that whereas in such pre-industrialized societies the male-headed home was at least conceivable as a social good, in post-industrialized contexts male headship has too often been co-opted in service of an inherently sexist ideology. Within the present framework, male headship—defined fundamentally in terms of modern and secular understandings of leadership/rulership—has been rightly identified as harmful and oppressive.

Not surprisingly, then, modern Western exegetes have commonly dismissed the contemporary relevance of Paul's proffering the concept of the man as "head" in relation to the woman. We will trace the history of this interpretive trend in the fourth chapter, "Revisionist Heads: Headship in Modern Interpretation." There I will demonstrate that the

---

19. For a helpful entryway into this basic point, see Meyers, "Was Ancient Israel Patriarchal?" Here Meyers helpfully complicates the term "patriarchy," demonstrating that it is insufficient as a historical descriptor of all male-headed societies. See also Rogers, "Female Forms of Power."

characteristically modern trend to disavow male headship is not so much the result of more careful or rigorous exegetical work (compared with earlier interpreters), but is rather the result of shifting theological foundations, distinguished by a new set of markedly modern and only quasi-theological methodological norms. To highlight these interpretive shifts, and demonstrate the inadequacy of the modernist methodological commitments with which they operate, I will outline two of the dominant modern approaches to questions of headship (termed loyalist and revisionist), concluding that modern scholars in these interpretive camps are by and large playing a losing game—either (1) seeking to rid Christianity of male headship or (2) seeking to fit male headship (defined in modern terms) within a secular frame where it simply does not fit. I will argue, however, that interpreters in the Nicene tradition of Christian orthodoxy are necessarily bound to affirm and receive rather than deny and dismiss the notion of the man as "head," rightly conceived.

In the fifth chapter, "Soteriological Heads: Headship in Canonical Perspective," we arrive at a more explicitly constructive chapter where I will define and develop the notion of headship figurally, according to its use within the scriptural canon. In this chapter I formulate my argument that headship functions as a *soteriological synecdoche*, i.e., as a means of denoting soteriological representation, with the salvation or damnation of the body mediated or accomplished by one's head. This will be demonstrated through a survey of various scriptural head "types," including Adam, Noah, Abraham, and, finally, Christ. In conclusion I will argue that the head in Scripture everywhere figures Christ and his headship with respect to his bride, the church. Accordingly, Christ's headship must determine the significance and contours of any and all creaturely modes of headship, whether within familial or ecclesial spheres.

In the sixth and final chapter, "Figural Heads: Toward a Constructive Theology of Gender," we explore possibilities for how a theological account of gender may take shape in contemporary contexts. Here we find that, whereas the man is identified as the head-representative of the one-flesh union, the woman, in a corresponding manner, is the "glory" of that union. Unpacking these figures, we arrive at a constructive theological vision for male and female unity-through-difference—man and woman together a symbol and foretaste of God's redemptive love for us, wrought in the one Christ, head and body.

CONCLUDING REMARKS

But I began by talking about women's ordination.

For many North American Christians, especially Protestant Evangelicals, the hermeneutics of "male headship" has become one of the key determinants for resolving the question of women's ordination. In short, it was argued that if the man is "head" of the woman, understood in terms of leadership and authority, the woman must not be eligible for ordination as elder/priest.[20]

Headship, however, is not primarily a matter of leadership or authority, as I will argue. Moreover, claims concerning the man's status as "head" are never made with reference to ordination in the OT or NT. For these reasons, I contend that the "head" figure needs to be engaged on its own terms—not simply as a tool in service of the question of women's ordination but as a matter of theological interest in itself. Accordingly, I seek to offer a theological account of headship that is not essentially tied up with the question of women's ordination. My hope in doing so is to offer a theology of gender which undercuts facile arguments—including those for and against women's ordination—providing instead a robustly theological framework within which a renewed discussion concerning matters of sexuality, gender, and ecclesial authority can occur.

More broadly, my hope is that this work will contribute to several areas of theological scholarship: (1) recovering and exploring a figural-christological reading of Scripture to serve as a case study in employing historic practices of theological exegesis; (2) providing a more robust understanding of the socio-theological meaning of the "head" within post-biblical Western cultural history; (3) reframing the headship discussion by developing the "head" in its canonical context as a soteriological figure; and (4) identifying the notion of "headship," scripturally defined, so as to recover a Christian vision of gender for contemporary life.

In "the strange new world within the Bible,"[21] the significance of each gender is determined and to be discovered within the creative plan of the Father, who sends his Son to be joined to a bride, united in the Spirit. Here, gender is given and to be received as a means of reflecting,

---

20. E.g., see Schreiner, "Valuable Ministries of Women," 284. Here male headship is understood as synonymous with male leadership and bound up with male authority in the church.

21. Barth, "Strange New World."

proclaiming, and participating in the divine life, whose purposes climax in the union of Christ and the church, God and his people.

To be sure, "headship" is not the only way to approach a theology of gender, but scripturally speaking, it is one way, and, I will argue, a useful way at that.

CHAPTER 1

Problems with Male Headship

Cultural Evolutions and the Matter of Sexual Difference

For the husband is the head of the wife even as Christ is the head of the church, his body.

But I want you to understand that Christ is the head of every man, and the man is the head of a woman, and God is the head of Christ.

—Saint Paul of Tarsus[1]

The statement that "the man is the head of a woman" (1 Cor 11:3) is, for most in our day, tactless and profane. And understandably so. First off, Paul's words seem to indicate—against strong cultural currents toward the equality of the genders—that the man is the leader, the authority, the ruler in relation to the woman, in a place of superiority and dominance in general.[2] Second, male headship seems to suggest that the genders are fixed and binary, implying that all men everywhere share a set of essential

---

1. Eph 5:23; 1 Cor 11:3.
2. In evangelical contexts in particular, the notion of "male headship" has been the cause of much controversy as it has been used to argue against women's ordination to ecclesial office, and to maintain and increase male power in the life of the church and family. Three recent monographs have sought to highlight the way dysfunctional and oppressive forms of masculinity have been touted in conservative Christian and evangelical contexts. See Barr, *Making of Biblical Womanhood*; Du Mez, *Jesus and John Wayne*; Byrd, *Recovering from Biblical Manhood*.

traits or characteristics—a claim which has likewise come under intense scrutiny in our day. With these objections, many have sought to dismiss the relevance of male headship for contemporary Christian faith and practice.

In this chapter we will consider these two most basic challenges to the contemporary notion of male headship. In the first section, "Male Headship and Male Dominance: Mapping Cultural Evolutions," we will consider the first of these objections: namely, that male headship serves a social vision of male dominance over women. Here we will find that male headship—once perceived as a rather benign culturally assumed social reality—has in fact been co-opted as a function of male dominance in the modern West.

In the second section, "Essentialism, Constructivism, and Realism: Mapping Gender Difference," I will address the second of the aforementioned challenges: namely, that the notion of "male headship" apparently commends a fixed and binary philosophy of gender in contrast to contemporary constructivist trends. In order to engage this challenge, we will consider two of the historically dominant approaches to gender—essentialism and constructivism—and propose a "gender realist" position as a middle way. Within this realist frame, I will draw out two positive affirmations: first, that humanity is irreducibly gendered; and second, that the genders are an irreducible duality, male and female.[3]

In a third section, entitled "Sexual Difference in a Theological Perspective," I will suggest by way of a brief and ad hoc engagement with Scripture that these "realist" claims correspond to the theological account of sexual difference to be developed in the forthcoming chapters.

Before proceeding further, a few words of caution are in order. There are admittedly dangers ahead in developing a theology of gender from the christological figure of Christ and the church. To say that the man corresponds to the divine element of the figure, Christ, and the woman to the human element, the church, suggests a male-favored gender

---

3. I use the terms "sex" and "gender" throughout in a manner aligned with the definitions provided by the APA: "*Gender* is used to denote the public (and usually legally recognized) lived role as boy or girl, man or woman, but, in contrast to certain social constructionist theories, biological factors are seen as contributing, in interaction with social and psychological factors, to gender development"; "*sex* and *sexual* refer to the biological indicators of male and female (understood in the context of reproductive capacity), such as in sex chromosomes, gonads, sex hormones, and nonambiguous internal and external genitalia" (DSM-5 451). While I will problematize a clear and stable distinction between two these terms, the APA's definitions in large part capture the nuance with which I employ them.

imbalance. To say that the man corresponds to the *head* of the body, and the woman to the *body* of the head, also suggests an imbalance, especially in light of the ways these terms have developed in the West (see ch. 2). These are significant challenges to our retrieval and use of the head and body figures.

For these reasons, it is important to note clearly, up front, that these figures, in their gendered dimension, are limited in their scope in accordance with the limits set for them by the Scriptures' own boundaries. The man, for instance, is not the "head of the woman" in every possible regard but only in those ways the Scriptures indicate, reflecting specified dynamics of the ways of Christ with the church. Moreover, the very idea that the woman, as a figure of the church, is in an inferior position to the man is complicated by the scriptural ascription of the church as the very "body of Christ"—an ascription which at least complexifies a simple divine/human male/female dichotomy.[4] This being the case, I suggest that we must evaluate these figures by engaging with them on their own terms, within their scripturally circumscribed scope.

To retrieve a theology of headship, as outlined above, will require us to engage the aforementioned challenges both with resolute honesty and tenacious hope: with honesty about the ways that this scriptural figure has been used to "tear" and "strike down"; yet with hope that the same figure, rightly conceived, might offer a way to "heal" and "bind up" (to use the poignant language of Hos 6:1).

MALE HEADSHIP AND MALE DOMINANCE: MAPPING CULTURAL EVOLUTIONS

"Are we still talking about this?"

The question is raised in bold letters, introducing a 2010 *Sojourners* article entitled "The Persistence of Patriarchy: Hard to Believe, but Some Churches Are Still Talking About Male Headship."[5] To the modern ear,

---

4. The notion of the church as a "divine" or "divinized" entity admittedly stands at odds with large strands of Protestant ecclesiology. Still, the Reformed tradition offers resources for a qualified understanding of the church as a communion of "partakers" in the divine, particularly through its doctrine of *Christus in nobis* and its emphasis on union with Christ, evident in Luther, Calvin, Watson, Edwards, and Kuyper, among others. For a brief history of this tradition, see Murphy, "Reformed *Theosis*?" See also Billings, "United to God."

5. Eggebroten, "Persistence of Patriarchy." See also Bishop, "Churches Teaching Male Headship."

the notion that the man is "head" of his wife or "head" of his household in not only outdated but, the article argues, is a matter of gender discrimination and oppression.

Throughout the history of Western civilization the title of "head"—more specifically the man's identity as head of the household—has been used to connote man's familial prominence, public prestige, and formal power, and has often been deployed as a synonym for "ruler" or "authority-figure."[6] In most times and places, at least until the advent of women's suffrage, such authority was not informal, but legislated and institutionalized.[7] Certainly, the nature of such rule and authority has been variously understood, sometimes with an emphasis on power and privilege, and other times on duties and constraints.[8] Still, male headship has been consistently conceived in the modern West in terms of male authority, particularly in relation to wife and household.[9] Such authority was once legally enshrined. Now, where accepted at all, it is construed as the man's informal "role."

In the present North American context, the man's informal role as "head" became largely defined, at least since the 1940s, in terms of male breadwinning—requiring female domesticity as its "complement."[10] Of course, the breadwinning ideals of the forties through the seventies now appear strikingly at odds with (if not manifestly inimical to) contemporary political, familial, and economic trends. In Canada, from 1976 to 2018, the percentage of women in the labor force rose from 37 to 48 percent, now nearly half of Canada's working population.[11] From 1987 to 2015 the percentage of female legislators and senior government managers and officials rose from 37 to 54 percent. Traditional norms and

---

6. "Headship," OED.

7. The legal authority of the household head entailed most basically the man's status as legal representative of the household, including, in most cases, his legal authority over wife and children, and ownership of all property and assets (a claim to be examined further below).

8. See Gallagher, "Reflections on Headship."

9. The nature of these claims will be illustrated and substantiated in what follows.

10. Stasson, "Politicization of Family Life," esp. 101–2.

11. Statistics taken from Statistics Canada, which defines the labor force as that portion of the "civilian noninstitutional population 15 years of age and over who, during the survey reference week [in which the employment survey was taken] . . . . were employed or unemployed" (Phillips and Poulin, "Labour Force," s.vv. "What Is the Labour Force?").

notions of the "male as breadwinner" have changed rapidly.[12] Similarly, in the United States women now comprise 47 percent of the total labor force, holding 52 percent of all management, professional, and related occupations.[13] If breadwinning is now the shared task of women and men, it would seem that headship as a male category has been neutered.

Indeed, at a time when the bygone norm and stereotype of the male-as-breadwinner and authority figure is dissipating, we may appropriately ask, *Why are churches still talking about male headship?* Such talk is all the more unseemly at a moment when the equality of the genders is globally acknowledged as a basic human right—including women's "full participation . . . *in all spheres of society*," the "*equal sharing of responsibilities for the family by men and women*," and the promotion of "*women's economic independence.*"[14] At such a time as this, whither male headship?

For millennia in the West, that the man was "head" of the home was a simple fact of social life, no more dubious than its characteristically collectivist or agrarian features. Enshrined as a scriptural claim, linguistically embedded in the church's liturgy and wedding rituals, the sociopolitical reality of the male-headed home became reinforced in and through the church as a spiritual, even metaphysical, claim, to be upheld as a matter of religion and conviction under God. A tradition of male household "headship" has thus persisted into manifold modern contexts—rural and metropolitan, agrarian and industrial, poor and wealthy, across continents to the present day. As we shall see in the third chapter, some form of a male-headed family seems to have taken its place, by and large, as a societal norm from the earliest emergence of human civilizations—a norm seriously and substantively redressed as a matter of gender justice beginning only in the nineteenth century.[15]

---

12. Catalyst.org, "Women in Workforce—Canada," s.v. "Summary."

13. Catalyst.org, "Women in Workforce—United States," s.v. "Summary." This is not to suggest that we have reached a state of economic equality for the genders. In Canada, e.g., in 2015 only 25.6 percent of senior managers in the private sector were women; in 2018 only 15.8 percent of TSX-listed companies, and 5 percent of S&P 500 companies, had a woman CEO.

14. United Nations, *Beijing Declaration*, art. 13, 15, 26; emphasis added. The document was received unanimously by 189 nations.

15. See Bennett, "Feminism and History," 264. John Stuart Mill's *The Subjection of Women*, first published in 1861, is considered one of the earliest and most influential works to have advocated for gender equality in distinctly modern terms. Of course, many challenges to the gendered status quo had arisen prior to the nineteenth century. One of the most striking examples comes from the *querelle des femmes*. Still, there is little evidence that the *querelle* represented a widespread change in attitude towards

How then did it come to pass that male headship became incommensurable with Western social norms and practices? At first glance, the answer seems obvious: In a post-patriarchal culture, where the equality of the sexes is everywhere presumed and pursued, to affirm that the man, by virtue of his maleness, is the head of the woman is a category mistake which necessarily undermines the equality of the sexes. As such it has no place in this, our secular age.[16]

However, a number of questionable assumptions underlie such a response. For one, it presumes that to affirm the male-specified "head" identity necessarily supports a patriarchal and male dominant ordering of society. It likewise presumes that all societies, ancient to contemporary, that affirm some version of the male-headed home are in favor, implicitly or explicitly, of a systemic sexism with the privileging of men. In what follows, such assumptions, while not altogether without warrant, will be problematized.[17]

To be clear, throughout this book I will be arguing that "male headship" as it is presently understood in Western contexts is by and large problematic. This is most fundamentally because by definition in the present context, the title "head" confers a status of superiority, necessarily placing women in subservience to men. Yet, as I will argue, the problem herein lies not with the "head" title (or "figure") per se, scripturally understood, but with a tradition which has developed culturally and linguistically to construe such a title chiefly in terms of male authority and female subservience. As I will argue, the scriptural "head and body" figure speaks a better word for women and men alike.

But problems with male headship are more far reaching still. The very idea of deeming the man *qua* man the "head" risks essentializing both genders into fixed entities in service of male dominance—the very thing feminist theorists have warned against. We are thus pressed to engage the fraught and complex question of the relation between gender

---

women. Such widespread social changes would begin only in the nineteenth and twentieth centuries. See Beauvoir, *Second Sex*, 21–22; see also Douglass, *Women, Freedom, and Calvin*, 67–71.

16. In a secular age, male headship shares a fate similar to that of theism: we have gotten past it, and it is embraced critically, if at all. In this context, to affirm male headship publicly is akin to a public affirmation of belief in the God of Christianity. See Taylor, *Secular Age*, 164–65.

17. Defining sexism, too, is not altogether straightforward, since it can be understood in terms of hostility toward women, or as inclusive of both hostility and "benevolence." See Glick and Fiske, "Ambivalent Sexism Inventory," 492.

essentialism and social constructivism. Is there room for fixed gendered identities of any kind—let alone the fixed identity of the man as "head"? Or, do gender identities of every kind show plasticity and instability?

ESSENTIALISM, CONSTRUCTIVISM AND REALISM: MAPPING GENDER DIFFERENCE

In truth, to go for a walk with one's eyes open is enough to demonstrate that humanity is divided into two classes of individuals whose clothes, faces, bodies, smiles, gaits, interests, and occupations are manifestly different. Perhaps these differences are superficial, perhaps they are destined to disappear. What is certain is that they do most obviously exist.

—SIMONE DE BEAUVOIR[18]

The irreducible duality of the sexes has been a shaping force in the creation and maintenance of social and cultural norms in every enduring human civilization. While some have emphasized the unity and others the differences within this duality, male and female have emerged in every place as distinct modes of being, involving gendered divisions in vocation and labor, skills, tools, speech, dress, spaces to inhabit, along with a great many distinct social and familial expectations in every place.[19] What is less established—even a matter of great contention in nearly all scientific and social-scientific fields at present—is whether, or to what extent, this gendered duality arises predominantly as a fact of nature (for "essentialists") or as a feature of social construction (for "constructivists"). On both sides of the debate, most admit that there is an interplay between nature and nurture when it comes to gendered social formation.[20]

Gender essentialists contend that each sex has an "essential" or underlying nature with concomitant properties. For instance, women's "essential nature" might be said to involve qualities of "nurturing and

---

18. Beauvoir, *Second Sex*, 14.
19. These claims will be elucidated and defended in the next chapter.
20. In this debate, "sex" typically denotes "the biological category," whereas "gender is the culturally shaped expression of sexual difference" ("Gender," in Blackburn, *Oxford Dictionary of Philosophy*).

caring" in distinction to the male's essential nature to be "aggressive."[21] Gender "constructivists," in contrast, posit that gender is "an artefact of social practices, including language and institutionalized ways of categorizing the world."[22] In its more radical expressions, gender is viewed as a construction that is only accidentally related to biological sex. For example, where nurturance of the young is characteristic of women in a given cultural context, gender essentialists will attribute this to an underlying "essence" characteristic of the female sex; and gender constructivists will attribute this same characteristic fundamentally to the powers of social practices and expectations.

Until relatively recently, a form of gender essentialism has been the dominant approach to gender in the West, where male and female have been conceived as biologically determined beings bound to their "natural capacities" as male and female.[23] "Gender essentialism" has been variously understood, both in a minimalist trajectory—where women and men are deemed equal in most, if not all, respects (the tradition of Plato)—and a maximalist trajectory—where women and men are deemed to be significantly different, with the male as superior (in the tradition of Aristotle). In either case, a relatively fixed duality of the genders has been generally assumed and reinforced throughout the West.[24]

Such assumptions became increasingly suspect in the post-industrial era (for reasons we will explore in ch. 3), culminating in a certain feminist unrest in the mid-twentieth century. It was at this time that Simone de Beauvoir's *The Second Sex* was first published (in 1949) with its provocative claim "One is not born, but rather becomes a woman."[25] This landmark statement would mark the beginning of a broad trend away from older essentialist notions of gender toward an attention to the socially constructed nature of gendered identities. Against the grain of Western gender essentialism, Beauvoir's claim would come to function as a rallying cry for generations to come, gaining traction in the American "second-wave" feminist movements of the 1960s.[26]

21. "Essentialism," in Blackburn, *Oxford Dictionary of Philosophy*.
22. "Social Constructivism," in Blackburn, *Oxford Dictionary of Philosophy*.
23. Bem, *Lenses of Gender*, 1–2.
24. Allen, *Aristotelian Revolution*.
25. Beauvoir, *Second Sex*, 301.
26. In the North American context, the first wave of feminism arose in the eighteenth and nineteenth centuries, and was ridden into shore with the Nineteenth Amendment to the United States Constitution of 1920, affording women the right to

In an era when certain male privileges were assumed and unquestioned, there was something extremely powerful about Beauvoir's claim. It came as a word of hope that women could overcome the oppressions they faced, past and present. Further, this notion of the existential freedom of the woman—to become what she desired to be—offered a compelling theoretical point of departure for many feminist theorists to follow. In fact, the denunciation of biological determinism has become one of the basic presuppositions undergirding much of the contemporary discipline of gender studies.[27]

This rejection of biologically determined gender identities in the decades following the 1950s was largely motivated by a common sentiment among feminists that biological determinism went hand in hand with women's oppression, and that in order to be free from past and present forms of male dominance, whether in the sphere of family or economics, women needed to be untethered from their biologically determined past.[28] The modern woman ought not be bound by any preestablished norms of "womanhood," since all such norms had been culturally constructed in cultures of male supremacy. In light of such a past, any attempts to identify a "feminine essence" would seemingly fall into the trap of reifying patriarchal patterns that were steeped in old socially constructed and oppressive norms. In short, many feminists feared that a determinate feminine essence would guarantee a subservient feminine destiny. Escape from the past demanded an escape from any namable feminine essence. A gender constructivist framing, in this way, seemed to provide a way forward for women to escape from the harmful labels and assigned identities of the past.

However, with much of contemporary gender discourse effectively uprooted from any essentialist foundations, many gender theorists have been brought face to face with a serious challenge. On the one hand, they must establish the *identity*, and thus *determinacy*, of woman—to maintain that the category of woman, whether acknowledged as an ontological

---

vote. The "second wave" typically refers to the American and British feminist movements of the 1960s and 1970s. The Second World War had ushered many women into the public workforce, and many of these women continued working in the wake of the war, thus challenging the "status quo" of the idealized "working man" and "domestic woman." Issues of gender inequality, stereotypes, sexual violence, workplace and reproductive rights, and female identity in the public sphere became central subjects of public discourse as women rallied together in the fight for social equality.

27. See Flax, "Postmodernism and Gender Relations."
28. Alcoff, *Visible Identities*, 153.

or nominal category, is an *identifiable category*. On the other hand, they must establish the *freedom*, and thus *indeterminacy*, of woman—to assert that *there is no "ideal type" called "woman"* which might serve as the rule according to which all women might be (inappropriately) measured. Feminist theorists have thus been caught in a conundrum, seeking to identify a stable identity for women, yet without capitulating to older forms of biological determinism. Simply put, the challenge has been to identify *what woman is* without at the same time identifying *what woman ought to be*.[29]

Theorists have tended to respond in one of two ways to this conceptual problem. For some, the problem is *not* that woman has been defined in distinction from man, but that *woman has historically been defined by men*, characterized and treated in ways that uphold male dominance. The solution here is not to do away with a stable feminine identity, but to have women reappraise the situation, to reclaim historically and culturally feminine characteristics in positive, pro-woman terms. This might involve construing woman's "passivity as her peacefulness, her sentimentality as her proclivity to nurture, her subjectiveness as her advanced self-awareness,"[30] and so on. Feminists who take this approach have been called "cultural feminists," who stand in contrast to the "poststructuralist feminists."[31]

For "poststructuralists," following Judith Butler, the problem is not simply that women have been defined and characterized by men to men's own benefit, but that women have been defined as a stable category at all. The solution here is to reject outright the very possibility of defining "woman as such." Alcoff explains,

> Feminists who take this tactic go about the business of deconstructing all concepts of woman and argue that both feminist and misogynist attempts to define woman are politically reactionary and ontologically mistaken. . . . Such errors occur because we are in fundamental ways duplicating misogynist strategies when we try to define women, characterize women, or speak for women, even while allowing for a range of differences with the gender.[32]

---

29. These concerns are addressed in a series of articles: Bachiochi et al., "Contemporary Feminism."
30. Alcoff, *Visible Identities*, 134.
31. Alcoff, "Cultural Feminism."
32. Alcoff, "Cultural Feminism," 407.

Alcoff identifies the former approach as gender essentialism ("there is such a thing as woman") and the latter as gender nominalism ("there is no such thing as woman"), and suggests a "third way," what she calls gender realism—a view of gender which, though rooted in certain biological differences, affirms that such differences are inevitably given their shape by, and interpreted within, particular cultural contexts.

For Alcoff, the dividing line between genders—the "objective basis for the category of sexed identity"—is located in their relationship to reproduction.[33] She explains: *"Women and men are differentiated by virtue of their different relationship of possibility to biological reproduction, with biological reproduction referring to conceiving, giving birth, and breast-feeding, involving one's own body."*[34] In this account, one gender (women)—whether prepubescent or menopausal, regardless of sexual orientation, health, or even physical ability—always bears a "relationship of possibility to reproduction" which the other gender (men) does not.

This biological foundation for gendered identity is not to be confused with an essentialist account of gender. Rather, though rooted in the biological "relationship of possibility to reproduction," Alcoff insists that gendered identities only emerge in concrete contexts, and so must be defined locally. In this account, gender identity can take many forms, although it is never untethered from bearing a particular relation to biology and hence reproduction. She elaborates:

> The possibility of pregnancy, childbirth, nursing, and in many societies, rape, are parts of females' horizons that we carry with us throughout childhood and much of our adult lives. The way these are figured, imagined, experienced, accepted, and so on, is as variable as culture. But these elements exist in the female

---

33. Beauvoir affirms the same: "Males and females are two types of individuals which are differentiated within a species for the function of reproduction; they can be defined only correlatively" (*Second Sex*, 33).

34. Alcoff, *Visible Identities*, 172; emphasis in original. She continues, "I want to capture the reality that this differential relationship of possibility to biological reproduction remains in place even for women who have had hysterectomies, women who have no desire or intention to reproduce, and women who are not fertile. Those classified as women will have a different set of practices, expectations, and feelings in regard to reproduction, no matter how actual their relationship of possibility is to it. That is, even infertile, prepubescent girls or postmenopausal women, and women who have no intention to reproduce *still* have a relationship to biological reproduction that is different from what males have."

horizon, and they exist there because of the ways in which we are embodied.[35]

Alcoff thus represents an important current in contemporary gender and feminist discourse, cutting through the divide between what she calls "a poststructuralist genderless subject" and "a cultural feminist essentialized subject."[36] By taking the inescapably material and embodied nature of existence as a given, and at the same time refusing to essentialize or universalize "kinds" of gendered existence, Alcoff provides a way forward in her insistence that our existence as humans is irreducibly gendered, while creating space to discern what this means in diverse cultural and historical contexts.

Moreover, Alcoff presses her readers beyond the mere facts of biological difference to consider the ways in which humans are further shaped by these differences. In her account, gendered differences are biologically rooted and have a force which cannot easily be diminished or refashioned according to the political or even ethical exigencies of a given time and place. There are, in this sense, real boundaries between the genders, which distinguish women from men in every place by virtue of their relation to reproduction.

From this realist framework emerges two foundational affirmations which, I will argue, correspond to the gendered framework that emerges from the Scriptures and the Christian tradition: namely, (1) that humans are *irreducibly gendered*; and (2) that the genders are an *irreducible duality* consisting of male and female.

According to Alcoff's realist framework, humans cannot escape our particular relation to reproduction. To be human is to be received into a world whose perceptions and expectations fit each individual into one of two biological categories, each entailing and ensuring a vast network of gender-specific possibilities. For women, for example, these include existential possibilities of pregnancy, childbirth, and nursing as well as unique possibilities of sexual exploitation and objectification, including greater risk for being physically assaulted. These possibilities inevitably shape the horizons, the decisions and values, desires and opportunities, of women in any given time and place.

None of this suggests for Alcoff that such biologically rooted differences produce the same results in any two places. However, it does

---

35. Alcoff, *Visible Identities*, 176.
36. Alcoff, *Visible Identities*, 145.

suggest that in every place such differential "relations of possibility to reproduction" will produce differences that can be mapped along gendered lines. These differences will be more exaggerated in some places than others, at times difficult to name or discern. Nevertheless, in every place there emerge "two classes of individuals whose clothes, faces, bodies, smiles, gaits, interests, and occupations are . . . different," to use Beauvoir's phrase.[37] Humans are, in this way, irreducibly gendered, male or female, tied to an inescapable "relationship of possibility" to reproduction.[38]

Understood this way, a second foundational affirmation emerges from a gender realist framework. Not only is humanity fundamentally gendered, but the genders, male and female, are an *irreducible duality* who together comprise a unified whole in their mutually dependent relation to reproduction.[39]

J. Budziszewski presents a simple analogy on this point. Each man breathes, making use of lungs and a diaphragm. Each woman can circulate blood by herself, with her own heart. "So it is with each of the vital functions, except one," says Budziszewski. "The sole exception is procreation." Compared to breathing, it is "as though the man had the diaphragm, the woman had the lungs, and they had to come together to take a single breath."[40] In this sense, it is in reproduction alone where we find the man and woman working together as a "two-body system," an irreducible biological duality.[41]

Even where the genders are acknowledged as a mutually dependent duality in relation to reproduction, there will be minimalist and maximalist accounts of this. For some, this "bare duality" is relevant only for

---

37. Beauvoir, *Second Sex*, 14.

38. Such a realist conception of gender, with its binary construal of sexuality, stands in contrast to certain transsexualist ideologies which posit that one's biological sex can be transcended. In the present account, one's gender expression always emerges as the expression of a gendered body, male or female. For a fuller discussion of transsexuality, specifically in relation to a Christian framework, see O'Donovan, "Transsexualism and Christian Marriage."

39. This claim is made most basically at the bio-sexual level, but might also be established psychologically, philosophically, anthropologically, sociologically, etc. (Alcoff, *Visible Identities*, 162).

40. Budziszewski, *On the Meaning of Sex*, 28.

41. The advent of new reproductive technologies might be thought to render such a male-female duality unnecessary. However, it should be noted that such technologies still require the use of both male and female bodies at some level. Moreover, they are available only to the elite, globally speaking. See Kissil and Davey, "Health Disparities in Procreation"; Harris et al., "Socio-Economic Disparities."

procreation. For others, such minimalist accounts will be too simplistic, failing to acknowledge a more extensive duality which is related to, or emerges from, such stable reproductive differences. In any case, at the very least, a realist account of gender will prioritize the male-female unitive duality at the level of reproduction, which itself may open into a broader vision of male-female partnership in child-rearing and long-term coupling.[42]

In sum, I contend that neither essentialism nor constructivism provide satisfying accounts of gendered embodiment. Essentialism tends to overestimate the stability of gender differences cross-culturally, even associating manhood and womanhood with sets of psychosocial characteristics which are purportedly consistent across time and cultures. Constructivism tends to underestimate the ramifications of distinctly sexed bodies for identifying distinctly gendered modes of being among human cultures. As an alternative, I have followed Alcoff's "realist" position which posits that the sexes are objectively distinguished according to their differential relations to reproduction; and, further, that these differential relations manifest themselves distinctly in every time and place.

Finally, I have argued that such a "realist" vision leads to two basic affirmations: first, that humanity is irreducibly gendered; and second, that the genders are an irreducible duality, male and female, in relation to reproduction. We have only briefly considered here some of the most basic ramifications of this reproductive duality. In the chapters to follow I will argue that this fundamental reproductive duality signals a still more far-reaching duality of the genders.

---

42. For this reason, Butler and others are critical of gender realist accounts, logically tied as they are to the prioritization of "heterosexual coupling." Alcoff tries to overcome this apparent limitation by claiming that gender realism "does not require *sustained heterosexual coupling*" (*Visible Identities*, 174; emphasis in original). However, this claim requires substantiation, since it runs contrary to much of the current social-scientific research, which affirms sustained heterosexual coupling for the well-being of children. See Ribar, "Marriage Matters for Child," 11. See also McLanahan et al., "Effects of Father Absence"; Wilcox, *Why Marriage Matters*. In this way, a realist account of gender relativizes a same-sex telos by insisting that males and females exist as a duality in relation to one another at the level of sex and reproduction. For a more philosophical discussion of these issues, see Scruton, *Sexual Desire*.

SEXUAL DIFFERENCE IN A THEOLOGICAL PERSPECTIVE

From a theological perspective, a gendered duality is presupposed by the creational categories of humanity made both "male and female" in the image of God (Gen 1:27). Here, the gendered differentiation that Western academics strain to locate is simply a scriptural given of creaturely life under God. Moreover, we discover not merely a bare bio-sexual "irreducible duality" between genders but a more robust and complex interdependence.

Gender differences are rooted, scripturally, in the order of creation: "For Adam was formed first, then Eve" (1 Tim 2:13; see also Gen 2:7, 21–22). Throughout the biblical narrative, gender is never depicted as an accident of creational existence—neither as something to be dismissed or grudgingly endured—but itself places us, as those who image God, in a particular relation to God and to one another. Here the man plays a founding, or beginning, role in the narrative of human formation, and the woman a completing, or culminating, role. Man is the beginning, woman the end; woman is the completion of man, the end to his beginning (Gen 2:20–23). As the apostle Paul recounts and applies the Genesis account: "The head of the woman is man.... For man was not made from woman, but woman from man.... Nevertheless, ... as woman was made from man, so man is now born of woman. And all things are from God" (1 Cor 11:3, 8, 11–12).

In this context, the assumed hierarchies of "firsts" and "seconds" are regularly engaged and upended. What is prior is sometimes superior (e.g., God in relation to creation) and other times inferior (e.g., the primordial "darkness" in relation to God's "light"). Often the first, who is presumed to be the favored one, is discovered to be in service of the second. Indeed, the basic plotline of Scripture unfolds along these lines: first to the Jew, then to the Greek. Or, first the blessing to Abraham, and only through him to the nations. First to Jacob's line, and only through him, to Esau, and all other families of the earth. Such an ordering, theologically understood, can only be taken as God's good and gracious ordering of the whole—the first for the second, one for the sake of all. The first-and-second relation of male-female comprises its own unique "orderedness," to be engaged on its own terms.

In First Corinthians, Paul uses the word "head" to describe the man's relation of "firstness" to the woman (11:3). While some have supposed that, in doing so, Paul is inserting something new into the scriptural world (viz. "male headship"), in fact Paul is affirming something old. He is taking up a concept familiar to all of Israel, throughout its generations, of the man's identity as household head.[43] Indeed, "headship" is one of the many ways the Scriptures approach and depict humanity's gendered difference, by commending man as "head" in relation to his sexual counterpart, woman, and woman as "body" (or "flesh") of his own body (Gen 2:23-24; Eph 5:23). And all of this, Paul says, is "from God."

While the scripturally extracted principle of "male headship" has indeed become a tool of oppression and division in many places, I will argue that the notion of the man as "head" in relation to the woman is not without scriptural warrant and theological significance. However, its significance is not discovered in *men* or in *men's actions*, per se, but in the One to whom men are created to signify: namely, the renewed man, the Second Adam, Jesus Christ. In this sense, headship is a story that begins "from above," whose earthly significance is determined by its heavenly substance. The meaning of headship will thus be located not in what *men do* as heads but in what *God has done* as "head," and what God is doing in and through human heads of all kinds—and preeminently in his Son as "head over all" (Eph 1:22; Col 2:10).

CONCLUSION

As we have seen, the notion of male headship has become problematic to modern hearers for at least two reasons in modern Western contexts: first, for the particular shape it has taken as a purportedly scripturally legitimized form of male dominance; second, for its apparent commendation of a fixed and binary gender essentialism—an essentialism which has tended to undergird sexist conceptions of the man as the superior sex. The first of these issues carries considerable weight, as affirmations of male headship in modern contexts seem very much to contradict basic definitions of gender equality. In response, I have already pointed forward to an argument that will unfold through the course of the chapters ahead: namely, that while the male "head" in contemporary Western contexts

---

43. Exod 6:14, 25; Num 7:2; 17:18; Josh 14:1; 19:51; 21:1; 22:14; Judg 10:18; 11:8–11; 1 Chr 5:24; 7:2, 7–10, 40; Ezra 8:1; Neh 11:13; Hos 2:2; Mic 3:1; etc.

indeed signals the legitimation and promotion of male dominance, it has not always been so. Moreover, the "head," scripturally defined, is in opposition to such modern conceptualizations of "headship."

With regard to the second of these issues, we have seen that both gender essentialism and the newer constructivism each fail to account for gender difference as both a biologically rooted and socially pluriform reality. As an alternative to these, Linda Alcoff's "gender realism" offers a more convincing framework for understanding the realities and complexities of gender difference. I have contended that a scriptural account of gender—even that suggested by the figure of the male and female as a head and body union—corresponds most fittingly with a realist framework. While many have taken the scriptural categories of male and female in essentializing directions—and many more have criticized the same from constructivist standpoints—I have suggested and will develop the argument that a scripturally delineated vision of gender avoids both constructivist and essentialist pitfalls. Instead, it offers an utterly "realistic" account of humanity as a gendered duality, male and female.

Theologically speaking, the man and woman are the "head" and the "body," respectively, and together in one-flesh union signify and reflect the one-flesh union of Christ and the church, bound together in covenant faithfulness and self-giving love. This has been a consistent theme in Christian theological reflection. However, the concept of the male "head" as it has developed in the West, generally, needs to be distinguished from the "head" as given in the Scriptures. "Headship," in its scriptural use, is not principally concerned with questions of authority, leadership, dominance or privilege but chiefly with *representative responsibility* after the pattern of Christ's relation to his body, the church. In this sense, the application of the "head" figure to gendered human identity turns out to be complex; it is concerned less with gender roles and more with Christian virtues and humanity's heavenly participation.[44]

Such a theological vision is made all the more complex in the face of the present ideological polarizations on questions of gender and sex. My hope is nevertheless that through deep theological engagement with the "head" figure, the basic contours of a theology of gender will emerge

---

44. I speak here of "heavenly participation" after the manner of the Epistle to the Hebrews—which speaks of the "heavenly things" (8:5), the "heavenly country" (11:16), the "heavenly Jerusalem" (12:22), all of which are "heavenly" forms in which we "share" (3:1). As I will argue, the male-female one-flesh relation, too, constitutes a locus of "participation"—in the "heavenly body" of Christ in union with his bride.

which do not simply supplant but rather engage these contemporary concerns—even offering a better word.

CHAPTER 2

On the Etymology of Headship: Defining the Head

Headship, n.: "The fact or position of being the head, or at the head, of something."[1]

There is a mutual relationship between ideas and language: and the influence is not in only one direction.

—Ernst Kantorowicz[2]

Male headship connotes male rule and superiority and so the inequality of the genders. But it has not always been so. The goal of this chapter is to demonstrate that in modern Western contexts headship has become so redefined as to render it incongruous with its antecedent usage in scriptural contexts.[3]

To contrast modern notions of headship in this way with their scriptural antecedents is by no means to suggest that headship in scriptural contexts is never associated with oppressive rule or patterns of male dominance. It is. Still, modern notions of rulership or leadership fail as substitutes for the scriptural title of the "head." As deployed in the OT, the head is not a term that denotes self-serving dominance but service-oriented prominence, emphasizing responsibility, representation, and

---

1. "Headship," *OED*.
2. Kantorowicz, *King's Two Bodies*, 21.
3. Primary attention will be given to English-speaking contexts, with most of the contemporary debates concerning the modern notion of "headship" centered therein. For a brief historical sketch on this point, see Lakey, *Image and Glory*, 6–36.

mutuality.[4] In its Hebrew scriptural use, reference to the head is not fundamentally about "leadership" as in modern evangelical debates or even "authority" as in most contexts throughout the history of the West, but about *representation*.

To demonstrate this disjunction between ancient and modern understandings, I will outline the etymological shifts which have led to the present-day notion of the "head" as it has developed in the West. Traversing through several related cultural-linguistic contexts, we will see how the notion of headship developed into the modern-day notion that now serves to bolster anti-scriptural sexist and male-dominant ideologies.

WESTERN ETYMOLOGIES OF HEADSHIP

Head, n.: "The uppermost part of the body of a human, or the front or uppermost part of the body of an animal."[5]

The Greeks of the Homeric age considered [the head] the location of a *psuchē* difficult to control and opposed to reason and judgment, which were located in the chest and heart.... The Pythagoreans localized sperm in the head... [as the] localization of life force.... Among the Celts... the head was the container of a sacred force, whereas in other ancient and traditional cultures, the head is conceived of as the seat of vital energy, the active principle of the whole individual.

—MICHEL MESLIN[6]

How the anatomical head is conceived in a particular culture inevitably shapes the way the term comes to be used metaphorically. Among the Homeric Greeks for whom the head was "opposed to reason and judgment," the word head (*kephale*) was rarely if ever used as an authority-connoting title.[7] Beginning with the Pythagoreans, however, for whom the head was believed to be the "localization of life force," the head becomes a title used

---

4. See, e.g., Josberger: "Between Rule and Responsibility"; "For Your Good Always."
5. "Head," *OED*.
6. Meslin, "Head," paras. 1–2.
7. *Kephale* in the sense of being the leader or ruler only finds its beginnings in the LXX (Heinrich Schlier, "κεφαλή," *TDNT* 3:73–75)

to identify someone as the "beginning," "origin," or perhaps the "source."⁸ Only with the Septuagint and later Greek writings does the head come to be associated with rule and authority.⁹

It is this final sense—headship as authority and rule—that has come to prominence in the modern West among the dominant Western language groups. Here, the head, as house to the brain, is conceived as the center and source of all knowing, willing, choosing, and acting.¹⁰ In the present social imaginary—where the uppermost positions of social authority are specifically conceived as "heads" (whether of states, schools, corporations, families, etc.)—there is no bodily counterpart equal in perceived prestige, proficiency, or prominence to the head.¹¹ In this context headship can mean only mastery and superiority.¹²

---

8. Quoted in Grudem, "Does κεφαλή Mean 'Source'?," 48. For the argument (contra Grudem) that *kephale* was at times used in this period to denote "source," see Cervin, "Does *Kephale* Mean Source?"

9. Wolters, "Head as Metaphor," 143.

10. The entire history of Western thought evinces a tug-of-war between a head-centered (encephalocentrist) and a heart-centered (cardiocentrist) anthropology, the former deeming the head (or brain, or part of the brain), and the latter the heart, to be the locus of the mind/soul, the "control center," or *hegemonikon* (Galen), of the body. Encephalocentrists typically trace their lineage to Plato and cardiocentrists to Aristotle. It was Aristotle's successors, however, who demonstrated the central role of the brain in psychophysiology, a claim further substantiated by Galen. Although the encephalocentrist position became dominant from the time of Galen onward in the West, the cardiocentric position gained prominence in the East among Arabic physicians, most notably Avicenna, and eventually made its way back into the West through the work of Albertus Magnus, who attempted to reconcile the views. Thus, the encephalocentrist view, though remaining dominant throughout Western history, secured a final victory over Aristotle's cardiocentrism only with the Enlightenment, when neuroscientists finally proved that "the hegemonikon and the true physical correlatives of emotion are to be found not in the heart but in the brain" (C. Smith, "Cardiocentric Neurophysiology," 12). See also Crivellato and Ribatti, "Soul, Mind, Brain"; Santoro et al., "Anatomic Location of Soul."

11. The "follow your heart" slogan, thematized in so many Hollywood films, remains a part of popular culture, to be sure. The prominence of this theme perhaps demonstrates the persistence of the cardiocentric view into the present (see previous footnote). Nonetheless, it remains aspirational and is rarely (even in Hollywood) commended as a trustworthy motto to normatively direct one's life. Rather, it functions as the exception that proves the rule, often subsumed within broader narratives of self-denial, taking responsibility, "using one's head," and "doing one's duty." See Doak, "Hollywood, Popular Culture."

12. The head as master of the body is a long-standing and prevailing metaphor in Western thought, beginning at least as early as Herophilus, who deemed the head the "command center" of the body (Herophilus, *Art of Medicine*). The metaphor was developed by Calcidius (mid-fourth century) in a commentary on Plato's *Timaeus* where

Contrast this with the ancient Hebrew imaginary of the OT, where the heart (*lebab*) is the source and center of all intellectual, emotional and volitional activity, "the center of life and the epitome of the person."[13] In such a context—where the source of one's being and acting is centered not in the head but in the heart—even while headship continues to denote a certain "prominence" vis-à-vis other bodily members, such prominence will more aptly be understood in terms of complementarity, not superiority. In this context, formal prominence is not synonymous with superiority, as though the prominent position of the head were somehow more objectively desirable than the concealed and more centralized position of the heart. Head and heart in this bodily metaphorical framework can readily be conceptualized as counterparts of equal regard.

In fact, in a Hebrew bodily metaphorical framework, the notion that the head might "order the body around" is rendered metaphorically incomprehensible, since the head cannot act on its own volition. Volition comes from the heart, with the head serving *its* interests. Here the head cannot "lead" the body; nor is it in "authority over" the body. Rather, the head is truly a *part of* the body. Moreover, the OT evinces no sense that the head is distinct from the body—no head-body duality.

In sum, when the head is conceived as the unequalled, supreme, and domineering part of the body, male headship suggests inequality, supremacy, and dominance of the head over the body, the man over the woman. This is where we find ourselves in the modern West.

---

he writes: "the order of the commonwealth imitates the divine order: the head occupies the chief place and holds dominion over the other members, being the seat of wisdom." The metaphor was taken up in the twelfth century by John of Salisbury, reflecting on and popularizing Aesop's fable "The Belly and the Members" (Harvey, *Body Politic*, esp. 12, 15).

13. A. Dihle, "ψυχή," *TDNT* 9:626. The ancient Hebrew heart-centric anthropology is to also be distinguished from the ancient Greeks for whom the "mind" (*dianoia*) or the "soul" (*psyche*) were most often deemed the center of being, not the heart. Only with the LXX does the Greek *kardia* become an equivalent of the Hebrew *leb* or *lebab* (heart), as "the focus of [man's] being and activity" (9:609). This observation helps to explain the apparent discrepancy between the *Shema Yisrael* as given in Hebrew (Deut 6:5 in particular: "You shall love the Lord your God with all your heart and with all your soul and with all your might") and the Shema as quoted in Greek, which adds "with all your mind (*dianoia*)" (Matt 22:37; Mark 12:30; Luke 10:27), arguably because in the Hebrew context, to love the Lord with all of one's heart (*lebab*) necessarily involved the intellect, whereas in a Greek context the "heart" (*kardia*) was more narrowly understood. Indeed, in Classical Greek the use of the word "heart" is almost entirely physiological. See Johannes Behm, "νοῦς," *TDNT* 4:954–56; F. Baumgärtel, "καρδία," *TDNT* 3:606–8.

But this was not always so. Headship has not always signified authoritative rule. As we will explore, it was instead conceptualized as a place of prominence, with the head as the representative member of the body. The implicit inequality now so bound to the notion of male headship is more than a matter of conceptual shift, however (from a heart- to a head-centric view of human personhood). The course had already been set for the present transmogrified sexist notion of male headship well before the move toward modern head-centered biologies, before the heart was ever demoted from its place as the "center of life and the epitome of the person."

The survey that follows will outline the etymological lineage of headship in the Western tradition. We will focus on three dominant Western language groups (Hellenic, Italic, Germanic), wherein headship became predominantly and narrowly defined in terms of rulership and dominance.[14] These transformations contrast with ancient scriptural (Hebrew and Greek) understandings and reveal that "headship," once a term that bespoke corporeal unity, representation, and responsibility—as of the head *with and for* the body—has in Western usage come to connote gender inequality—the head *over* the body—the man *over* the woman.[15]

A. Hellenic Heads: Late Ancient Developments

The word for "head" in each of the three dominant Western language groups is etymologically linked to the Greek *kephale*.[16] As noted above, the Greek term was not used as an honorific title in Homeric Greek and did not denote authority or rule. Only in the process of Roman Hellenization did the term develop a "Hebrew-like" titular use, exemplified

---

14. In order to prove this pattern in Western language groups I include considerations of proto-Germanic origins along with examples from the three dominant strands of Indo-European languages in the West—namely, Hellenic (considering developments in Greek), Italic (considering developments in Latin and French), and Germanic (considering developments in German and English).

15. Whereas Western cultures have developed an increasingly specified understanding of "headship" as a category, it is important to note that the OT offers a diffuse and unelaborated depiction of the "head," variously and flexibly deployed as a title within a context of comprehensive corporeal figures. Only later in Western history does the "head" become an official office ("headship"), shaped by a melding of NT language with antique political, ecclesial, and legal concepts, such that by the modern era "headship" has become concretely defined in terms of rule and dominion, as we shall see.

16. Kroonen, *Etymological Dictionary of Proto-Germanic*, 173.

and codified in the Septuagint and later in New Testament writings.[17] Indeed, until the Septuagint, the Greeks did not deem a family's chief representative or leader the "head" (*kephale*), but characteristically the "ruler" (*archon*). It was only from the third century BCE onward that *kephale* came to be increasingly used as a synonym for *archon* and was popularly used to denote the family's chief representative.[18]

Whereas for the ancient Hebrews the father, chief, judge, or king—even God—was defined and titled as "head" of a corpus, the Greeks defined these same "uppermost" persons principally as "rulers over" a people. The prominent position in and for the family was not the *kephale*, but rather the *patriarch*—the *ruler* (or *beginning*) of the family. Only with the Septuagint did this begin to change. When the Hebrew Scriptures were translated into Greek, in each place where the Hebrew term *rosh* (head) was used to denote a person's title it came to be translated as either *kephale* or *archon*. In this way *rosh* came to be deployed generally in the Greek language as a synonym for *archon* (ruler). Whereas for the Hebrews "head" remained the dominant term to denote the father's function in the family—a term that bound the notion of prominence to notions of unitive love and responsibility—when translated into Greek, Hebrew headship came to be taken captive under the aegis of *rule and authority*, defined explicitly as "rulership."[19]

The Greeks indeed upheld a gendered hierarchy conceived explicitly in terms of male rule and female subordination, codified in the laws of ancient Greece and traced back as early as Aristotle.[20] According to Aristotle's infamous sexual hierarchy, men were deemed whole beings, closer to perfection than women, less emotionally vulnerable, more resilient, truthful, courageous, and reasonable, of better mind, stronger, and

---

17. See Wolters, "Head as Metaphor," 142."

18. See Bedale, "Meaning of κεφαλή," 211.

19. See Parmentier, "Greek Patristic Foundations." See also Ruether, "Sexism and Misogyny," 84.

20. According to Aristotle (384–322 BCE), "The relation of male to female is by nature a relation of superior to inferior and ruler to ruled" (*Politics*, 1245b12). Plato has the Greek general Meno depicting man alone as "competent to manage the affairs of his city," whereas woman's duty was that of "ordering the house well, looking after the property indoors, and obeying her husband" (Plato, *Meno*, 71e, 72a). Legally speaking, in Homeric and classical times, Greek women had no personal legal status generally but were subsumed within the *oikos* (household) headed by the male *kyrios* (master). See Foxhall, "Household, Greek." See also Cantarella, "Greek Law and Family"; MacDowell et al., "Marriage Law, Greek."

more fit to rule.²¹ It is no surprise, then, that when *kephale* finally came into use to denote the Greek *patriarch*, such headship was understood and expressed explicitly in terms of male superiority and rule.

B. Italic Heads: Medieval Developments

A similar development occurs in Latin, from late antiquity through the High Middle Ages. Just as the Greek term for head was rarely if ever used as a title of prominence before its scriptural refashioning, the same is true of the term in Classical Latin. Only in post-classical Latin (from the third century CE onward) does head (*caput*) take on a semantic range nearly identical to the *kephale* of Hellenized Greek. This is the direct result of Latin engagement with the Jewish and Christian uses of the term "head," as the Scriptures and concepts of the church are translated into Latin. In fact, *caput* is rarely ever used as a title that denotes an office until the period of Rome's Christianization, beginning under Constantine.²²

In its Latin use, however, the "head" title quickly becomes subsumed and redefined within preexisting Roman notions of the "rule" or "power of the father" (*patria potestas*). During the post-classical period the household "head" becomes synonymous with the Roman *paterfamilias*, the "father of the family," wielding an extraordinary power of life and death over his dependents.²³ In this way, Hebrew and early Christian notions of headship were baptized into the Latin linguistic world of Rome, now reconceptualized in terms of dominical power—the *caput* as the *paterfamilias*.

The notion of the household head thus took to itself all of the preestablished Greco-Roman connotations of patriarchy as "rulership." Here, man's headship *is* his rulership (*patria potestas, dominica potestas, pater patriae*). Head (*caput*), as a title, here sheds its corporeal and inherently organic dimension—as prominent member of the body—and becomes increasingly reduced to a synonym for "ruler."²⁴

---

21. See, e.g., Aristotle, *History of Animals*, 9.608b.

22. See Charlton Lewis and Short, *New Latin Dictionary*, 289. See also Wolters, "Head as Metaphor," 150; Kantorowicz, *King's Two Bodies*, 21.

23. The Roman *paterfamilias* has its own distinct character and history, involving a stricter form of patriarchy relative to the Greek patriarch and the Hebrew head. See also Bradley, *Discovering the Roman Family*; Dixon, *Roman Family*; Saller, *Patriarchy, Property, and Death*; Grubbs, "Promoting *Pietas*," 379, 382.

24. Much the same would happen later in the French language with the Latin-derived

In time, this Romanized version of headship—*caput* as *paterfamilias*—is extended from the *familia* to the *ecclesia*, and from the *ecclesia* to the *politia*. This extension of Roman headship into ecclesial and imperial polities would develop over several centuries. For the first thousand years of the Western Church's existence, *caput* was rarely used ecclesially to denote human rule or to designate an ecclesial office, but instead was almost always reserved as a title for Christ in relation to the church.[25] From the outset, the Roman Church was *corpus Christi*—Christ's own bodily presence in the world, of which Christ alone was head. The most prominent ecclesial leaders, including the bishops of Rome, Antioch, Alexandria, Jerusalem, and Constantinople, were deemed *episcopus*, *patriarchae*, or *papa* of their respective ecclesial jurisdictions, never *caput ecclesiae*.[26] Likewise, the emperor was conceived primarily as *princeps* of an empire (among his legion of titles), never *caput* of a body.

---

chef, where its corporeal meaning becomes largely eclipsed by its authority-connoting use as a title. The French *chef*, originally meaning "a head" (derived from the Latin *caput*) is largely eclipsed by the term *tête* for denoting the anatomical head, with *chef* taking on connotations of leadership and authority almost exclusively (as with the English derivatives, "chef" and "chief"). In this way the head (*chef*) becomes an authority-connoting title that is practically disentangled from the corporeal dimension. See Brachet, *Etymological Dictionary of French*, 11–12, 84, 383. This is borne out in the Cambridge French-English dictionary, where *chef* is translated "personne qui dirige" (person in charge), "chief, leader, boss." This transition from *chef* as anatomical head of a body to *chef* as leader over others vividly illustrates one of the challenges with certain modern Western notions of headship. Where the head has become synonymous with authority—the head ruling *over* the body—and loses the corporeal dimension—the head as a *member of* the body—headship becomes stripped of its unitive dimension, with the mutuality and responsibility it implies. So, while Eph 5:23 (*ho Christos kephale tes ekklesias*) affirms Christ's prominent position vis-à-vis the church in a corporeal dimension, the same verse in standard French translations (e.g., la Bible de Jérusalem) loses this dimension, resulting in a claim about Christ's authority over the church ("Christ est le chef de l'Église") instead of about his preeminent place in union with the church, as head (*tête*) of the body. The more recent "thought-for-thought" translation, la Bible du Semeur, seeks to correct this: "Christ est la tête, le chef de l'Église."

25. See Schaff, *Mediaeval Christianity*, 218–24.

26. In the late sixth century, when the patriarch of Constantinople was deemed "universal bishop" at a Constantinopolitan synod in 588, Gregory the Great, bishop of Rome, was repulsed by the title. Gregory demanded that his successor renounce "the wicked title," writing that "whosoever calls himself universal priest, or desires to be called so, was the forerunner of Antichrist" (*Ep.* 7.13, cited in Schaff, *Mediaeval Christianity*, 220). In contrast Gregory "called himself, in proud humility, the 'servant of the servants of God'" (221). According to Schaff, Gregory "regarded the four patriarchs of Constantinople, Alexandria, Antioch, and Jerusalem . . . as co-ordinate leaders of the church under Christ, the supreme head, . . . yet after all with a firm belief in a papal primacy" (219).

In the twelfth century terminological changes created new possibilities for reconceptualizing Roman polities, beginning with shifts in the terms of ecclesial polity, from christic (the church as "the body of Christ") to generic (the church as "a body politic").[27] The church, which had heretofore been deemed *corpus Christi*, was now deemed *corpus mysticum*—a term which had to this point designated the eucharistic host. This latter term now effectively disentangled the church from its unique christic identity, bound as a body to Christ as its head, and instead rendering it a generic, "mystical," sociopolitical body, comparable to any other. "In short," Ernst Kantorowicz explains, "the expression 'mystical body,' which originally had a liturgical or sacramental meaning, took on a connotation of sociological content."[28]

As long as the church remained *corpus Christi* it made little sense to deem any bishop or pope its "head."[29] However, once redescribed as the more generic *corpus mysticum*, the church as "body politic" now stood in need of a political head.[30] In this way, the title of pope as *caput ecclesiae*, which had been so strongly opposed a few centuries earlier, was accepted and soon "summarized and dogmatized" by Pope Boniface VIII at the start of the fourteenth century.[31] As Hermann of Schilditz would write shortly thereafter, "Just as all the limbs in the body natural refer to the head, so do all the faithful in the mystical body *of the Church* refer to the head of the Church, the Roman Pontiff."[32] Prior resistance to deeming the pope *caput ecclesiae* was thus overcome, to be further formalized

27. See Lubac, *Corpus Mysticum*, 106, 109–12, 117–18.

28. Kantorowicz, *King's Two Bodies*, 196. Kantorowicz explains further, "[Until the twelfth century] it had been the custom to talk about the Church as the "mystical body of Christ" (*corpus Christi mysticum*) which sacramentally alone makes sense. Now, however, the Church, which had been *the* mystical body of Christ, became *a* mystical body in its own right . . . a mystical corporation . . . a juristic abstraction. . . . Above all, that originally liturgical notion, which formerly served to exalt the Church united in the Sacrament, began to be used in the hierarchical Church as a means to exalt the position of the emperor-like pope" (201–2; emphasis in original).

29. The title *caput ecclesiae* as applied to bishops and popes seems to have arisen for the first time only in the eighth century, and not dogmatically, but in a personal letter with clear political motivations, when John VI of Constantinople addresses Pope Constantine as the head of the church (Schaff, *Mediaeval Christianity*, 456). When in the eleventh century *caput* is used more formally as a papal designation it is met with opposition. See Lubac, *Corpus Mysticum*, 115.

30. See Lubac, *Corpus Mysticum*, 115; Kantorowicz, *King's Two Bodies*, 211.

31. Kantorowicz, *King's Two Bodies*, 194.

32. Hermann of Schilditz, *Contra Hereticos*, 11.c.3, cited in Kantorowicz, *King's Two Bodies*, 203.

and ratified at the Council of Florence (1431–49) when "the pope was acknowledged not only as the successor of Peter and Vicar of Christ, but also as 'the head of the whole church.'"[33]

Such terminological changes were no accident. As the Roman Church was seeking to establish its authority as a supranational entity with centralized power in the pope, recasting the pope as head of this "mystical body" would certainly serve this end. But it would also serve to politicize the title of "head" when used as a symbol of papal power. The Roman-styled *caput* thus secured for itself through the pope a body larger than ever.

It is only with this reconceptualization of the *ecclesia* as a "body politic" that the Roman *politia* follows suit, reconceptualizing the emperor now as head of a body.[34] Indeed, only in the fourteenth century was the person of the king finally and fully recast as head of a body, mimicking the pope's headship of the church. As Lucas de Penna would write later in the fourteenth century, "Just as men are joined together spiritually in the spiritual body, the head of which is Christ . . . . so are men joined together morally and politically in the *respublica*, which is a body the head of which is the Prince."[35] It is Lucas de Penna who thus first redefines the Roman *politia* in ecclesio-corporational terms, with the prince recast as *caput regni*.[36]

---

33. Schaff, *Mediaeval Christianity*, 285, citing Hefele. Moreover, by the time of the Tridentine Council, the papal titles would escalate from the primitive *vicarius Petri* to *vicarius Christi* to *ipsius Dei in terris Vicarius*, i.e., from vicar of Peter to vicar of Christ to the vicar of God himself (*Mediaeval Christianity*, 204). The pope's title as head of the church was thus irreversibly dogmatized, reiterated at the Second Vatican Council, when the pope was again named the bishop of bishops, vicar of Christ, and head of the church. See Schaff, *Creeds of Christendom*, 1.151.

34. To be sure, the head and body metaphor had ancient precedent as a political metaphor—at least as early as Plato—but only in the thirteenth century did it gain widespread acceptance *as* a political metaphor, initially through John of Salisbury's *Policraticus*; and only in the fourteenth century is it used of the king as such. See Kantorowicz, *King's Two Bodies*, 14–17, 22.

35. Lucas de Penna, on *Codex Justiniani*, 11.58.7n8 (Lyon, 1582), quoted in Kantorowicz, *King's Two Bodies*, 216. Lubac explains this same dynamic: "Once the Church had triumphed over the empire and in some way succeeded to its title, Christian Rome made wider use of this [body] metaphor . . . replacing [Rome] and its Caesar, in the role of head, with regard to the universe—or rather now with regard to the universal Church—which played the role of body" (*Corpus Mysticum*, 86).

36. "The Church as the supra-individual collective body of Christ, of which he was both the head and the husband," says Kantorowicz, "found its exact parallel in the state as the supra-individual collective body of the Prince, of which he was both the head and the husband—'The Prince is the head of the realm, and the realm the body of

The sacramental-christological language of the church is henceforth co-opted for political use among the Roman-shaped realms of the Western world, a dynamic soon to be inherited among the English.[37] The two most powerful figures of the medieval West, pope and emperor, are recast as political and mystical "heads" of their respective "bodies," with the power struggles between them recast for the first time as a struggle for "headship" over the church. In this way, the title of "head" is eventually swept up into an ecclesio-political jostling for power—a battle of heads to secure the rights of the *caput ecclesiae*, conceived as the *paterfamilias* over the transnational ecclesial body.

In sum, as Rome was Christianized, Roman Christianity perpetuated a Greco-Roman-styled tradition of "headship as rulership"—a far cry from the sacramental union of Christ and the church and from the scriptural and christological articulation of the head as one with, bound to the interests of, the body in self-giving love.[38] As the Hebrew notion of the head was translated and received into the Greco-Roman world and carried into the Christian era of the Roman Empire, headship became a synonym for rulership, dominical power, and supremacy in political governance.

To be clear, to contrast the Hebrew "head" title with Roman headship in this way is not to suggest that the "head" in Hebrew was devoid of "rule" or "authority" in its range of meaning; yet it could never have been reduced to this. While the titular use of *rosh* maintained, at least in principle, the significance of the head's *union with* and *responsibility to* the "body," headship came to be a matter not so much of *union with* and *responsibility to* but *rule over*, a notion increasingly associated with and defined as political "rule," as became clear in the medieval and early modern church.

---

the Prince.' In other words, the jurist transferred to the Prince and the state the most important social, organic, and corporational elements normally serving to explain the relations between Christ and the Church—that is, Christ as the groom of the Church, as the head of the mystical body, and as the mystical body itself. . . . [Such] arguments exercised a surprisingly great influence in later times [e.g., in sixteenth-century France and England]" (*King's Two Bodies*, 218).

37. Kantorowicz notes that, by the sixteenth century, during the reign of Henry VIII, "the analogy between the body and the state had by now become something of a cliché" (*King's Two Bodies*, 229).

38. That the scriptural "head" title suggests a corporeal (unitive, self-giving) framework, is not lost on Augustine (*WSA* 3.2:41).

Thus, a Greek patriarchalized headship, styled as the "rule of the father" in its Roman-Christian trappings, came to permeate the entire empire, and has become the established norm in various permutations in and through the expansion of Western cultures for nearly two millennia. This strand of Greco-Roman headship is indeed the direct ancestor of headship as conceived in the modern West.

C. Germanic Heads: Early Modern Developments

Among the Germanic languages, the word for "head" finds a common proto-Germanic root, *habuda*. The various German adaptations of this term (*habuda* > *houbit* > *houpt* > *hauft* > *kopf*) evidence a definite semantic borrowing from the Greek *kephale*, with a nearly identical semantic range.[39] As with the Greek term, the Germanic head title denotes the chief or leader; and it is from the Germanic that the English "head" first emerges, likewise with an almost identical semantic range.[40]

From the era of early Old English (ca. 650–900) onward, the title (*heafod*, *heafd*, etc.) is used to designate a "person or thing holding the senior or most important position; a chief or leader, and related senses," most commonly referring to scriptural and ecclesial figures.[41] By the fourteenth century, the use of the term as a title consistently centers on the question of who is "head" of the church on earth, whether Christ or pope—a point of vigorous political debate that persists through the nineteenth century.[42]

In England this debate gained particular momentum when Christ and the pope were joined by a third candidate in vying for the role of "head of the church"—namely, the English monarch. Henry VIII dubbed himself, and those who would succeed him, *supremum caput*, "supreme

---

39. Kroonen, *Etymological Dictionary of Proto-Germanic*. Indeed, from the eighth to eleventh centuries, the German language was significantly shaped by the Scriptures. See C. Edwards, *Beginnings of German Literature*, esp. his first essay, "Tohu Wabohu."

40. See Healey, "Old English Head," 175; Kluge, *Etymological Dictionary of German*, 137; "Head," in Engeroff, *English-German Dictionary of Idioms*, 115.

41. See "Head," *OED*.

42. E.g., John Wycliffe emphasizes that *Christ*, not the pope, is "Heed of þis Chirche" (ca. 1384) (Wyclif, *Select English Works*, 3:339). The Swiss Reformer Joachim Vadianus (1484–1551) argues against his opponents' claims that the "chyrche of Rome should be hed chyrche of all other[s]" (*Of the olde faythe*, 36). The English historian John Foxe remarks, "Thus began first Rome to take an head aboue all other Churches" (*Actes and Monuments*, 2:4).

head," of the church in the 1534 Act of Supremacy, a bold political statement supplanting the pope as head of the church in England and asserting the king's divine right to rule.[43] The title was short lived, however, among the English monarchs. It was passed on to Henry's son, Edward VI (1547–53) only to be repealed in 1555 by Edward's half-sister Queen Mary I, who sought to restore unity between England and Rome.[44] Even when Elizabeth I (another half-sister) took the crown and reinstated a renewed Act of Supremacy (1559), Elizabeth took the title of Supreme Governor rather than Supreme Head. She did this apparently for three reasons: first, to appease Roman Catholics for whom the pope was the head of the church; second, to fend off Protestant concerns that the title of Supreme Head of the Church was to be reserved for Christ alone;[45] and third, because Protestants and Catholics alike claimed it improper for a woman to take the title "head" of the church.[46] In this way, with Elizabeth's renewed Act of Supremacy what was disputed theologically in England became determined by formal polity—that the designation "head of the church" was unacceptable for any person, male or female, monarch or pope, save Christ himself.

Looking back at the course of these sixteenth-century English debates it becomes clear that the meaning of the "head" had developed in divergent directions. The English Roman Catholic priest Thomas Harding (1516–72) demonstrates this well. For Harding, the head needed to

43. The official Roman Catholic position that the pope is head of the church is traced at least as far back as the Second Council of Nicea (787 CE) where it was asserted that "the holy Roman Church" is "the head of all the Churches of God." Moreover, it refers to Peter, the first bishop of Rome, as "the supreme head of the Apostles." Still, even here it is only Christ who is given the explicit title "head of the Church." See Schaff, *Seven Ecumenical Councils*, 4.

44. Queen Mary had asked at one time, "How can I, a woman, be Head of the Church, who by scripture am forbidden to speak in the church?" (Marshall, *Heretics and Believers*, 420).

45. "It was, in fact, a necessary concession to the Queen's more fervent Protestant supporters. Some were mindful that Calvin had described Henry VIII's supreme headship as 'blasphemy'. But a vein of English Protestant unease about the title can be traced back to Tyndale" (Marshall, *Heretics and Believers*, 430).

46. See Neale, "Elizabethan Acts," 308. When the first "bill of supremacy" passed under Elizabeth's rule, it assigned her the same title as her father and brother, "supreme head." In response, another bill was passed to modify this title. One spokesperson, Archbishop Heath, noted that because of Elizabeth's sex this title was a stumbling block to radicals as well as to conservatives. "'Her highness beyinge a woman by birthe and nature, is not qualyfied by God's worde to feed the flock of Chryst'; and he went on . . . to quote St. Paul for confirmation" (Strype, *Annals*, 1.2:399–407, quoted in Neale, "Elizabethan Acts," 321).

be understood in two respects. On the one hand, the title could be understood in terms of an "inward influence," whereby the power and virtue of the body is "derived from the head" and involves the "power to justify" its members. Headship of this sort emphasized the corporeal dimension of headship and was attributable to Christ alone. On the other hand, being "head" could be understood in terms of an "outward government" with "power and authority" over the "outward acts" of its members. Headship in this sense was a matter of political power and was shared by Christ with the Roman pontiff and other earthly authorities.[47]

In this way, Harding clarifies what had happened with the use of "head" as a title in the Western Church: the head as a designation for earthly rulers had been dislodged from its corporeal-christological meaning. The title of head could only be attributed to humans in respect of their "outward government," involving "power and authority" over the "outward acts" of their members. Headship, as a sociopolitical term, was a matter of power and outward influence, now devoid of any "inward" or corporeal connectivity to the body.

Thus, through scriptural-ecclesial discourse in highly politicized contexts, the meaning of the "head" as a position or title was forged in the English-speaking world. And it is precisely in this context of political debate over the propriety of deeming pope, king, or Christ as "head" of the church that the term "head*ship*," newly coined, comes into being, specifically denoting "supremacy, primacy; leadership."[48]

But what use did the developing English-speaking world have for such a novel term? The title of "head" was beginning to change from an ontological category to a category of social performance, from a person-defining title to a title that designated a set of functions. In the scriptural context, the man "is" the head (1 Cor 11:3; Eph 5:23). Now, the man had to carry out a task or a role, an office, called "headship."

With no direct cognates in Hebrew, Greek, Latin, or in any of the Indo-European languages, it appears that this new noun, "headship," evolved uniquely in the English language.[49] Only in 1565, in an interaction between Thomas Harding and Bishop John Jewel (1522–71) do we find the term "headship" explicitly deployed.[50] Here Harding uses (coins?)

---

47. T. Harding, *Confutation*.

48. "Headship," OED.

49. An early equivalent, "Heedhode" (viz. "Headhood"), is first reportedly used by Reginald Pecock, bishop of Chichester, ca. 1449 ("Headhood, n.," *OED*).

50. Harding's *Confutation* is written in response to Jewel's 1562 *Apology*.

the term in order to discuss the relationship between *Christ's* status as head and "humaine [i.e., the pope's] headship." Their correspondence sets off a short chain of responses,[51] a debate between Roman Catholics and Protestants centered precisely on the question of who is the rightful head of the church—a debate that would be carried on and codified on both Roman and Protestant sides.[52]

Until this time, being the "head," whether of household, church, empire, or whatever, was defined not as an abstract concept but always *in relation to* something or someone. However, with the early modern invention of the term "headship" came the advent of an abstract position, a universalizable role, divorced from being the head *of* something (or someone). In abstraction from a particular "body," "headship" denotes a position of rule and authority over an entity (of whatever sort). This new term, hitherto undefined, was quickly filled with meaning by those who invented it. And for early modern English Christians, like their predecessors, headship could only mean power and authority over another.[53] This meaning is evident in all three contexts in which the term "headship" is most commonly used: in the church, school, and home.

In the church, as noted above, "headship" came into being and was popularized through arguments over who was its true head—Christ, king, or pope—and at the bottom of this argument was the question of authority. To whom is the Christian ultimately to submit? Whose voice is finally authoritative: Christ speaking in the Scriptures, Christ speaking through the pope, or Christ reigning through the king? This conflict

---

51. Jewel responds directly to Harding, and is in turn addressed by Thomas Stapleton, an English Roman Catholic historian. The following year, Jewel issues another response; and after a final published response from Harding and a related comment from Theodore Beza, this original "headship debate" apparently comes to a close. See Jewel, *Defence*.

52. For Protestants the debate became codified in the Westminster Confession of Faith (1646): "There is no other head of the Church but the Lord Jesus Christ. Nor can the Pope of Rome, in any sense, be head thereof" (WCF 25.6). For Roman Catholics it appears the concluding magisterial word to this debate is given at the First Vatican Council in 1870: "If anyone says that the blessed Apostle Peter was not established by the Lord Christ as . . . the visible head of the whole militant Church . . . let him be anathema" (Pius X, "Pastor Aeternus," 3.2)

53. The earliest English publications containing the word "headship" connect it to concepts such as supreme authority, supremacy, universal jurisdiction, power, rule, domination, lordship, privilege. By the seventeenth century these word associations persist, even as the concept becomes increasingly codified (e.g., with talk of "the doctrine of headship") and is increasingly associated with political power—with words such as preeminence, royal, infallible, honor, kingship. See "Headship," EEBO.

over authority was only exacerbated as the debate centered on papal rule, where headship as rule, not as mystical union, became the focus.

Outside of ecclesial contexts, teachers and principals in educational settings were designated "heads," with headship thus denoting authority over the educational establishment.[54] Likewise, within the family, headship came to refer to the husband's position of authority in relation to his wife and children. This use became especially prevalent in American Protestant communities following the Reformation, with a characteristic emphasis on the husband's rule of the home and the wife's subordination.[55]

We have thus observed that among each of the major Western language groups (Hellenic, Italic, Germanic) the term "head" came to share a similar semantic range, originating with a semantic borrowing from the Hebrew (*rosh*, as the principal or representative member in relation to the body), refracted through a Greek social imaginary (*kephale*, as the *archon*, the ruling member), and then carried forward into Italic and Germanic languages, primarily denoting supremacy, rule, and authority. Some of these contexts have retained the corporeal dimension of the head and body metaphor, thus uniting supremacy, rule, hierarchy, and authority with complementary senses of responsibility, unity and mutuality. What is common throughout these languages, however, is that headship comes to denote superiority and rule vis-à-vis the body. "Male headship" at present cannot but signify the supremacy of the man over the woman.

We now turn our attention to the ancient Hebrew (OT) use of the "head" title in order to compare and contrast it with its present use in the West.

---

54. This is the secondary meaning provided in the *OED*: "The position or office of head of an educational institution; a headmastership or headmistress-ship; a principalship." From the sixteenth century onward it became common to speak of one's "headship" of/over a particular school. The *OED* records the earliest use of "headmaster" in 1545 and "headmistress" in 1632.

55. Marilyn Westerkamp narrates the history leading to this dynamic, specifically in the early American colonial household. With the Reformation prioritization of marriage and family, each family becomes conceptualized as a "little church" with the men as patriarchs, priests, and kings, and women "destined . . . to subject themselves to the rule of their husbands" (*Women and Religion*, 4–5).

HEBREW HEADSHIP:
A NEAR EASTERN SEED PLANTED IN WESTERN SOIL

In the OT, the head (*rosh*) refers to the top- or front-most anatomical part of a human or animal, the "top" or "height" of an object, or the "beginning" of a period of time. As an OT title, it most often indicates the relation of the father (*av*) to his household.[56] Ancient Israel traced its history back through prominent male householders—"heads"—beginning with Abraham, Isaac, and Jacob. Each of the twelve sons of Jacob was accordingly deemed head of his tribe (Num 1:1–16; Exod 6). In this way, the meaning of *rosh* as the anatomical head, "the uppermost part," is extended to describe the "uppermost" or most "prominent" person of the family, normatively the father. It is thus the father, in and through Israel, who becomes the paradigm for "heading" tribes and nations.[57]

Within Israel's Scriptures, the meaning of the head title is thus closely tied to the man's identity and function as father. Here the head (viz. father) does not "play the role" of the head; he *is* the head. As such, women, other men, children, and servants were ultimately under his legal care and responsibility. At times they were grouped together as part of his wealth (e.g., Gen 12:20; 13:1; Exod 20:17), at times subsumed within his name and identity. In him the family might rise or fall. His status was the status of the family, his shame the shame of the family, his salvation the salvation of the family. As such, the household head was indivisibly joined together with his household, his responsibility to them as to his own body.[58]

Surveying the standard lexicons, most biblical scholars agree that *rosh* is a synonym for "chief" or "leader."[59] While *rosh* is not without these connotations, however, I contend that in the OT context *rosh* is most fundamentally about *representation*, not leadership or chiefdom.[60] This

---

56. This is the most common though not the only use of *rosh* as a title. It is also used to denote officers in Israel's judiciary, priestly and military contexts. See "rōš," in R. Thomas, *NAS Exhaustive Concordance*; BDB.

57. E.g., Exod 6:14, 25; Num 1:4, 16; 7:2; 17:3; 31:26; 32:28; 36:1; etc.

58. Paul Heger argues that the man functions throughout the Hebrew Bible as legal representative of the household and of the woman in particular, the two comprised as a one-flesh union and thus a singular identity (*Women in the Bible*, 504).

59. E.g., see "rōš," in R. Thomas, *NAS Exhaustive Concordance*.

60. Stephen Bedale acknowledges that translations of *rosh* need to be constrained by the head metaphor, "connected, not with the controlling influence of the head over the limbs, but with the idea of priority." He goes on to note that *rosh* in the Hebrew Scriptures is clearly distinguished from the *qatsin* as "ruler" or "commander" (e.g., Judg

becomes clearer when the head is set in the context of Hebrew organ symbolism.

The head is one part of a broader Hebrew anatomy of emotion and thought, of being and doing, in which bodily parts represent more than mere vehicles for the inner psychic life. Bodily organs were understood as intimately tied to human emotions and actions. "Rage, lust, hunger, joy, compassion, and so on were once considered not as abstract moods or psychological states but as passions associated with specific anatomical parts."[61] In this living anatomy, the innards were typically presented as the locus of emotion, with compassion coming from the bowels, joy from the liver, and discomfort from the kidneys. Hands were associated with power and ability (Gen 16:6–12), and the face with encounter and presence (Gen 32:21; Exod 33:14–15). Various anatomical parts also manifested a moral dimension. Eyes, for example, can be haughty, greedy, or benevolent (Prov 21:4; 22:9; Matt 6:22–23), while the healing of one's "navel" and "bones" comes from turning one's eyes from evil (Prov 3:7–8). "Fat (Pss 17:10; 119:70; Jgs 3:22) serves as a metaphor for human unreceptivity.... Kidneys are the bodily part that Yahweh examines for human malice or goodness (Pss 7:10; 11:2; 26:2; 73:21; Jer 11:20; 17:10)."[62] It is not incidental, in this perspective, that the foreskin of the male sex organ is associated with "the flesh" of sinful nature, needing to be cut off.[63]

If joy resides in the liver, mercy in the bowels, goodness (or malice) in the kidneys, and if thinking, feeling and acting all arise from the heart, what role, then, does the head play in the schema of this living Hebrew anatomy?

Here *the head principally functions as a synecdoche for the whole person, the representative member of the body*.[64] As the most prominent

---

11:11) ("Meaning of κεΦαλή," 213). For him, Paul's use of *kephale* is an extension of *rosh*, "signifying not mere 'overlordship', but rather a certain relationship of one to the *being* of another" (215).

61. Peters, "Bowels of Mercy," 28.

62. M. Smith, "Heart and Innards," 429.

63. For more on the Hebrew anatomy of emotion, see Schroer and Staubli, *Body Symbolism in Bible*; M. Smith, "Heart and Innards." For a broader survey of Indo-European organ symbolism, see Onians, *Origins of European Thought*.

64. In Israel, the human head "represents, as *pars pro toto*, the whole person. When a crowd of people has to be counted, one counts heads" (Schroer and Staubli, *Body Symbolism in Bible*, 83). Admittedly, here I am at odds with the majority opinion that understands *rosh* fundamentally as a synonym for chiefdom. As I have sought to demonstrate, however, this position fails to relate the titular-metaphorical use of *rosh* to

(topmost) member of the body, the head *represents* or "sums up" the rest of the body (see Exod 30:12; Num 1:2, 49; 4:2, 22; Ps 139:17; Prov 8:26).[65] So, when a census is taken, men are counted "head by head" (*legulgolotam*), the head indicating the whole person (Num 1:2). Each "father's house" is represented by a single "head" (*rosh*), the "head of the household" functioning as the representative member for the whole familial body (Num 1:4). The whole body is in this sense present in and with the head. This is why Moses, for example, can say of "all Israel" that *they* heard the voice of God and *they* came near to Moses, when in fact it is the "heads" of the tribes who drew near (Deut 5:1, 23). The head is the representative member who sees, hears, draws near on behalf of the whole body.

The OT head thus entails more than itself, not as a part divisible from the whole but rather as one part (or aspect) that includes the whole, the "sum" of the body.[66] The head, in this sense, is a synecdoche for the whole body; and the "body" always includes its head.[67] In this way, the

---

its most basic "literal" meaning—i.e., that the head is the anatomical member which represents the body as a whole. This is not to say that the head does not play a central or even "chiefly" role, but that *rosh* as chief is secondary to the more basic meaning of *rosh* as representative. It is not because the head is chief that the head represents the body. Rather, it is because the head represents the body that it has a chiefly function. The significance of this observation seems to be missed by most of the modern scholarship, which envisions headship fundamentally as leadership, not representation.

65. Isaiah 9:14–15 makes this representative function of the head more explicit: "The LORD will therefore cut off from Israel head [*rosh*] and tail. . . . The elder and face [*panim*], he is the head" (AT). Here *panim* (lit. "faces") denotes those who stand "before" or "on the surface of" the people, and could well be rendered the "representatives [of the people]." Indeed, the face in Hebrew symbolically denotes the presence of the whole person. As elder and "face," the household head was responsible to represent his whole family in the sacrificial and cultic life of worship in preexilic Israel. See Sklba, *Teaching Function*, 53; Hahn, *Kinship by Covenant*, 215.

66. James Dunn speaks similarly, that "while Greek thought tended to regard the human being as made up of distinct parts, Hebraic thought saw the human being more as a whole person existing on different dimensions." He speaks of Greek anthropologies as "partitive" (the body made up of distinct parts) and Hebrew as "aspective" (the bodily members conceived as aspects of the whole). For instance, God's hand is never seen as detached from God but rather as centering the attention on one aspect of God's total being (*Theology of the Apostle Paul*, 54).

67. A "head and body union" is a concept foreign to OT anatomy, as any talk of the body includes the head as one among many parts (e.g., Lev 4:11). The head-body contrast is a later Greek development. See Michael Baumgärtel, "σῶμα," *TDNT* 7:1047–48. In fact, the notion of the "body" as it came to be understood in the West (related closely with the Greek *soma*) is foreign to the Hebrew language. There is no Hebrew equivalent to the Greek *soma*. Rather, it is the Hebrew word *basar*, which corresponds closely with

OT head title retains its corporeal dimension, as it is everywhere depicted as one with and inseparable from the body.

These observations impose certain conceptual limits on how Hebrew "headship" might be understood. To start, whatever power is held by a head is bound up with the interests of the body. When applied to OT male heads and their female counterparts, the individuated identities of both man and woman are subsumed within a larger "one-flesh" whole. The woman loses her individuated identity, becoming part of a single body, represented socially, legally, spiritually and covenantally by the man. The man likewise loses his individuated identity, becoming a member of a larger body of "flesh," as the representative of it. (Such "conceptual limits" will be further explored in ch. 5.)

While a head and body corporeal duality is only explicitly developed in the NT, still there are hints of such a concept in the OT. The Gen 2 speech of *Adam* identifies the woman as the man's own "bone" and "flesh," "from" him and "of" his own body (2:22–23). With "one-flesh" union here given as a paradigm for marital bonds in Israel, this union extends from this most fundamental union to other blood relations. Brother, uncle, nephew—indeed the whole people of Israel—will later be described as being of the same "flesh" and "bone" (37:27; 29:14; 2 Sam 5:1; 19:12–14; Neh 5:5; Isa 58:7). In these ways, the man's place as "head" of household is part of a broader conceptual network which envisions the household as a "body" of shared flesh. This is implicit throughout the OT and named as such explicitly in the NT (Rom 12; 1 Cor 12; Eph 4).

---

the Greek *sarx*, which is at times translated *soma*, but infrequently and only where *basar* is used to indicate the "totality of a person." Only in Greek writings does *soma* denote an "anthropological dualism." "For the translators of the LXX and the authors of the original Greek works σῶμα offered a Greek concept that had not yet been developed in Hebrew" (7:1047–48). Indeed, rarely is the person dichotomized in any sense in the OT. There is no head-body dualism, no head-heart dualism. Instead, body parts are almost invariably used synecdochally. When the OT speaks of a head it speaks of the whole person; the heart is the whole person; the flesh is the whole person. If there is any notable intrapersonal dichotomy it is not between head and body but between heart and flesh (Pss 16:9; 73:26; 84:2; Prov 4:21–22; 14:30; Eccl 11:10; Jer 17:5; Ezra 44:7–9; Dan 5:21; Nah 2:10); still, never are these contrasted or juxtaposed, but only put together to emphasize the totality of the person. (The same can be said of the Hebrew phrase "heart and soul"; e.g., Deut 4:29; 6:5; 10:12; 11:13, 18; 30:2, 10; Ps 84:2; Prov 2:10; etc.) The great contrast in Israel, then, is not the heart and the head, or the heart and the flesh, but the stony heart and the fleshy heart (Ezra 11:19; 36:26), the heart (viz. person) closed to God and neighbor and the heart of love toward God and neighbor. Thus, in the Hebrew imaginary there is no anthropological dualism as we find in Greek thought but only the dualism between Creator and creature, and between the unseen realm of God and angels, and the seen realm of fleshly existence.

Not only is the "head" title used in Israel's familial contexts, but from the exodus onward Israel is explicitly organized in its military and judicial processes according to representative "heads."[68] Upon entry into the promised land, for example, God raises up national representatives, the "judges," who are also called "heads," to bring salvation to Israel.[69] Later, when the kingship is first established in Israel, the king is explicitly defined as "the head of the tribes of Israel" (1 Sam 15:17).[70] David is later deemed "head" likewise of the nations gathered into his kingdom (2 Sam 22:44; Ps 18:43).[71] The eschatological vision proclaimed by Hosea is one of a renewed union of Judah and Israel as one body united under "one head" (Hos 1:11).

In all of these depictions of heads in Israel there is a common theme: the head is the representative of the body, to serve the interests of the body. Indeed, ideal heads are explicitly associated not with unjust rule but described explicitly as "men who fear God, men of truth, those who hate dishonest gain" (Exod 18:21), who serve the interests of the whole.[72]

---

68. The two extrafamilial contexts where men are most frequently deemed heads are judicial and military contexts, these two overlapping considerably. And in each of these contexts, whether as military or judicial judge, the head is portrayed as a head on behalf of a body, whether as military or judiciary savior. Such a position is portrayed as a great responsibility, even a burden, and yet a necessary burden to be borne for the sake of the whole. For more on this tripartite division of heads along familial, military, and judicial lines, see Bartlett, "Use of Word *ROSH*."

69. E.g., Abimelech comes to judge Israel as its head (Judg 10:18)—identified as the "bone" and "flesh" of his people, Shechem (10:2)—and Jephthah also (11:8–11). While not all of the judges are explicitly deemed "heads" they each fulfill analogous roles in Israel as those who are.

70. Before Israel appointed Saul king, Samuel had appointed his sons as judges over Israel. "Yet his sons did not walk in his ways but turned aside after gain. They took bribes and perverted justice" (1 Sam 8:3). It was precisely his sons' inability to serve Israel's interests that disqualified them from acting as Israel's head (8:1–4) and moved Israel to opt for a new head, a king. Interestingly, Samuel warns Israel of the abuses of the kingship, all the while himself representing a counterexample of an ideal head who always acted on behalf of the people (12:1–5).

71. Before David is declared king we are told that "all the tribes of Israel came to David," saying, "Behold, we are your bone and flesh" (2 Sam 5:1). See also 2 Sam 19:12–14 where David says to the elders of Judah, "You are my brothers; you are my bone and my flesh.... 'Are you not my bone and my flesh?'" In response, "as one man" they called the king to return and lead them. See also the royal cry, "How I bear in my bosom all the many peoples" (Ps 89:50).

72. It is significant that though Israel certainly had their own terms for ruler (*shallit*), captain (*shalish*), chief (*alluwph* or *sar*), leader (*nasiy*), none of these come to characterize the role of the father as household representative, but instead *rosh*. Moreover, every leader in Israel who is raised up by God to be "head," whether as warrior, judge, or

It is as "head" that Jephthah brings salvation to Israel (11:32–33) and as head that David strikes down Israel's enemies (2 Sam 5:1–5; 17–25; 6:12–15).

None of this is to suggest that the heads of ancient Israel always, or even often, live up to their designations as heads. Nevertheless, the head in Israel, whether father, judge, priest, or king, is consistently identified as one who stands in relation to a particular collective, given for the good of that collective.[73]

Moreover, alongside the various depictions of Israelite "heads" stands a vast array of corresponding corporeal language used for Israel—personified as a son (Hos 11:1–7), a daughter (Isa 10:32; 37:22; 52:2; Lam 2:10–15; Mic 4:8; Zeph 3:14; Zech 9:9), a bride (Isa 49:18; 61:10; 62:5; Hos 4:13–14), and a servant (Isa 52:13; 53:11).[74] All of this personified language has led some to identify Israel as a "corporate personality," wherein Israel is understood most fundamentally not as a collection of

---

king, is raised up on behalf of, for the good of, Israel. Indeed, prior to the establishment of the kingship in Israel (and arguably after), never is a leader raised up for his own sake but always for the salvation of the whole. E.g., Saul's first act as king and "head of the tribes" is to bring salvation to Israel over their enemies (1 Sam 11:1–11; 15:7); and this *rule on behalf of the people* is precisely what secures his kingship throughout Israel (1 Sam 11:12–15). David also is later raised up precisely as one who brings salvation to Israel (1 Sam 17:46–54; 2 Sam 5:17–25). This dynamic is made particularly clear in the idealized kingship of Solomon, where the king professedly reigns not as ruler over slaves—"of the people of Israel Solomon made no slaves" (1 Kgs 9:22)—but as one who led his people into the life of freedom and rest (4:25) by exercising justice and righteousness on the peoples' behalf (10:7–9).

73. This is precisely the point argued by Daniel Block and later tested and expanded by Rebekah Josberger: that "the biblical presentation of the ideal role of the Israelite *av* 'father' is not that of privileged rule but of profound responsibility" (Josberger, "For Your Good Always," 166). (For Block and Josberger alike, the Israelite *av* is synonymous with the "head of household.") See also Block, "Marriage in Ancient Israel." Josberger suggests that much of modern scholarship, in focusing on the appalling nature of situations where men had such power over women, misses the fact that the words spoken to men in this context are restrictive for them and protective for the vulnerable ("For Your Good Always," 166). Indeed, she maintains that where the woman is in a place of extreme vulnerability and the man in a place of power and privilege, the texts' purpose is specifically to limit the rights of the head for the sake of the woman (185). See also Wright, *Deuteronomy*, 234.

74. We might note also that Israel is at times described as a people gathered "as one man" (e.g., Judg 20:1, 8, 11; 1 Sam 11:7; Ezra 3:1; Neh 8:1). As noted, kin relations more broadly are described in terms of being of one body, or of the same flesh (Gen 29:14; 37:27; Neh 5:5; Isa 58:7). For close kin relations the phrase *sh'er basar* or "flesh of flesh" is used (Lev 18:6; 25:49).

disparate individuals but as a unified whole, a corporeal solidarity.[75] Indeed, the very fact that the people are constituted as God's people under the name Israel reflects this corporeal dimension. God's people are his people because Abraham is his person (Gen 12:1–3; 15:1–21; 17:1–22), and Abraham's benefits are extended to Isaac, and to Jacob, and to all of Jacob's children (35:9–12).[76] It is by virtue of a person's inclusion "in Israel" that a person receives the blessing *of* Israel, as all of the blessings and promises of God are given to all who are part of this ever-growing body.[77]

To summarize, the household head in Israel becomes the prototypical "topmost" position within the social structures of Israel. As Jacob's own family grows, his twelve sons become the twelve tribes according to which Israel organizes its life under representative heads (albeit, with the tribe of Levi set apart from the other twelve, and Joseph divided into the "half-tribes" of Manasseh and Ephraim; see, e.g., Num 1:1–16). As the society expands, the name "head" is applied not only to household heads, but to tribal chiefs and judges.[78] With the increasing stratification of so-

75. The classic scriptural texts that gave rise to this notion of "corporate personality" include the story of Achan (Josh 7:1–24; 22:20), along with the corporeal imagery of Israel in Ezek 16–23 and in Isaiah's Servant Songs (Isa 42:1–4; 49:1–6; 50:4–7; 52:13—53:12). The language of "corporate personality" was first popularized by H. Wheeler Robinson, *Corporate Personality in Israel*. This work was greatly influenced by the anthropological theories of Lévy-Bruhl, who argued that primitive Semitic psychologies had no sense of the self as an individuated being but only as part of a more fundamental corporate whole. While Robinson's work has since been criticized for its psychological reductionism, Jurrien Mol has argued for the continued usefulness of "corporate personality" as a notion that can clarify "the understanding of the relationship of the individual to the collective (which bears responsibility)" (*Collective and Individual Responsibility*, 2; see also 257–58). Using Ezek 18 and 20 as a test case, Mol explains, "The distribution of responsibility is indicated from the family structure. The family is the unity of responsibility. Individual responsibility is constituted within the family. The individual derives his identity from the collective of the family and these two are indissolubly connected. There are no two different systems of attribution of responsibility, of which Ezekiel 18 would reflect the one and Ezekiel 20 the other" (262).

76. "The land which I gave to Abraham and Isaac, I will give it to you, And I will give the land to your descendants [lit. 'seed'] after you" (Gen 35:12).

77. Israel as an ever-growing body connects with the image of Israel as the "vine" (Isa 5:7; Hos 10:1).

78. The titles of "judge" and "head" are at times interchangeable. E.g., after Moses was instructed to set "judges" over the people, "Moses chose able men out of all Israel and made them heads over the people, chiefs of thousands, of hundreds, of fifties, and of tens" (Exod 18:25); "[Moses said,] 'How can I bear by myself the weight and burden of you and your strife? Choose for your tribes wise, understanding, and experienced men, and I will appoint them as your heads.' . . . So I took the heads of your tribes, wise and experienced men, and set them as heads over you, [as] commanders . . . throughout your tribes" (Deut 1:12–15).

ciety, as each layer is added to Israel's social ordering, the "head" always, fittingly, remains on top, so that when Israel comes to appoint a king, that king too is deemed "head";[79] and the God of Israel is determined to be the great "head" over all (1 Chr 29:11).

Here, the meaning of the man's identity as "head" is determined chiefly by the head's symbolic anatomical function—namely, the head *represents* the "body" synecdochally, whether in reference to the individual, family, tribe, or other collective.[80] The head is one who acts on behalf of its members. Their good is his good. Their welfare is his welfare. The status, shame, and salvation of the head is altogether bound up with that of the body.[81]

Finally, we have seen that Israel is likewise depicted as a "body," or a "corporate personality" (son, daughter, bride, servant). As we have noted, however, the notion of Israel as a head and body duality is nowhere made explicit in the OT. Instead, there are "heads" in Israel and there is "flesh" in Israel, but these two are never spoken of together explicitly as a corporeal duality. In this way, the OT offers no well-developed model for a gendered head and body duality. Instead, what becomes well defined in the NT here remains diffuse and unelaborated.

CONCLUSION

In this chapter I have argued that the modern notion of "headship" developed in the West as a term that primarily denotes *rule* or *leadership*. This is a departure from the meaning of "head" as set forth in the OT. In the ancient Hebrew context, the head was located within an informing matrix distinct from later Western conceptions, suffused instead with connotations of unity, responsibility, and, most fundamentally, representation.[82] In ancient Hebrew, it was not the head *as leader* who represented

---

79. Samuel, in appointing Saul as Israel's first king, says to Saul, "Though you are little in your own eyes, are you not the head of the tribes of Israel?" (1 Sam 15:17).

80. All three of these senses are given in Num 1:1–16: first, those "able to go to war" are numbered "head by head" (i.e., person by person) (1:2–3); second, each "head" is identified in relation to "his father's household" (1:4; see also Exod 6:14, 25); third, the representative of the tribal divisions is referred to as the "head" (Num 1:16, 44).

81. The apparent decoupling of the individual from the family in Ezek 18 seems to stand against such claims. Mol has argued however that Ezek 18 must be understood in the context of Ezekiel as a whole (esp. ch. 20), where individual responsibility is upheld within the context of corporate responsibility. See n75 [X-REF].

82. As I have argued, while the OT concept of "head as representative" carries

the household, but the head *as representative* who had certain leadership functions, delineated according to his status as head of a body.

The OT "head" thus stands in contrast to "headship" as it comes to be conceived in the West, where the notion of headship is too often disjointed from its corporeal dimensions. While the "head" once included (as a corporeal metaphor) connotations of unity, responsibility, mutuality, and representation, in the Western tradition these are largely overshadowed, if not entirely eclipsed, by notions of headship as rule, connoting supremacy and authority, defined in modern secular terms.[83] In short, the "head," originally understood as *the representative member of the body*, has evolved into "head*ship*," *an office denoting leadership and rule over an entity distinct from itself*. In this way, the endorsement of *male headship* in the present context naturally bolsters a sexist ideological framework.

Admittedly, the insistence that headship means "representation," scripturally defined, does little to change the fact that affirmations of male headship remain problematic in the present cultural-linguistic contexts of contemporary Western cultures. Whether conceived as "leadership" or "representation," the result appears to be the same: men qua men are offered a distinctive status which privileges men in relation to women. Such gender-based distinctions are generally unwelcome, if not abhorrent, in a modern and secular age.

But this has not always been the case. Such a gender-based distinction has not always been perceived as problematic. Rather, as we shall see in the next chapter, it is through specific and significant cultural transformations that male headship, however conceived, has been rendered incommensurable with modern Western notions of gender equality.

---

accompanying connotations such as leadership, authority, prominence, etc., such connotations are not central but peripheral to its meaning.

83. Though the "authority" of the head is almost always construed as "servant authority" or "authority on behalf of" in contemporary headship debates, nevertheless it is construed in terms of authority. One might wonder at this point whether there is any great difference between headship as authority and headship as representation. Admittedly, in practice it is difficult to tell and historically complex (a matter to be taken up in the next chapter). In principle, however, "representation" is the language of democracy and "authority" the language of autocracy. A fuller engagement with this difference will be explored in ch. 5.

CHAPTER 3

On the Genealogy of Heads
Headship in History

Ours is a civilization concerned to relieve suffering and enhance human well-being, on a universal scale unprecedented in history, and which at the same time threatens to imprison us in forms that can turn alien and dehumanizing.
—Charles Taylor[1]

The past is a foreign country: they do things differently there.
—L. P. Hartley[2]

Given the ways in which the meaning of headship has developed etymologically in the West, male headship has come to denote male dominance and female subservience in the present age.[3] Male headship is thus largely unwelcome, conceptually and practically, in our increasingly egalitarian global contexts.

But the problem with male headship runs deeper still. Not only has headship become redefined in terms of "authority over," thus rendering male headship repugnant to a post-patriarchal age, but the very

---

1. Taylor, foreword to *Rivers North of Future*, xiii.
2. Hartley, *Go-Between*, 1.
3. See the previous chapter where I argue that in Western contexts the meaning of the term "head" has been largely, though not wholly, reduced to a matter of "authority over"—and thus "male headship" to a matter of male dominance.

suggestion that the genders might be distinguished along vocational lines has itself become largely unacceptable.[4] The problem with male headship, then, is not simply that it connotes male dominance, but that it suggests fixed gender-differentiated identities at all. We have entered into an era where male headship is not only problematic for its dominical flavor but also for its inherently gender-essentializing and identity-differentiating claims.

Such gender-based vocational difference was once ubiquitous—not judged to be prohibitive or harmful, but a necessary ingredient to social flourishing for the good of women and men alike. *How is it that gender-differentiated identities generally have become incommensurable with present notions of gender equality and justice?* In this chapter we will uncover the foundations upon which gender-differentiated modes of living were once based but which are now eroded. This erosion has rendered notions of male headship doubly inadmissible, both as a term denoting male dominance (as described in ch. 2) and as a category that establishes gender-differentiated identities as culturally fixed and binary (in the present chapter).

In what follows I will demonstrate that gender-differentiated identities in general and the gender-differentiated identities of male heads in particular are not, historically speaking, inherently sexist gendered arrangements. Rather, such gender-based vocational differences only became sexist and oppressive through cultural revolutions that have radically transformed modern conceptions of the self.

In order to demonstrate these claims, we will examine some of the sociohistorical shifts which have led to the incommensurability of gender-based identities generally, and male headship in particular, with our secular age. We will begin by bringing headship into relation with patriarchy as a historical phenomenon, in order to distinguish headship and patriarchy in their Western developments. Here we will find that although, scripturally speaking, they are distinct in important ways, male headship and patriarchy have become conflated in the Western tradition, where headship has become "patriarchalized." This conflation has sorely complicated modern discourse concerning male headship, with headship now conceived as an affront to gender equality and women's rights.

---

4. While gender-based vocational differences have been culturally normative for the majority of human cultures, to be sure, the social and material factors that made such gender differences so prevalent and far reaching have largely eroded, as we shall see. For a description of some of the key philosophical and material conditions that have led to such cultural transformations, see Trueman, *Rise of Modern Self*.

Within this first section we will embark on a "genealogy of gender," charting out the journey from a male-headed and patriarchal past to our more egalitarian present. Following Ivan Illich's genealogical account of gender, we will explore the ways in which household and tribal heads functioned in a gendered (pre-industrialized) world, and how headship lost its familial and societal place in a relatively genderless (post-industrialized) world. The goal in this section will be to identify the onset and spread of wage labor as a seismic societal shift that has, along with other linguistic, cultural, and technological transformations, rendered male headship incompatible with the reigning social values and norms of the contemporary West. To affirm male headship in the present age has come to mean affirming an inescapably sexist gendered framework.

This first section will lay the groundwork for a subsequent section on "Depatriarchalizing Headship" in which I will then present an alternative way of conceptualizing male headship not as a tool of patriarchy but as a feature that fits within a gendered society of equal regard. Following the anthropological insights of Susan Carol Rogers, we will find that whereas in industrialized contexts in general male headship is inherently sexist, in preindustrial contexts male headship can be discerned as part of a broader gendered framework that serves the interests of women and men alike. My goal in this final section will be to disentangle male headship, conceptually and practically, from notions of patriarchy and male dominance.[5]

PATRIARCHALIZING HEADSHIP: ON THE ORIGINS AND SCOPE OF PATRIARCHY

During the neolithic revolution . . . man's mind was directed along the path of technological advance and discovery, while woman's remained linked to immediate realities. . . . Because of this, genetic adjustments took place that emphasized the intellectual divergence between them. . . . During [this time], man experienced an enormous surge of self-assurance, became certain of

---

5. Throughout I use "patriarchal" and "patriarchy" to denote the broad swathe of institutionalized forms of male-dominant social hierarchies—wherein men predominantly occupy the "upper places" of the hierarchies—in which "men have more power and access to resources than women, and some men are dominant over other men"(Wiesner-Hanks, "Forum Introduction," 320). See also Lerner, *Creation of Patriarchy*, 53.

his own superiority. After it, by the time humanity emerged into the light of recorded history, there was no question but that man was the master.

—REAY TANNAHIL[6]

In *The Creation of Patriarchy* (1986), Gerda Lerner identifies patriarchy as a primordial global phenomenon coinciding with the rise of civilization, whereby the male-headed family became institutionalized as an aspect of state power.[7] Although the form and extent of patriarchy has differed greatly across time and cultures, according to Lerner the "father-ruled" home has been a basic structural norm at the foundation of almost every enduring civilization.

Many have argued, however, that concrete historical contexts are too complex to be described with a single category—"patriarchy"—as though male dominance has been a monolithic feature of all cultures in the same ways and to the same extent.[8] To be sure, the patriarchy Lerner speaks of (specifically in the Western context) is far from monolithic, taking on diverse forms in which "male rule" is never absolute.[9] While men have been sovereign in certain regards, in certain spheres, they have not been sovereign in every regard or in all spheres. The kind of "patriarchy" that depicts women as the powerless puppets of men has been exposed as the mythmaking of certain "radical feminists."[10] What of women's agency,

---

6. Tannahil, *Sex in History*, 13. This represents one of many theories of male dominance that seek to explain the pervasiveness of male-headed families and social institutions in history. Others have argued that male dominance is not a *social* phenomenon but a development dependent upon *psychophysiological* differences between women and men. See Goldberg, *Why Men Rule*. For an evolutionary-biological perspective, see Kraemer, "Origins of Fatherhood."

7. Lerner argues that the male head of household served as the primitive organizing social unit for later patriarchal societies, codified and solidified in the ancient Near East through a 2500-year process (ca. 3100 BCE to ca. 600 BCE), beginning with the commodification of women's sexuality and reproductive capacities in emerging agricultural societies. In this account, the archaic state is the genealogical precursor to "patriarchy" as it came to be established in ancient Mesopotamia and as later embraced and promulgated throughout Western civilizations (*Creation of Patriarchy*, 50–54, 212–16).

8. The July 2018 issue of *Gender & History* focuses on the question of patriarchy as a historical descriptor. All contributors agree that as a descriptor of the relation of men to women in general, "patriarchy" is inappropriate, as it obscures the more complex and varied realities experienced cross-culturally. See Wiesner-Hanks, "Forum Introduction." See also Hendrix, "What Is Sexual Inequality?"; Bourguignon, "Sex Bias."

9. Lerner, *Creation of Patriarchy*, 217. See also Poska, "Agentic Gender Norms," 354.

10. See Amussen, "Contradictions of Patriarchy," 350; Dialeti, "Patriarchy as a Category," 331.

leadership, autonomy, sovereignty, expertise in particular spheres? What of established patterns of dominant women, female leaders and rulers of nations?[11]

Still, Lerner observes, "There is not a single society known where women-as-a-group have decision-making power *over* men or where they define the rules of sexual conduct or control marriage exchanges."[12] Despite the assured facts of women's agency, authority, relative autonomy and rulership in every place, Lerner insists that patriarchy—in this more constricted sense—remains a useful descriptive category for characterizing most of the enduring civilizations our world has known, and certainly in the West. Following Lerner and others, in what follows I hold that patriarchy—defined as a male-dominant hierarchical social system wherein men in general hold more power and access to resources than women—remains an apt category of historical description and analysis.[13]

What then is the relation between patriarchy and male headship?

As noted, for Lerner, the two, while distinct, are coincident: patriarchy is the institutionalization of the male as head (viz. chief) of family and society, conceived as a form of male dominance. This is no surprise. As outlined in the previous chapter, in both ancient and modern contexts male headship has largely been conceived as a subset of, or synonymous with, male dominance.

But as I argued in the last chapter, male dominance is not the same as male headship, at least in its primal Hebraic literary expression—the latter being fundamentally about representation, not dominance or "authority" or "leadership." In its scriptural enunciation, headship is a position vis-à-vis the household which is altogether bound up with the interests of the household. In the Hebrew context from which Western notions of headship emerge, and in the broader scriptural-canonical

---

11. For treatments of the history of women as rulers in early modern European contexts, see Jansen, *Monstrous Regiment of Women*; Monter, *Rise of Female Kings*.

12. Lerner, *Creation of Patriarchy*, 30; emphasis in original. For similar claims in a medieval context, see Hanawalt, *Good and Ill Repute*, esp. 79. The "matriarchal" cultures of the Khasi of India and the Mosuo of China may represent genuine exceptions to Lerner's claims. Still, if they are exceptions, the matriarchy of these cultures cannot simply be understood as the obverse of patriarchy but rather must be defined according to their own standards and norms. See Goettner-Abendroth, "Re-Thinking 'Matriarchy'"; Kelley, "Myth of Matriarchy"; Ledgerwood, "Khmer Kinship."

13. See Dialeti, "Patriarchy as a Category," 332; Amussen, "Contradictions of Patriarchy," 345; Bennett, "Feminism and History," 266.

context in which it is later transfigured and codified, headship cannot be reduced to a term for rule or dominance. Instead, the corporeal image of the "head," especially when articulated in the heart-centric context of Israel's socioreligious imaginary, necessarily denotes a relationship of mutuality and responsibility—the head as *representative member of the body*.

Again, to define the head fundamentally as "representative" of the body is not without connotations of "authority." Still, the authority of the head as representative is different from that of the *patriarch* or *paterfamilias*; the authority of the former is conceived not in terms of rule but in terms of corporeal representation.

By no means is this clarification offered to suggest that heads as representatives are immune to abusing the power afforded them. Whether headship is conceived as "representation" or "rulership," in history we observe only broken forms of headship, muddled together with patterns and practices of male domination. This is no less true of Hebrew heads than of Greco-Roman or modern ecclesial heads. As will be explored in later chapters, the only ideal "head," historically instantiated, is the person of Jesus Christ.

Although tidy distinctions between male headship and male dominance cannot easily be made, conflated as they are in their historical manifestations, it must be noted that all oppressive forms of male power are, scripturally speaking, betrayals of the very meaning of headship. In the scriptural framework, the head's position vis-à-vis the body is to serve the interests of the body. Male headship in its scriptural mode must thus be differentiated from patriarchal male dominance.[14]

Yet modern society has failed to perceive these distinctions. Into the modern era the church, and society as a whole, has continued to deploy the title of head as denoting rule, leadership, and authority. Moreover, and as a result, with the feminist reforms beginning in the 1950s and 1960s, male headship as a category was swept into debates over women's economic and political emancipation—debates centered on male-female power relations. Accordingly, headship was denounced as a symbol and progenitor of male power and female oppression.

14. I do not presume that distinguishing between headship and patriarchy semantically or theoretically will disentangle headship from patriarchy practically. The "formal power differential" offered to heads comes with opportunities and proclivities to abuse that power. Still, the purpose of distinguishing headship from patriarchy remains salient: the two terms are not identical in meaning: the latter foregrounds the rule of the father; the former corporeal prominence and responsibility.

Moreover, for most early feminists it simply was not the case that male headship, if simply disentangled from patriarchy, would become an acceptable feature of social life. Even if all notions of rule and authority were completely eradicated from the "head" title, there still remained the problem that this title was reserved for men only. Indeed, to offer any title or privilege to one gender had become problematic on its own terms in an increasingly egalitarian age—not least because such "difference" had for so long been construed in Western tradition in terms of the ontological subordination of woman to man.[15] It was therefore *gendered difference itself* that needed to be overcome, and male headship with it. Little did anyone realize, well before the 1950s and 1960s the process of deconstructing gender difference had already begun.

A. On the Genealogy of Gender

As we have seen, throughout most human civilizations, and certainly in the West, men have consistently and normatively functioned as heads of household, tribe, and nation. This was a fact of social life that only came to be challenged in a widespread, sustained, and enduring way in the recent past.[16] The radical and unprecedented social changes of the last several centuries set in motion a serious, substantive, transcultural challenge to patriarchy (and hence to concomitant notions of "headship"), a challenge which has gained widespread adherence and traction over the last hundred years or so, evidenced and concretized in the British and American feminist movements beginning at the turn of the nineteenth century.[17] In the wake of these movements, heterarchy is finally and unprecedentedly coming to replace patriarchy as the Western cultural ideal. In this context, the individual's rights, capabilities, and desires have come to be the chief indicators and determiners of social roles rather than one's sexuality. That one's gender necessarily imposed social demands

---

15. See Cere, "Marriage, Subordination."

16. In Lerner's account, patriarchy did not come under serious criticism until the rise of "feminist consciousness," emerging in the late nineteenth century (*Creation of Feminist Consciousness*).

17. It was during this time, from the 1950s through the 1980s, when several seminal feminist works were published, including Beauvoir, *Second Sex* (1949; English, 1953); Saiving Goldstein, "Human Situation" (1960); Friedan, *Feminine Mystique* (1963); Trible, *God and Sexuality* (1978); Russell, *Liberating Word* (1976); Ruether, *Religion and Sexism* (1974); Ruether, *Sexism and God-Talk* (1983); Schüssler Fiorenza, *In Memory of Her* (1984); Trible, *Texts of Terror* (1984).

and limitations was once taken for granted. Today, such gender-based demands and limitations are called discrimination.

Such a radical break from what it means for humans to be human does not simply happen.[18] These changes have been set in motion by such seismic shifts as the onset and spread of wage labor and the shifts toward individualism and secularism of the seventeenth and eighteenth centuries, along with the great health transition and rapid development of contraceptive and reproductive technologies of the nineteenth and twentieth centuries. Only in the wake of the convergence of such vast social transformations and technological innovations has the pervasive patriarchy of the past, and the notions of male-female distinctness which underlie it, come into view as a system capable of deep criticism. In short, the power and influence of these shifts and movements cannot be easily overstated.

One result of these shifts has been the minimizing and obscuring of culturally embodied sexual distinction. The significance of sexual distinction as a basis for ordering families and communities is eroding as sexual difference is coming to mean something quite different for us today than it has meant to any human culture before the twentieth century. For instance, the claim that women can and should function in society in ways indistinguishable from men is a decisively novel claim in the history of the human species. The novelty of this claim evinces a definite break with a fundamental tenet of what it has always meant to be human—namely, for men and women to live within the contours of their given familial and societal vocations, culturally assigned according to their sexuality, whether as male or female.

All of this has obvious ramifications for the "headship debate." In a world where gender justice is articulated as a matter of ensuring that a woman and man ought to be able to do and to be "the same thing" in most every respect, a head and body gendered metaphor finds no easy fit. Where *gender difference* as a fundamental feature of creaturely life is replaced with *gender sameness* as a controlling social value, the notion that humans might be limited in any way according to our gender—whether in terms of how we relate or in terms of what a given gender might or

18. Some have argued that the last two centuries mark a period of unprecedented sociocultural newness in the landscape of human history, which some have dubbed the "Anthropocene" epoch—an era identified by radical ecological and sociocultural changes involving transformations in geography, health and lifespan, and social identity. See S. Lewis and Maslin, "Defining the Anthropocene." For a critical evaluation of the term, see Ruddiman, "Anthropocene."

might not do or be—becomes a matter of injustice. In this framework, viewing man as "head" in relation to the woman as "body" indeed almost inevitably bespeaks injustice.

In order to understand this shift we turn now to the Roman Catholic philosopher, polymath, and cultural critic Ivan Illich, who locates this transformation principally in the onset and spread of wage labor.[19] Described as one of the preeminent thinkers of the twentieth century, whose work it was "to uncover . . . the deeper strata of Western culture,"[20] Illich has received accolades of praise for his incisive, if controversial, inventories of modernity and its apparent social and technological advancements.[21] While not without its critics, Illich's book *Gender* likewise presents a challenging, insightful and realistic account of its subject matter. Here Illich describes a movement from a gendered to a genderless world—hence, a movement away from a world where a head and body gendered framework finds a fit. As he says early on, "I describe [gender] from the perspective of the past. About the future, I know and say nothing."[22]

B. From the Reign of Gender to the Regime of Sex: Illich's Genealogy of Gender

Gender bespeaks a complementarity that is enigmatic and asymmetrical. Only metaphor can reach it.

From afar, the native can tell whether women or men are at work, even if he cannot distinguish their figures. The time of year and day, the crop, and the tools reveal to him who they are. Whether they carry a load on their head or shoulder will tell him their gender. If he notices geese loose in the harvested field, he knows a girl must be nearby. . . . If he comes across sheep, he knows

---

19. Identifying the spread of wage labor as a crucial moment in a history of gender is well established. See, e.g., Wagner et al., "Male Dominance"; Medick, "Proto-Industrial Family Economy"; Agassi, "Theories of Gender Equality."

20. Bruno-Jofré and Zaldívar, "Ivan Illich's Late Critique," 585.

21. See Taylor, foreword to *Rivers North of Future*, 9, 13. See also C. Miller, "Ivan Illich"; *Utne Reader*, "100 Visionaries"; Ertman, "Exchange as a Cornerstone," 405; Murata, "Feminine Spirituality," 218–19; Levi, "Radical Nemesis." Giulia Frova identifies Illich as an important "alternative thinker" for catalyzing human flourishing from an international development perspective ("Development Debate on Sustainability," 277).

22. Illich, *Gender*, 21. For a brief personal and intellectual biography, see Hoinacki, "Trajectory of Ivan Illich."

he will find a boy. . . . Gender is in every step, in every gesture, not just between the legs.

—IVAN ILLICH[23]

For Ivan Illich, humanity is irreducibly gendered, with every culture throughout human history ordered clearly along gendered lines—that is, until the recent past. In preindustrial societies, from infancy each gender experienced the world differently and was perceived—even "gazed upon"—differently, each habituated to a uniquely gendered mode of conceptualizing the world.

> The duties befitting each gender are inculcated at an early age. By the time she is nine, a Bemba girl knows how to distinguish forty mushrooms, while the boy knows the calls of many birds. The most fundamental cognitive division in the evolution of concepts is that based on gender.[24]

Illich defines gender as "the eminently local and time-bound duality that sets off men and women under circumstances and conditions that prevent them from saying, doing, desiring, or perceiving 'the same thing.'" "Gender not only tells who is who, but it also defines who is when, where, and with which tools and words; it divides space, time, and technique." He aptly names this duality "asymmetric gender complementarity."[25]

Far from essentializing the genders, Illich insists that what is "essential" about gender is not "maleness" or "femaleness" per se, but rather the duality of the genders. Illich explains, "Gender . . . bespeaks a social polarity that is fundamental and in no two places the same. What a man cannot or must not do is different from valley to valley."[26] Gender is "vernacular": as particular to a culture as its vernacular/regional dialect. Such a gendered duality, according to Illich, was culturally pervasive. There was no genderless humanity, but only humanity as male or female, expressed variously across cultures.

But something has happened, according to Illich—a shift in our self-understanding, whereby gender's social significance has been all but

23. Illich, *Gender*, 4, 67–68.
24. Illich, *Gender*, 127.
25. Illich, *Gender*, 20, 99.
26. Illich, *Gender*, 68.

lost in the contemporary West. He calls it the transition from "the reign of gender" to "the regime of sex," with sex now redefined as a category in service of economic interests. He explains the difference between sex and gender this way: "Economic sex is the duality of one plus one, creating a coupling of exactly the same kind; gender is the duality of two parts that make a whole which is unique, novel, nonduplicable."[27] Under the reign of gender we had "asymmetric gender complementarity"; under the regime of sex we have the singular, ungendered "human," who, regardless his/her given genitalia, is expected to be and to do the same things—with the "minor" exceptions of carrying, birthing, and nursing infants, the only truly feminine functions that remain under the present regime.

How did this happen? How did it happen that gender difference became boiled down to genital difference, along with related maternal pre- and postnatal processes? Illich roots this transformation in the Industrial Revolution, arguing that the Industrial Revolution was, in its own way, a sexual revolution.[28]

Consider this story, told by Illich: Between 1800 and 1850, the surprising number of four dozen divorces were documented in the small community of Württemberg, Germany over the period of less than fifty years, in a time and place where divorce happened rarely, if ever. This was unprecedented.[29] What were the underlying causes? Was there war, famine, disease, and/or political or economic crisis?

At this time industrialization was well under way in this region, and most of the town's families found themselves pushed out of agricultural subsistence lifestyles into industrial labor—from keeping family farms, with crops and gardens, to working in large-scale production. Their world was changing. Commodities were multiplying—new tools and clothes, newly convenient ways to prepare food—and in order to participate in this new economy, families were forced to change the way they worked.[30] The center of production would no longer be the household but the factory. And this was not only the case in Württemberg. This was happening

---

27. Illich, "Sad Loss of Gender," 4.

28. See Davidoff and Hall, *Family Fortunes*. With the rise of industrialization and capitalism came the withdrawal of middle-class women from what was perceived as productive labor; the outer world of politics and work became the domain of men, giving rise to the modern dichotomization of the public (male) sphere and the private (female) sphere. See also Wagner et al. "Male Dominance."

29. Illich, *Gender*, 173–74. See also Sabean, "Intensivierung der Arbeit"; Lottin, "Vie du couple."

30. Sabean, *Kinship in Neckarhausen*, 263.

across the Western world. "Work" was being radically redefined as something that happened "out there."[31]

This was, for Illich, the beginning of "genderless work." Until the eighteenth century work had been predominantly divided and ordered along explicitly gendered lines. By and large, there was no "neuter" or genderless "human" work. Instead, there was male work and female work—what men did and what women did—with distinct gendered domains, spaces, tools, forms of knowledge and expertise.[32]

With work displaced out from the home and into the factory, everyone, both men and women, could now be funneled into the same jobs and carry out the same work for the first time.[33] And alongside genderless work came the novel idea of genderless education, as men and women now needed to learn all of the same things; and with this came the onset of genderless institutions of all kinds—genderless health care, genderless religious worship, genderless space, public and private, and genderless roles within said institutions and spaces.

With this revolution, within a single generation in this small region in Germany, women were suddenly forced to join men in men's work in order to earn enough to survive. These same women, however, had to continue carrying out their previous household duties, but now "faster and more furiously" than ever. Illich explains the situation this way:

> The divorce proceedings reflect how deeply disturbing these innovations were for both men and women, how helpless each felt, how unable to understand the implications of their seemingly rational decisions. Women complained that men suddenly ordered them around at work, a totally new experience for them. No matter how much the gender-defined work of women might seem subordinated to that of men, the notion that men could direct women in the work itself had so far been unimaginable. Women resented the loss of domain.... Envy of a new kind, envy

---

31. The advent of capitalist economies has often served to disrupt gender relations in traditional societies. Women typically suffer most as a result. See, e.g., Bould, "Development and the Family," 47.

32. Illich, *Gender*, 67–68. See also Baulant, "Scattered Family." Preindustrial examples can be found of women inhabiting male domains, of course, and vice versa. Even so, where one sex enters into the work and space of the other, this happens precisely as an exception to the rule. E.g., even when a woman rose to power and inhabited "male" spaces and roles in ancient Athens, the male-female gendered stratification and idealized gendered distinctions remained. See Davidson, "Bodymaps"; Van den Heuvel, "Gender in the Streets," 698.

33. Illich, *Gender*, 103–4.

for the other gender's schedule and rhythm, thus appeared, an envy destined to remain as a central characteristic of modern life, an envy fully "justified" under the assumptions of unisex work but unthinkable under the shield of gender.[34]

As Illich recounts, this transition from the "reign of gender" to the "regime of sex" posed great challenges to women and men alike, and therefore to households and communities. As households were displaced from the center to the periphery of economic life, greater value was vested in the economic capabilities of the individual. The male head was vested with greater power and prestige than ever before, now conceived as the primary or "sole wage earner." With this came the concomitant decentering of "family interests" as an organizing principle of family life, as the interests of the individual took center stage.[35]

Coincident with the increased prestige of the wage-earning worker came the diminishment of the domestic worker. Women's work and men's work had in times past been conceived as equal in importance, even if unequal in prestige.[36] But with the displacement of work from the home, women's work became what Illich calls "shadow work"—that unpaid labor which "complements" wage labor.[37] The wife was turned into a "housewife" who was no longer conceived chiefly as a producer but as a consumer, taking what the husband provided through his wage-earning work and helping to make it usable, edible, or functional for the household. Her role was perceived less and less as meaningful to a complementary partnership, and more and more as inferior.

In these ways, according to Illich, in the wake of the Industrial Revolution, the division of labor became explicitly and inherently sexist. Women were now required to spend their lives doing work that could only be deemed "shadow work."[38] Moreover, outside the realm of this

---

34. Illich, *Gender*, 174. Illich is by no means suggesting that prior to the Industrial Revolution most wives were happy or most marriages healthy. Certainly spousal abuse was prevalent in preindustrial societies, perhaps with greater frequency and intensity than in postindustrial contexts. For a critical analysis of Christian engagements with violence against women in medieval and modern contexts, see Nienhuis and Kienzle, *Saintly Women*.

35. See Liu, "Patrimoine magique."

36. See Segalen, *Love and Power*.

37. Illich, *Gender*, 46n31.

38. To name women's work as "shadow work" under the new economic regime has misled some to think that Illich is deeming said work simple and unimportant. Nothing could be farther from the truth. Instead, the unpaid and in-house labor that became normalized as women's labor was often more, not less, challenging, more lonely, and

shadow work, in the realm of wage labor, women were now in direct competition with men in male-dominant economic spheres.

For Illich, the chief problem of this new cultural context was that of everything economics measures, women always get less. "Under the reign of gender, men and women collectively depend on each other; their mutual dependence sets limits to struggle, exploitation, defeat." However, under the "economic regime . . . both genders are stripped and, neutered, the man ends up on top."[39] For Illich, the modern housewife is a novel, subservient, and impoverished form of existence, and the modern scarcity-based economic system an inherently sexist system.

Illich set forth these ideas in the early 1980s. Certainly, progress has been made since that time in terms of women's relative income, with women occupying more highly paid, powerful, high-status positions than ever before. However, as many have noted, a gender pay gap remains that relegates many female-led households to strictly limited, if not impoverished, lives. There indeed remains surprising income disparity between the genders even in the most developed of nations.[40] Moreover, while advancements toward gender equality have been made since the 1980s, sexism persists in many ways beyond the gender pay gap, still very much a part of our social and economic fabric.[41] The chief problem Illich raised thus persists—an inevitable and ubiquitous sexism under the present economic regime.[42]

necessarily stripped of its dignity and perceived importance—even while remaining necessary to the flourishing of the family and society.

39. Illich, *Gender,* 178–79. See also Huws, "Hassle of Housework."

40. From Illich's perspective, and by his time of writing, policies had been in place for some two decades in many Western countries, seeking to secure women's equality in the workplace, but with little effectiveness. While significant progress was made in closing the gender pay gap through the early 2000s, by 2010 these trends plateaued and even mildly reversed, with the gap remaining "quite large" even across developed nations, in ways "disappointing" and difficult to explain. See Kunze, "Gender Wage Gap," esp. 388. See also Blau and Kahn, "Gender Wage Gap," 852–53; Hegewisch, "Gender Wage Gap: 2017."

41. Sexism in the workplace remains through negative stereotyping, "disturbingly frequent" acts of sexual violence, discrimination against gaining employment, sexual harassment on the job, and being "perceived less favorably than men when enacting leadership roles in a masculine manner or domain" (Glick and Fiske, "Ambivalent Sexism Inventory," 492). See also Connor et al., "Ambivalent Sexism."

42. Illich's claims were supported by the results of a cross-cultural study, which concluded that "in societies which preserve some flavor of a vernacular gender-role structure, the position of women in the family implies autonomy in many fields, which is not threatened immediately by men's competition and vice-versa." Moreover, "male power in societies structured according to mutually interchangeable sex-roles entails

In sum, Illich has argued that prior to the onset and spread of wage labor ours was a radically gendered world. As long as production was centered in the home, male and female work tended to be comprehensively complementary—a claim which we will explore further below. While the reign of gender entailed distinct gendered paths—each with its own sense of vocation, goals, values, and ways of seeing the world—the regime of sex involves an economy of competition, envy and dehumanization. Wage labor replaces family subsistence, resulting in a redefinition of human worth in terms of economics and public power. Under this "economic regime" a particularly insidious form of male domination becomes possible. Work itself is neutered and women disadvantaged in their access to this supposedly "neutral" work. Women and men are forced to compete in a male-centric economic domain where sexism is inescapable—the man ever remaining "on top."

Where women and men are neutered in service of the economic flourishing promised by industrialization, there can be no male head and female body without damage done to the latter. In such a context, there can be no essentializing of gender roles and no gender duality, but only the singular, genderless human, *homo economicus*. Under this regime, male headship is a euphemism for male domination.

DEPATRIARCHALIZING HEADSHIP: ON THE MYTH OF MALE DOMINANCE

The husband is always the *chef d'exploitation*. . . . Well, that's what the law says. What really happens is another matter, but you won't find that registered in the *Codes Civils*.

—Marc Hantelle, former mayor, retired farmer

Most of the wives here really control their husbands,
even if it doesn't look like it.

—Peasant woman in rural France[43]

---

a competitive relationship and high interdependence between men and women. This quasi-egalitarian competition finally provides the soil for what is experienced as sexual discrimination" (Wagner et al., "Male Dominance," 66). See also Epstein, "Women and the Law"; T. Williams, "Demystifying Male Dominance."

43. Quoted in Rogers, "Female Forms of Power," 738, 747.

Thus far we have followed Illich's argument that with industrialization comes a particularly insidious and inescapable form of sexism. Of course, acknowledging that the dissolution of the gendered duality of our past has made possible the inherent sexism of our present by no means establishes the essential goodness of gendered duality, much less of male headship. Indeed, male headship remains patently undesirable in a post-patriarchal age since it appears from the start to place man in a position of prominence and control vis-à-vis the woman. Rather than offering a gendered vision that places man and woman side by side as selfsame independents, it places the man "above" (corporeally speaking) and the woman "below" as part of an interdependent and variegated whole. This is indeed an affront to contemporary notions of gender equality.

Admittedly, a certain inequality is presumed—inescapable even—under the aegis of gender. Here we are not speaking of two "equals" vying to be "on top" but of two variant counterparts together comprising a totality—not of two competing melodies, but of a melody and a harmony; not of two beginnings, but a beginning and an end. "Inequality" (in its literal sense of "not the same") is basic to the fundamental duality of the sexes, and such duality is foundational to the naming of man as head. Put bluntly, to affirm the duality of the genders is to assume a kind of inequality. The genders are "not the same." And this is not a problem.

Still, it seems wrong, or arbitrary at best, to offer man the more prominent role in this so-called "complementary" vision. Is "male headship" not merely a guise for male dominance, regardless of the cultural and conceptual context in which it is deployed? Or might it be that male headship can be conceived as an element in a truly complementary framework, a counterbalancing title which serves to achieve balance and justice between the genders?

To explore male headship as a feature of gender complementarity we will turn our attention to the work of anthropologist Susan Carol Rogers, who focused her studies on peasant households of pre- and postindustrial Europe. Rogers's work, I contend, opens up a way of conceiving male headship as part of a complementary system of equal regard. As defined in the previous chapter, the "head" functions here as legal and political representative of the household. For Rogers this title entails public prestige and final decision-making authority within the family.[44]

44. To be clear, in identifying the peasant household as a locus where male headship is not necessarily sexist is not to suggest some idyllic historical instantiation of headship. Rather, the peasant household offers a lens for reimagining headship as a force for

74 TRANSFIGURING HEADSHIP

In her influential article "Female Forms of Power and the Myth of Male Dominance" (1975), Rogers argues that a nonhierarchical power balance is maintained between men and women in some peasant societies by acting out a "myth" of male dominance.[45] This myth, she explains, is expressed "not in legends or folktales, but in patterns of public deference toward men, as well as their monopolization of positions of authority and prestige."[46] Accordingly, in such contexts "males do not actually dominate, nor do either males or females literally believe them to be dominant." Rather, it is the formal attribution of men as "dominant" that serves to maintain a social power balance which serves the interests of both women and men alike, giving men "the appearance of power and control over all sectors of village life, while at the same time giving [women] actual power over those sectors of life in the community which may be controlled by villagers."[47] Rogers explains that "the two sex groups, in effect, operate within partially divergent systems of perceived

---

social balance and counterbalance between the genders. See Rogers, "Female Forms of Power," 747.

45. In a later critical reflection (1999), Rogers notes that in this and other earlier work she tended to overgeneralize her findings, as though her research in twentieth-century rural France was indicative of peasant societies in general ("Once upon a Time"). While I follow Rogers's earlier work throughout this section, I do take into account her own self-criticisms, using her work not to uncover general principles but as an example of gendered duality in particular contexts.

46. Rogers, "Female Forms of Power," 729. On her use of "myth" she explains, "I assume myth to be the expression of an idea which may be demonstrated to be factually untrue." Rogers speaks of male dominance as "myth" in the sense that it is not all-encompassing and often formal and vacuous in terms of lived power and influence. She thus understands male authority as severely circumscribed. What Rogers here calls "the myth of male dominance" is what I have been calling an "equal-regard gendered duality" wherein prestigious roles and titles (e.g., the man as "head") serve as counterbalancing forces in a complementary gendered framework. Whereas Rogers distinguishes between *male dominance as reality* (patriarchy) and *male dominance as myth* (patriarchy "in name only"), I have been distinguishing between *male dominance as reality* (patriarchy and life under the regime of sex) and *male headship* (as part of a complementary duality, scripturally defined).

47. Rogers, "Female Forms of Power," 733–34. Rogers defines power in terms of "having considerable input into, or control over, important decision-making processes" (728) and distinguishes between "formal" and "informal" power. Peggy Reeves Sanday, studying hunter-gatherer contexts, distinguishes between outward (male) power (hunting, killing, power seeking) and inward (female) power (childbearing and power containing) (Sanday, *Female Power*). Glick and Fiske distinguish between "male structural power" and "female dyadic power" in modern contexts ("Ambivalent Sexism Inventory," 492).

advantages, values, and prestige, so that the members of each group see themselves as the 'winners' in respect to the other."[48]

Rather than a means of oppressive rule, male headship in such contexts is a counterbalancing force. Men may occupy the uppermost positions of society and even monopolize the formal positions of political power, but in such domestic-centered contexts it is the women who maintain considerable power de facto.[49] It may be that a woman is expected to submit to her husband as head, but she does so in a context where the man has already submitted himself to many of the goals, desires, and expectations of the woman.[50]

To posit that the patriarchal peasant culture has its own built-in measures for balancing gendered power relations admittedly runs contrary to certain strands of the anthropological literature on peasant modernization—then and now—much of which Rogers claims "rests on false assumptions regarding the role of women."[51] According to Rogers, anthropologists until her day had been working with an ill-founded assumption that women virtually everywhere play a subordinate role to men. Rogers's argument was that this was the result of widespread "androcentrism" in the field, with power defined exclusively in male-centric

---

48. Rogers, "Female Forms of Power," 729. Rogers later elaborates on this dynamic: "Because extra-household activities are given highest prestige, it is to men's advantage to claim the village sphere as their own. It is to the peasant woman's advantage as well, because it leaves her in control of the domestic sphere, which is the central unit of the community and the only sphere over which villagers may have much control" (747).

49. "In peasant societies," Rogers explains, "the domestic unit is of primary economic, political, and social importance.... In addition, it has been found that women have significant channels of power, quite apart from their households" ("Female Forms of Power," 733). "In a domestic-oriented community, the fact that men monopolize high prestige extra-household positions is insignificant. The power attribution in the private, not the public domain, is of primary importance" (746). See also Friedl, "Position of Women."

50. Elizabeth Fox-Genovese argues that female submission in domestic-centered contexts is part of a historical development of reciprocal submission between women and men. For her, the institutionalization of patriarchy "did more than subordinate women to men: it began a centuries'-long project to subordinate men to society." See her review of Lerner's *Women and History*, 612.

51. Rogers, "Female Forms of Power," 752. See also Rogers, "Once upon a Time," 156–57. While such claims remain contested in certain strands of feminist discourse, this is now taken for granted among classicists, who began as early as the 1960s to argue that terms like "patriarchy" and "male dominance" were inappropriate as general descriptors for all premodern cultures. See, e.g., Crook, "Patria Potestas"; Y. Thomas, "Vitae necisque potestas"; Saller, *Patriarchy, Property, and Death*. See also Meyers, "Was Ancient Israel Patriarchal?"

terms according to male values in male domains.[52] Rogers contended that "traditional women, at least in peasant societies, are by no means uniformly the downtrodden, subordinated creatures they have been assumed to be."[53] Once androcentric definitions of power have been abandoned, it becomes clear that women in such settings wield considerable power.[54]

For Rogers, moreover, "power" is not the only operative concept for understanding social fairness between the genders. Instead, one needs to account for other crucial factors such as autonomy, reward, and prestige, along with desired goals and the ability to attain them. Further, all of these factors must be evaluated with attention to the way each gender relates to differing spheres, whether economic, domestic, political, or religious.[55]

To identify any given culture as male dominant evidently requires more than simply identifying whether the positions of formal power are monopolized by men. It entails dynamic engagement with the inner workings of family and social life, accounting for the goals and desires of individuals, and whether each has the means to achieve its goals. It entails studied analyses of where decision-making power is located, and the ways each gender negotiates with the other to gain "structural" or "dyadic" power.

> What we see operating in peasant society is a kind of dialectic, a delicately balanced opposition of several kinds of power and authority: overt and covert, formal and informal, direct and indirect. For this reason . . . the model of one sex group in a "primary" or dominant role and the other in a "secondary" one is specious and ignores the complexity of the situation.[56]

52. Rogers, "Female Forms of Power," 728. See also R. Cohen, "Political System," 491.

53. Rogers, "Female Forms of Power," 748. She continues, "This first assumption having been challenged, the second one—that traditional women are emancipated in the process of modernization—is left in an awkward position. If women do not actually play such a subordinated role in the traditional setting, what happens when they become modernized?" (748–49). See also Greenough, "Women, Men, Children."

54. See, e.g., Desray, "Holistic Society."

55. Alice Schlegel suggests that power is in fact an insufficient category for understanding sexual rank and equality. Rather, evaluating sexual rank is three dimensional, including reward, prestige, and power ("Theory of Sexual Stratification," 3). See also Agassi, "Theories of Gender Equality," 168; Stockett, "Importance of Difference"; Stephens, *Family in Cross-Cultural Perspective*.

56. Rogers, "Female Forms of Power," 746.

Framed this way, a title such as "household head" does not indicate, by itself, an imbalance in power; and the "male head" does not indicate, by itself, male domination. Instead, the man's title as "head" (i.e., representative; figure of public authority/prestige) in such contexts can serve as a counterbalancing measure, a response to the woman's de facto power in such domestic-centered cultures.[57]

While her notion of male dominance as "myth" is certainly not true of all societies, Rogers suggests that it may yet apply not only to peasant societies but to a number of non-peasant contexts as well, providing they share the following six "essential elements":

1. Women are primarily associated with the domestic.
2. The society is domestic oriented.
3. Most ordinary and important interactions occur in the context of a face-to-face community, where informal relationships and forms of power are at least as significant a force in everyday life a. . . . authorized relationships and power.
4. Men have greater access to jural and other formal rights.
5. [Men] are occupied with activities which may at least be overtly considered important.
6. Men and women are approximately equally dependent on each other economically, socially, politically, or in other important ways.[58]

Contemporary Western societies largely fall outside of such a framework. Indeed, under the "economic regime" of an industrialized age, male dominance is all too often not "mythical" but actual.[59] And where male domineering rule is actual, male headship, even as a purportedly Christian ideal, all too easily aids oppression.

In both Rogers's and Illich's accounts, the transition from domestic-oriented toward wage-oriented societies marks the end of gender

---

57. Rogers suggests this exactly: "Within the domestic sphere, it is also to the woman's advantage that her husband be a figure of authority. . . . In this way, . . . if he is allowed to be the overt decision maker, his status as 'head of the family' is preserved, and with it, his—and his family's—image in the community. Here, the exchange, probably unconscious, is between power and image: 'I'll give you credit for making the decisions here, if you'll make the ones I tell you to'" ("Female Forms of Power," 747).

58. Rogers, "Female Forms of Power," 730.

59. Rogers, "Female Forms of Power," 749. E.g., Segalen, *Historical Anthropology of Family*, 218.

complementarity as a culturally given path toward flourishing. Still, both accounts offer an opportunity to envision male headship, at least theoretically, as a counterbalancing force within the lived dynamics of a given marriage, household, or society. This reveals a way that headship might be understood (conceptually, if not practically) as a function of gendered reciprocity and mutuality and part of a balanced network of give-and-take which serves the interests, needs, and goals of male and female alike.

CONCLUSION

The notion of male headship is an affront to the modern *homo economicus*, whose habitat is a genderless world under the regime of sex. Under the present regime male headship is necessarily a sign of inequality. But this has not always been so.

According to Illich, under the reign of gender, a gendered duality is simply a given of life under the sun. In such contexts, male heads have characteristically been part of the cultural fabric basic to familial and societal subsistence. Rogers has shown that within such frameworks, attributions of formal power (e.g., the male "head of household") can serve as balancing measures between the genders. Accordingly, I propose that male headship needs to be differentiated from male supremacy/dominance and reconceived as—at least potentially—a feature of an equal-regard gendered framework.

In such a framework the apparent inequality of deeming the man head of the woman is but one of a thousand "inequalities," each serving to balance and counterbalance a boundless network of give-and-takes which ebb and flow between women and men. And herein lies one of the great challenges in establishing "male headship" as part of a broader complementary vision for an egalitarian age: strictly speaking, a social vision that espouses the duality of the genders offers no genderless standard to which *this man* or *this woman* can be held, no final arbiter of equality between unequals. There is no tit-for-tat tally to be added and assessed, only countless acts of love and mercy, or the contrary, to be judged finally by the one who says, "The last shall be first, and the first shall be last."

CHAPTER 4

Revisionist Heads

Headship in Modern Interpretation

Far from seeking, like Homer, merely to make us forget our own reality for a few hours, [the Bible] seeks to overcome our reality; we are to fit our own life into its world, feel ourselves to be elements in its structure of universal history. ... Everything else that happens in the world can only be conceived as an element in this sequence; into it everything that is known about the world ... must be fitted as an ingredient of the divine plan.

—Erich Auerbach[1]

For millennia the Scripture of Israel offered its adherents a realistic and incisive vision of the world, including its depiction of humanity in our gendered dimensions. In the first creation account, the man and woman are together presented as the culmination of a great chain of created dualities—light and darkness, the skies above and the ground below, the dry ground and the gathered waters, and, finally, humankind emerging as male and female, the pinnacle of God's reciprocally ordered world (Gen 1:1–27).

In the second creation account, with the man made from dust (2:8–20), and the woman from the rib of the man (2:21–23), there is nothing especially flattering about the origins of either gender. Still, throughout the history of its reception (at least until the latter half of the twentieth

---

1. Auerbach, *Mimesis*, 15.

century) these Scriptures offered origin stories which were utterly realistic in their depictions of the genders, naming the human condition with profound explanatory power. Humanity was created from and for God and in turn, the male and female from and for each other. Even the respective judgments on Adam and Eve for their sin—the man toiling "in pain" (3:17) and the woman being "ruled" by the man (3:16)—for all their bewildering unfairness, stated the case of human life as it genealogically unfolded.[2]

When the apostle Paul then came to write of the man as "head" (viz. representative) of the woman, he was naming a reality that was, scripturally speaking, utterly plausible and consistent with the lived realities of Israel's social life. In a world of patriarchs, priests, and kings, of male heads of households, tribes, and nations, there was nothing remarkable about Paul's household codes—or of Jesus's all-male apostolate for that matter. Following these scripturally inscribed patterns, moreover, it is no surprise that the church came to affirm an all-male priesthood—a norm fixed in its tradition for nearly two thousand years, in Catholic, Orthodox, and Protestant Churches with near global unanimity.[3]

How, then, did it come to pass that the scriptural account of humanity, in its gendered dimension, came to be seen as implausible, unrealistic, even deplorable within certain sectors of the modern church? More specifically, how is it that the normatively male-headed church and family came to be seen as excisable from contemporary mainstream expressions of Christianity?

Some have argued that such modern objections have come about largely, if not wholly, as a result of the advances of feminist ideologies, facilitated by secularist presuppositions and modern social-scientific findings. In this perspective, the overturning of the church's male-headed tradition among certain Protestant denominations is the result of an

---

2. There is a sense in which the story of Israel, with its patriarchal social life, is the story of God's curse (Gen 3:13–24) genealogically unfolding, where the woman's desire would be for her husband, and he would "rule over" her—not in unitive love but in disharmony as one *over* the "other." It is also noteworthy that, with distinct yet unified origins—the man "from the dust" and the woman "from the man" (Gen 2:7, 21–22)—the subsequent judgments of God over their respective sins follow the logic of their distinctly ordered beginnings. The man is judged in relation to the ground from which he was made and the garden that he governed (Gen 2:8–20; 3:17–19); and the woman judged in relation to the man from whom she was made and with respect to the children of their union (2:21–23; 3:16).

3. See 1n1. [X-REF]

"alien ideology" infiltrating this strand of the church.[4] Certainly, the burgeoning feminisms of the 1960s onward have had their influence on Western cultures and the church at large. But feminist ideologies, especially in their more radical enunciations, would never have found a home in the church apart from the church's own transformations from within—namely, transformations in theological method and plausibility structures which enabled certain sectors of the church to reshape the dogmatic task, and thus reshape Christian dogma.[5]

From this perspective, the present challenge with notions of "male headship" has little if anything to do with the need for "better exegesis" or the employment of new "hermeneutical procedures";[6] rather, it requires coming to terms with an unprecedented transformation in our social imaginary—coming to terms with a new set of "plausibility structures"—which have reset the boundaries for the present gender debates, both within the church and without.

To be clear, the goal of this chapter is not to enter into the contemporary headship debate so much as to interrogate the structures on which the debate rests, along with its methodological presuppositions—and to point to a better way. In order to understand the present gendered framework in relation to the past, we will chart out two paths which will eventually converge. First, I begin by telling the story of the coming of age of a new theological paradigm—modern Christian theology—noting the ways in which theology's modernization created space for "alien claims" to enter into the realm of Christian faith and practice. Second, we will follow a parallel path exploring the modernization of work, with special attention to those factors that have given shape to modernized sexual identities and, ultimately, the construction of the modern self. What we will find is that these newly established sexual identities, forged in part through the modernization of work, have found a home within modern theology, broadly conceived, resulting in an odd marriage between feminist theory and Christian faith—and sidelining fundamental elements of a scriptural account of gender and human personhood.

---

4. See, e.g., Kassian, *Feminist Mistake*.
5. See Kathryn Greene-McCreight, *Feminist Reconstructions*.
6. Hays quotes an apt simile by Oliver O'Donovan: "Interpreters who think that they can determine the proper ethical application of the Bible solely through more sophisticated exegesis are like people who believe that they can fly if only they flap their arms hard enough" (Hays, *Moral Vision*, 3).

Ultimately, we will find that nothing short of the construction of a new and modern "self" has rendered scriptural gender arrangements (traditionally understood) untenable.

MODERNIZING THEOLOGY: FOUNDATIONS FOR FEMINIST HERMENEUTICS

As I have noted, a scripturally depicted gendered duality has become implausible not only within modern Western cultures at large but also within the Western Church. Such a transformation within ecclesial cultures in particular was made possible by the establishment of new plausibility structures which have rendered older assumptions concerning distinctly gendered identities untenable. These new plausibility structures will be the focus of the next section ("Modernizing Work").

In this first section, our focus is on the modernization of theological method, whereby the enterprise of "modern theology" has become uniquely vulnerable to the influence of alien ideologies. In order to explain this methodological shift, I begin by (1) setting the contemporary headship debate within the context of feminist hermeneutics, then (2) identifying modern methodological developments which have reshaped the theological enterprise such that feminist programs have found their seat at the table of modern Christian theology.[7]

A. Feminist Hermeneutics and the Headship Debate

The canonical writings have not only been subject to patriarchal interpretation through the centuries but are themselves products of patriarchal hermeneutics. The Bible is permeated with the language, symbols, and ideas of female inferiority and sub-humanity. Whatever the historical reality, the biblical authors, influenced by political and cultural tendencies, composed thoroughly patriarchal documents.

—Mary Ann Tolbert[8]

---

7. I define "feminist hermeneutics" as that enterprise which seeks to engage the biblical text and/or Christian tradition from the standpoint of feminist theory, such that the central tenets of feminist theory function as the ultimate standards by which the Scriptures are judged.

8. Tolbert, "Bible and Feminist Hermeneutics," 123.

In her 1983 article "Defining the Problem: The Bible and Feminist Hermeneutics," Mary Ann Tolbert expresses some of the key concerns of early feminist biblical scholars and theologians. For these scholars the "problem" was not simply a matter of a few patriarchal passages here and there. Rather, the blatantly patriarchal "texts of terror" were only the tip of the iceberg.[9] Since the Bible was written in an age of incontrovertible patriarchy, not only did the text stand in need of feminist interrogation, but so did the biases of the authors behind the text, along with the entire history of interpretation, grounded as it was in social and philosophical frameworks that espoused female subordination. The nearly two thousand years of androcentric readings of androcentric texts were almost exclusively through androcentric lenses, and therefore needed to be challenged and overcome.

These concerns first gained widespread traction at the outset of the American and British feminist movements of the 1960s and 1970s, commonly known as second wave feminism.[10] These movements first gave rise to the discipline of "feminist biblical hermeneutics," grounded in feminist theory. In the words of Gerda Lerner, feminist theory consists

> (1) of the awareness of women that they belong to a subordinate group and that, as members of such a group, they have suffered wrongs; (2) the recognition that their condition of subordination is not natural, but societally determined; (3) the development of a sense of sisterhood; (4) the autonomous definition by women of goals and strategies for changing their condition; and (5) the development of an alternate vision of the future.[11]

The principal task of the Christian feminist was to relate feminist theory to the Christian tradition. This involved coming to terms with the Bible as a patriarchal book, the church as a patriarchal institution, and the Scriptures as a potential tool for sexism and misogyny.

By the 1980s there was an explosion—both in terms of a proliferation and fragmentation—of feminist hermeneutics, with two dominant

---

9. See, e.g., Trible, *Texts of Terror*.

10. Thiselton, *Hermeneutics*, 283–87. From the 1950s through the 1980s several works were published that would serve as catalysts and sources of inspiration for the next generations of feminist theorists. See 64n17.

11. Lerner, *Creation of Feminist Consciousness*, 14. As Greene-McCreight has argued, feminist theory is the "practical parent" of feminist theology, which offers its own distinctive theological narrative: the "fall" into patriarchy, the already-not-yet redemption from patriarchy through feminist consciousness, and the eschatological vision of gender equality as the ultimate salvation of humanity (*Feminist Reconstructions*, 34).

approaches emerging: a hermeneutic of loyalty, and one of revision.[12] We will engage the first ("loyalist") approach only briefly, as it has generally been dismissed for not representing a genuinely "feminist" hermeneutic. The second ("revisionist") approach we will then engage more critically, before finally interrogating the very grounds on which these debates have taken place.

(1) The Hermeneutic of Loyalty

Many early Christian feminists claimed that biblical interpretation needed to conform to the doctrinal standards of "women's experience." For the loyalist, however, such an approach gets the theological task backward. In this perspective, all truth claims, including those of feminist theory, are to be evaluated in light of the Christian Scriptures, not the other way around. Feminist theory, with all of its claims, is ultimately to be judged by the Bible.[13]

The main stream of feminist biblical interpretation rejects the loyalist hermeneutic for its apparent failure to address and remedy the kinds of criticisms raised by feminist theorists.[14] Loyalists are accused of taking a "supranaturalistic" or Docetic approach to the Bible, in which its words are understood as untouched by the human cultural assumptions of its authors. Where feminist theorists assume that the patriarchal culture in which the Bible is written, received, and redacted necessitates a critical reception of these Scriptures, loyalists assume that these same Scriptures escape such (sinful) patriarchal pitfalls. Or, if the Scriptures do contain patriarchal teachings, it is because the kind of patriarchy promoted is not inherently problematic. Of course, when the latter tact is taken, the loyalist tends to affirm traditional hierarchical functional differences between men and women, even the place of the man as "ruler over" the woman. For this reason, most feminist interpreters have found the loyalist interpretation untenable, for its failure to reckon with the apparent disparity

---

12. See Osiek, "Feminist and the Bible." Among early feminist approaches were also "rejectionists," as a third major type, who sought neither loyalty to the text, traditionally conceived, nor a revisionist reclamation of the text, but rather rejected it outright as a dangerous source standing against women's liberation. E.g., Daly: *Church and Second Sex; Beyond God the Father.* See Letham, "Hermeneutics of Feminism," 6.

13. See, e.g., Kassian, *Feminist Mistake*, esp. 47–48, 116–18, 292–98; Elliot, *Let Me Be Woman.* See also Schottroff et al., *Feminist Interpretation*, 37–38.

14. Schottroff et. al., *Feminist Interpretation*, 38. See also Osiek, "Feminist and the Bible."

between the patriarchal norms presented in the Bible and the egalitarian norms assumed and sought in the present age of the modern West.

Some loyalists contest these criticisms, of course. In my estimation, however, where the loyalist approach typically falls short is in promoting a vision of gender that is too often and unwittingly shaped by a Western male-dominant ideology which is in fact sexist.

(2) The Hermeneutic of Revision

In contrast to the loyalists, the feminist revisionists accept the central tenets of feminist theory as basic to the biblical interpretive task. Here the pervasiveness of patriarchy in the text can neither be affirmed as good nor as a matter of indifference; rather, it must be challenged at every point through the lens of "women's experience." The goal is not to undercut the authority of the Scriptures as a whole or in part, but to relativize all parts in relation to the Christian feminist's central motive—namely, women's full inclusion in the promise and realization of liberation.[15]

There are at least two key problems with such an approach, however, from the standpoint of historic Christian orthodoxy. First, such an approach shifts the hermeneutical center away from the church's long-standing interpretive center—namely, the "rule of faith," a creedal summary of the faith which centers on Christ as the substance and fulfillment of the Scriptures. The rule of faith has served to anchor the interpretive task within the comprehensive structure of the whole of the scriptural arc. Interpreting Scripture according to another "central motive"—no matter how important, just or "scriptural"—inevitably displaces the particular narrative content that has served to orient and anchor Christian interpretation for two millennia. In this way, the revisionist approach marks a departure from the hermeneutical approaches of the apostolic and Nicene traditions.[16]

Moreover, not only does such an approach replace the church's historic interpretive "rule" with a new one, thereby tethering Christian interpretation to a new set of goals and interests, but even when the interpretive conclusions of revisionists seem to cohere with historic orthodoxy, such conclusions themselves stand in need of interrogation. For

15. Tolbert, "Bible and Feminist Hermeneutics," 122.
16. Greene-McCreight makes this same point in *Feminist Reconstructions*. For a discussion on the "rule of faith," see Radner and Sumner, *Rule of Faith*; Ferguson, *Rule of Faith*.

example, when "women's liberation" is posited as the new hermeneutical center, the revisionist—centered now on "liberation"—is prone to filling in the meaning of such liberation with content that is untethered to the message concerning Christ. The "liberation" which is so central to the scriptural narrative is thus itself redefined in service of the modern aspirations of "women's liberation." The Scriptures, however, offer their own positive vision of what liberation entails, most fundamentally conceived as freedom from the bondage of sin and death and from the dominion of darkness (Rom 6–8; Gal 5; Col 1:13), accomplished in Christ, by grace, through faith, and *for* obedience, even conceived as a new kind of "enslavement," as disciples become "slaves" of God (Rom 6:15–19; Gal 5:13). A properly Christian articulation of liberation must not be stripped of these particularities.[17]

Thus, whatever hermeneutical center the feminist revisionist chooses—whether a "liberationist" center, or "women's experience" or a more egalitarian history "within" or "behind" the text—in each case the problem remains the same: namely, an interpretive center is chosen other than a "rule" (or "guideline" for faithful interpretation) which tethers all interpretation to the substance, the narrative content and center, of the Scriptures themselves.

A number of Christian feminists were unsatisfied with the kinds of early revisionist approaches described above. It was not enough to simply reorganize the Christian story around a feminist center; rather, an entirely new interpretive framework was needed within which to understand the Christian story as a whole. For this, some took their cue from the "demythologizing program" of Rudolf Bultmann.

For Bultmann, the central problem for modern interpreters was that the scriptural texts were outdated, according to the standards of modernity, and thus the mythological character of the Bible needed

---

17. To speak of liberation in this way is not to spiritualize it so as to render it inconsequential in relation to, e.g., the oppression of women, institutional slavery, or any other form of social bondage; rather, such a "spiritual" liberation from bondage is always necessarily an embodied liberation, with physical and social consequences. Its goal is indeed to "set the captives free," body and soul. But, again, such freedom is to be understood in light of the central plot of the Christian story—namely, that God in Christ is reconciling all things to himself by establishing a kingdom, a royal priesthood, in all the earth (Col 1:20; 1 Pet 2:9). God has determined to bring his "peace on earth" (Luke 2:14)—that we might have "fellowship" one with another. "And our fellowship is with the Father, and with His Son, Jesus Christ" (1 John 1:3). This "fellowship," in the power of the Spirit, is the meaning, the means, and the goal of liberation, scripturally speaking.

"demythologizing." Some discerned in Bultmann a modernizing method that could be applied to the feminist cause, where the problem was not so much the *mythological* but the *patriarchal* character of the Bible, which needed "depatriarchalizing."[18]

What many such revisionist feminists failed to see, however, was that their preferred (Bultmannian) kernel-husk dualism was not simply "one way forward" for feminists. Rather, as we shall see, a modern form-content dualism had become the methodological foundation for modernizing the theological enterprise as a whole, and remained the only ground on which the feminist-revisionist edifice could stand.

(3) New Plausibilities: Interrogating the Grounds for Debate

Having briefly outlined "loyalist" and "revisionist" approaches to the challenge of a feminist interpretation of Scripture, we have seen that there is no simple way to reconcile the basic affirmations of feminist theory with the scriptural corpus without either undermining the equal status of women with men (as the loyalists tend to do) or undermining traditional scriptural claims and interpretations (as the revisionists tend to do). In this loyalist-revisionist tug-of-war both sides are playing a losing game, as each tries to merge scriptural claims with a secular framework within which such claims simply do not fit—the loyalist forcing "male headship" (viz. rulership, leadership) into an alien modernist framework, and the revisionist forcing an alien social framework onto the Scriptures.

All the while, the greatest challenge in this controversy remains hidden beneath the surface. Even as each side has offered arguments for and against the ongoing relevance of male headship in the contemporary church, neither has sufficiently acknowledged the underlying challenge—namely, that the ground on which the debate has taken place has shifted tremendously. The very social landscape that once made male headship an unquestionable given—even a social good(!)—has given way to another set of plausibility structures which, I will argue, have made historic theological accounts of gender, including notions of male headship, an unseemly cultural fit for most in the modern West.

Some may quip that this lost "social landscape" is simply the loss of "patriarchy," and that with the passing of patriarchy, a scriptural account of gender (including "male headship") loses its place. However, as

---

18. See Tolbert, "Bible and Feminist Hermeneutics," 125–26.

we have seen, our Western past, even where the norm of the male head has prevailed, cannot be construed too broadly in terms of "the rule of the father" and female subjugation—as though male-occupied authority structures have always entailed male dominance and the absence of female agency (see ch. 3). Neither can the historic place of the man as "head" be dismissed as a mere function of patriarchy or a feature of male dominance (see ch. 2). We have seen that the male head, scripturally defined, is at least potentially a social good, a counterbalancing force, under certain social and economic conditions.

But, again, what was once a given, scripturally and traditionally, has become utterly implausible to contemporary Western sensibilities. We will now consider how it came to be that a scripturally gendered duality became implausible, even within the life of the church.

B. The New Methodological Substructure

In *Feminist Reconstructions of Christian Doctrine: Narrative Analysis and Appraisal*, Kathryn Greene-McCreight argues that feminist theology would appear "incongruous" with Christian theology if not for certain innovations in Western theological method. As it stands, however, modern theology has provided a home for the feminist theological program. An interpretive approach at odds with premodern exegetical practice is now fully compatible in the realm of modern biblical hermeneutics.[19]

Central to this story is the separation of form from content that has so shaped the modern theological enterprise—a dichotomy often traced back to the "grandfather" of modern theology, Immanuel Kant (1724-1804).[20] In his 1793 *Religion Within the Boundaries of Mere Reason*, Kant articulated what would become a characteristically modern notion of the separation of philosophy from theology, of rationality from the realm of ethics. Here, the true meaning of "religion" (ethical content)

---

19. For one telling of the transition from premodern to modern engagements with Scripture, see Frei, *Eclipse of Biblical Narrative*, 1-65.

20. See Greene-McCreight, *Feminist Reconstructions*, 30. Here she identifies Kant, Schleiermacher, Feuerbach, and Bultmann as the four "fathers" of modern theology. Alternately, Peter Leithart locates the beginning of the modern theological form-content dichotomy with the Dutch Lutheran Lodewijk Meyer, in his 1666 work entitled *Philosophy as the Interpreter of Holy Scripture*. It is here, according to Leithart, where theology becomes a subcategory of philosophy, representing a break from the Protestant Orthodoxy of Meyer's forebears and from the broader interpretive tradition stretching from John Cassian through John Calvin (Leithart, *Deep Exegesis*, 7-22).

is severed from the form in which it is delivered (the scriptural text), offering "a hermeneutical method for stripping the chaff from the kernel of Christianity."[21]

Though the form-content dichotomy had found some traction among theologians prior to Kant, such a methodology largely remained on the theological fringes, until Friedrich Schleiermacher (1768–1834). For Schleiermacher, religion consisted most fundamentally in the "experience" or "intuition" of the divine. Dogmas, as with Kant, were the "shell" of religious life, add-ons to make sense of the ineffable—"abstractions... useful for persuading to moral action," in the end to be discarded.[22] The text was a husk, giving way to the kernel of religious experience, consummately described as the "feeling of absolute dependence."[23]

Although few theologians would come to adopt Schleiermacher's theological program wholesale, his theological method nevertheless gained widespread acceptance.[24] One particularly powerful propagator of this methodology was Rudolf Bultmann (1884–1976), who was seeking to rehabilitate Christian faith for the modern era. For Bultmann, the basic problem with Christian faith in the modern world was that there were outdated "mythic" elements in Scripture. He aimed thus "to remove the unnecessary stumbling blocks for the modern reader which are present in the ancient writers' mythological worldview."[25]

What became paramount for Bultmann was not to understand or believe the text in its literal expression, clothed as it was in mythic language and presuppositions, but to understand and believe the kerygma—the gospel—discerned within the text. The text was to be "demythologized," stripped of its mythic-historic form, in order to arrive at the more basic underlying transhistorical message of Christ. The "special motive" in interpreting the Scriptures was "to hear in the Bible authoritative words about our existence." Here the good news is that humans can move from "inauthenticity" to "authenticity" by moving from unbelief to

---

21. See Leithart, *Deep Exegesis*, 24, 29. See also Oman, introduction to *On Religion*, xxii–liv; Palmquist, "Immanuel Kant," 71.

22. Oman, introduction to *On Religion*, xlii; for Schleiermacher's own words, see Schleiermacher, *On Religion*, 15–16.

23. Schleiermacher, *On Religion*, second speech, 22.

24. See Braaten and Jenson, *Map of Twentieth-Century Theology*, 5.

25. Greene-McCreight, *Feminist Reconstructions*, 30. As Bultmann says, the aim of demythologizing is "not to eliminate the mythological statements but to interpret them. It is a method of hermeneutics" ("Demythologizing," 293).

the life "under faith." This anthropologically centered "existential appeal" is what calls us to faith and leads to our "justification."[26]

Bultmann thus reinterprets the gospel, scripturally and dogmatically articulated for "modern man," and reconceived in existentialist terms. For all his efforts to move beyond a conservative-liberal divide, however, Bultmann remains methodologically within the ideological framework of theological liberalism. In fact, he is bolstering its program by enshrining in theological discourse a Kantian form-content dualism in his treatment of the text as a husk and the kerygma its kernel.[27]

Such an approach is fundamental to modern revisionist theologies of gender generally, and feminist theologies in particular, and remains at odds with Nicene orthodoxy.[28] Moreover, as we shall see, this separation of the textual form from its content will render all such modern theologies unstable—vulnerable to housing alien claims.

MODERNIZING WORK: THE INDUSTRIAL REVOLUTION AS A SEXUAL REVOLUTION

In chapter 3 we observed that the Industrial Revolution was in its own way a sexual revolution. To use the categories of Ivan Illich, Western civilization has undergone a transformation, out from the "reign of gender," now under a "regime of sex" where, as Illich puts it, "both genders are stripped and, neutered, the man ends up on top."[29]

For Illich, sexual identities (which is to say *human* identities) are irreversibly transformed through this process of industrialization. The dual spheres of woman and man are transmuted into a uni-spherical economic hierarchy, consisting characteristically of male paid and female unpaid labor, the latter of which Illich calls "shadow work."[30]

---

26. See Bultmann, "Demythologizing," 298, 327–28.

27. See Porter and Robinson, *Hermeneutics*, 232–33, 238; Mueller-Vollmer, *Hermeneutics Reader*, 36.

28. As Greene-McCreight argues, apart from this modernizing theological movement many feminist theologies could hardly have been recognized as "Christian" except as a subset of modern liberal theology. She cites Feuerbach, *Essence of Christianity*, as the climax of this modernizing trend (Greene-McCreight, *Feminist Reconstructions*).

29. Illich, *Gender*, 178–79. For a critical engagement with this claim, see ch. 3.

30. Compared to preindustrial domestic labor, Illich describes shadow work as "that entirely different form of unpaid work which an industrial society demands as a necessary complement to the production of goods and services. This kind of unpaid servitude does not contribute to subsistence. Quite the contrary, equally with

Building on Illich's claims, we will now consider more specifically the ways in which the process of industrialization served to modernize sexual identities, transforming the economic sphere into a male sphere, and "women's work" into a denigrated form of work, resulting finally in a crisis in women's identity.[31] We will then find that the newly established sexual identities of women and men alike have become determinative for modern theology, demanding a thoroughly revisionist account of gender from within. The theologian is thus tasked with accommodating newly fashioned sexual identities within the realm of Christian theology.

In short, the modernization of work has led to modernized sexual identities—requiring the interchangeability of the sexes—which were in turn received into modern theology, rendering possible an odd marriage between feminist theory and the Christian faith.

A. The Elevation of Wage Labor as Supreme Status Symbol

In order to understand the importance of the modernization of work for the construction of modern identities it is instructive to begin by noting the ways in which work was practically and conceptually reconceived through the Protestant Reformation. As Ulrich Beck has argued, during the Reformation work became reimagined as no longer a means to an end—namely, subsistence—but as an end in itself, vested with ultimate significance. It thus became an appropriate identity marker and status symbol for constructing the modern self. "Work, and work alone, determined status, merits, and the usefulness of both subjects and communities."[32] Following the Reformation, the individual's status and worth would be determined most fundamentally not by wealth, religion,

---

wage-labor, it ravages subsistence. I call this complement to wage-labor 'shadow-work'. It comprises most housework women do in their homes and apartments, the activities connected with shopping, most of the homework of students cramming for exams, the toil expended commuting to and from the job. It includes the stress of forced consumption, the tedious and regimented surrender to therapists, compliance with bureaucrats, the preparation for work to which one is compelled, and many of the activities usually labelled 'family life'" ("Shadow Work," 37).

31. Matthews points to the 1963 publication of Friedan, *Feminine Mystique*, as an early articulation of and response to this crisis (Matthews, *Just a Housewife*, 14).

32. See Beck, *Brave New World of Work*. Philip Rieff makes a similar argument, marking out the transformation from the medieval "religious man" to the industrial "economic man" (*Triumph of the Therapeutic*). See also Shafi, "Caregiving, Work, and Debate."

or interests, nor by familial or social titles and functions, but by one's economic labor and the status conferred by it.[33]

Where labor would be redefined as "paid labor," the individual's status and worth would be dependent on his or her participation in the market economy. And where the market economy excluded women—functioning by default as a *male* economy—women's access to social status and dignity were severely limited. In short, where work as wage labor became definitive of one's status, and work as such became a male prerogative, women suffered a loss of dignity—a loss of "status, merits and [perceived] usefulness." The transition from economic partners to housewives performing forced, unpaid labor thus marks a devastating change in women's status.

B. The Rise and Fall of Domesticity: From Economic Partner to Unpaid Laborer

In *Just a Housewife: The Rise and Fall of Domesticity in America*, Glenna Matthews narrates the story of the effects of industrialization and secularization on the American colonial household. According to Matthews, from the eighteenth through the twentieth centuries, the proliferation of household commodities and new technologies brought a radical shift in cultural perceptions of domesticity and its societal status. The status of the "housewife" (and domesticity in general) went through a transition: from esteemed in 1750 to highly esteemed in 1850 to disesteemed in 1950 and beyond.[34]

"In 1750," Matthews writes, "the colonial American home was an essential locus of production for the entire society." Domestic tasks were productive tasks, essential to subsistence. "Soap required home manufacture, bread must be baked at home, bacon cured, and clothing

---

33. Beck explains, "The extent to which work is part of the modern European's moral being and self-image is evident from the fact that, in Western culture, it has long been the only relevant source and the only valid measure for the evaluation of human beings and their actions. Only those things which are proven and recognized to be work count as valuable" (*Brave New World of Work*, 10). See also Shafi, "Discourses of Work."

34. For Matthews, the denigration of domesticity coincides not with industrialism but with material factors in the postindustrial era. For reasons outlined below, domesticity had a brief rise in prestige following industrialization in America, before it would be relegated to the inferior standing as "subeconomic." Like the brightening of a lightbulb before its sudden burnout, the housewife's newfound nineteenth-century luster would soon turn dark.

pieced together for growing families, because consumer goods were not commercially available."[35] The woman was man's economic partner, sharing in the toils of life. Over the course of the next century the domestic sphere only increased in esteem, gaining unprecedented social, political and religious significance. Following the American Revolution, the home became the mainstay for the socialization of American citizens, deemed "crucial to the success of the nation" by politicians and pundits. The mother was redefined as "Republican Mother," the chief source and symbol of the nation's moral and social well-being and the bedrock of national interest whose "sphere could influence the outcome of history." Further, with this new "intermingling of the domestic and the political," women's education was "taken much more seriously than ever before," with girls almost as likely as boys to be found in school. "All of this represented a sharp break with the colonial past."[36]

This politicization of the home coincided with a suffusion of religious transcendence in the home, encouraged and propagated within the Romantic Evangelicalism of the mid-nineteenth century. This movement created "a religious role for the home that made it an even more important institution . . . seen as the front line of action to produce virtuous citizens." Each home came to be conceived as a "little church."[37]

With these and other changes, Matthews argues, an unprecedented dignity was popularly afforded women precisely for their maternal and domestic functions, which now secured them cultural authority and a public voice.[38] With the housewife newly afforded this high social standing, Matthews determines that the nineteenth-century "cult of domesticity" was by and large good for women. "Simply put, the epic style of domesticity empowered women both inside and outside the home."[39]

Such high esteem for domesticity would not last, however. Following the first World War and the Technological Revolution (ca. 1870–1914), the American home would undergo a postindustrial revolution. Within a decade or so the image of the idealized home would shift from "the Victorian domicile of some remote ancestor" to "the servantless home of the 1920s, filled with electrical appliances and brand-name products."

35. Matthews, *Just a Housewife*, 3–4.
36. Matthews, *Just a Housewife*, 6–7, 21, 35. See also Kerber, "Republican Mother," 61.
37. Matthews, *Just a Housewife*, 19–21.
38. Matthews, *Just a Housewife*, 28, 65.
39. Matthews, *Just a Housewife*, 34–35.

Matthews remarks, "The distance between those two homes was traversed with remarkable speed, so that by 1930 the 'home of consumption' was firmly entrenched in American culture."[40]

At first glance, this new "home of consumption" seemed a welcome change for the housewife. New technologies promised less work and more leisure. Along with these cultural and technological transformations, however, a new and impoverished identity was being shaped for the housewife, whose role had turned chiefly from a producer to a consumer.[41] Matthews goes on to demonstrate that this devaluation of the domestic was further reinforced by the concurrent process of secularization, bolstered by Darwinian evolution, resulting in the loss of a religiously suffused "transcendent home."[42]

In relation to the strongly Protestant cultural undercurrent in America at the time, Darwinism offered a radically different conceptualization of the world, and one which served to reinforce the woman's domestic identity even while diminishing her at nearly every point. Matthews summarizes:

> Darwin and many of his followers explicitly stated that women are biologically inferior to men. This, too, had a negative impact on the status of the home. Perhaps most damaging to the home was the fact that Darwin's theory of sexual selection located the source of evolutionary change in male struggle for mates, making men and male activity the "vanguard of evolution." Finally, Darwinism helped promote the secularization of American society, and thus served further to undermine the religious role of the home. All of this eroded the interest of American intellectuals, including women, in domesticity.[43]

In an attempt to salvage the sphere of domesticity, a turn-of-the-century discipline emerged—"home economics"—which would reconceptualize the home as an industrial workplace and the housewife as a workplace professional. It was thought that if the home could be made respectable according to the standards of the new economic regime "it would not matter so much if one sex was assigned the public world of

---

40. Matthews, *Just a Housewife*, 172.//
41. Matthews, *Just a Housewife*, 192.
42. Matthews, *Just a Housewife*, 144.
43. Matthews, *Just a Housewife*, 117. See also Fleming, "Charles Darwin, Anaesthetic Man."

work and the other sex was consigned to the home."⁴⁴ In this way, the economic production that had been dislodged from the home and reshaped in industrialized terms was creeping back into the home to refashion the home in its image and likeness and to afford it a measure of capitalist dignity.

With this economic refashioning, however, the home was only to be further denigrated. Now not only was housewifery unpaid work but its value was to be judged by the standards of professionalized industries. What was once valued as a counterpart to and refuge from the domain of industry professionalism and commodity production was now becoming another territory for industrial expansion. What had been sorely overlooked was the fact that, until this time, the home was important precisely *because* its purview lay "outside the cash nexus." Domesticity marked the celebration of values "in opposition to marketplace values."⁴⁵

It was through the burgeoning of "home economics," then, that "the devaluation of the female craft tradition . . . was greatly accelerated." The celebrated new discipline of home economics rendered all older generations of women more irrelevant than ever. Whereas the domestic craft, with all its demands, was once handed down from one generation to the next, it was now placed decisively in the hands of "professionals," "experts" who were bringing science and new technologies to bear on the home.⁴⁶ Housewives no longer needed to learn from their mothers and grandmothers but from "home ec" professionals.

Matthews concludes, "Thus the complex of social, political, and cultural factors that had created the ideology of domesticity and an enhanced possibility for self-respect on the part of the housewife had dissolved by the mid[-]twentieth century."⁴⁷ Labor had become the central determinant of one's status, yet with labor dislocated out of the home, women were left to the domestic sphere even as it was transformed from a productive to a consumptive sphere. With the woman as housewife cut off from participation in economic production, she was thereby cut off from the chief cultural sources of meaning and status. All of this produced a crisis in women's identity—what Betty Friedan would call "the problem that has no name," a problem that Matthews describes as "the

---

44. Matthews, *Just a Housewife*, 171.
45. Matthews, *Just a Housewife*, 171.
46. Matthews, *Just a Housewife*, 146, 193.
47. Matthews, *Just a Housewife*, 222.

emptiness of many housewives' lives," stripped of their prior dignity and status.[48]

C. Responding to the Fall of Domesticity

For many, it seemed the most straightforward response to the "unnamed problem" was for women to reclaim their rightful and historic place as full economic partners and co-producers with men. In an era of wage labor, this would entail women earning wages and joining men in the now male-shaped and male-dominant economic sphere. For others, conversely, the crucial need was not for women's "liberation" (understood by some as a euphemism for women's capitulation to the economic sphere of men), but rather the rehabilitation of the domestic.[49] In the latter perspective, capitulation to the super-valuation of "the workforce" would have widespread detrimental effects on women, especially those of the lower and middle economic classes. The pressing need was to re-dignify the domestic sphere—not to abandon it.[50] Sadly, construed in this way as a zero-sum game, victory for either side would amount to a net loss for women.

As is now becoming clearer, what was needed was not a capitulation to one side or the other—to women's economic equality with men

---

48. Matthews, *Just a Housewife*, xiv–xv. To illustrate, two women spend their days preparing meals and cleaning up after themselves. The first does so as a wealthy family's personal chef, the second as a wife and mother. Even if they perform identical tasks with comparable levels of competency, the former is esteemed as a contributor to the workforce, an economic competitor. The latter is "just a housewife."

49. See, e.g., Washburne, "Masculine and Feminine Occupations," 555; Abbott, "Women Do Not Wish Suffrage."

50. These divergent approaches would collide in the protracted battle over the Equal Rights Amendment, designed in the 1920s to remove all gender-based distinctions in federal and state laws that would discriminate against women. In 1971 the ERA was finally approved by the US House of Representatives as "a largely uncontroversial amendment." In 1972, however, a conservative coalition arose against the amendment, led by Phyllis Schlafly, the activist and self-described housewife who argued that "[women's] domestic roles actually freed them from the drudgeries and dangers of the office, the factory, and the military, among other male-dominated venues." Schlafly's STOP ERA coalition would play an important role in the eventual denial of the ERA's ratification in 1979. See E. Miller, "Phyllis Schlafly's 'Positive' Freedom," 279. Miller argues, "The central tension in the ERA debate may not have arisen between feminists who favored freedom and antifeminists who did not. It may rather have constituted a disagreement about what freedom means, or *which* freedom is most congruent with American identity" (279–80). See Schlafly, *Power of Positive Woman*. For a brief overview of Schlafly's life, see Martin, "Phyllis Schlafly, 'First Lady.'"

or to reclaiming the dignity of domesticity—but rather a fundamental restructuring of social values and the current economic structure.[51] As Monica Shafi has argued, such a restructuring involves most basically the reclamation and rehabilitation of domestic "care work."[52] By narrowing individual worth to a category of economic productivity, a great disservice is done to all whose livelihood and work falls outside of the cash nexus. And this has, by default, had a disproportionately negative effect on women.

Some might fear that such a "rehabilitation of the domestic" is a step backward and threatens to undo some of the progress of the women's movement. Shafi argues otherwise:

> Emphasizing the importance of care work and its impact on political, economic, and social arrangements is not to be seen as a strategy of relegating women to traditional concepts of femininity. On the contrary, acknowledging the significance is critical . . . for women's equality.[53]

For Shafi, one of the great shortcomings of the women's movement has been its failure to invest domesticity with dignity at the same time as affording women equal rights and opportunities in the economic sphere. Indeed, as Matthews says, "A disproportionate emphasis on one realm at the expense of the other impoverishes the whole of life."[54]

This story of the modernization of work thus comes to its climax with the elevation of paid labor and its correlate—the depreciation of domestic labor. Rather than fighting to recover the dignity of the domestic, the feminist mainstream joined the force of the new economic regime. Accordingly, the newly restrictive female domains were only further devalued and denigrated. Women's "equality" now meant that women were to be on an equal footing with men in the economic sphere. In spite of important advances made in women's economic equality at this time, the great majority of women would nevertheless remain disproportionately tied to the domestic. In this way, the women's movement would leave the majority of women behind.

By centering on economic equality, a new shape was given to women's identity; they were now economic neuters in the newly designed

---

51. See Held, "Gender Identity"; Slaughter, "Can't Have It All."
52. Shafi, "Caregiving, Work, and Debate," 152, 161.
53. Shafi, "Caregiving, Work, and Debate," 154.
54. Matthews, *Just a Housewife*, 225–26.

sphere where male and female workers are considered interchangeable. With women's social identities largely reframed and reshaped in the mold of economic man, many women began to reject any association with or semblance to historic forms of femininity; they needed to distinguish themselves from the traditions of womanhood in order to forge a new identity as the economic woman. While her foremothers and forefathers had shared a singular economic sphere in gender-differentiated ways, the modern woman would now enter the male-centric world of modern work and strive to perform the same tasks as the man in the same ways. Any gender difference that might hinder her success in the economic sphere was now seen as a threat to her reclamation of dignity. Economic woman would no longer be man's complement, but man's equal—no longer a counterbalancing force, but a competing force. Under this regime there could be no head and body duality, but instead a series of head-to-head maneuverings and collisions, as each would strive to do the same things in the same efficient, economically productive manner.

In the end, the modernization of work has led to the elevation of work as a male-centric sphere and, correspondingly, to an inflated male identity as the exalted "head" of the home. Conjointly, modernization has led to the denigration of women's work and a correspondingly diminished identity as the "heart" of the home. The social identity of the man as "head" thus became infused through the early twentieth century with a newly afforded grandeur and import made possible only by the supervaluation of work as the preeminent social value. Men were now deemed "workers" (and thus valuable) while women were deemed "housewives," a newly impoverished form of existence.

There is no easy way out from the brokenness of the gender-based challenges of our present social and economic structures. Rather, the road beyond will involve, at the very least, a recovery of the domestic sphere in order to honor the full range of human values and provide a refuge from the heavy demands of the present meritocratic marketplace values centered on material productivity. As Matthews puts it, "We cannot go back—nor would we want to—to the nineteenth-century home. But we can learn from history"—namely, that "the good society and the good home are inextricably intertwined."[55]

---

55. Matthews, *Just a Housewife*, 226. See also Goodman, *Gender Work*; Nussbaum, *Frontiers of Justice*.

THE MODERNIZED SELF AND THE HEADSHIP DEBATE: BEYOND A FEMINIST HERMENEUTIC

The historic duality of male and female spheres in which each is afforded its own dignity is no longer possible under the present structures of the new economic regime. There is instead now a singular and neutered economic sphere which welcomes into its grasp women and men alike, all the while favoring men. Since the mid-twentieth century, sexual identities have been reshaped to fit into this regime, and women's identities refashioned to fit into the newly male economic mold.

The woman is now required to be and to do all that the man is and does. Whatever "feminine features" are deemed unsuitable to the (male) economic task are to be shed from her identity. She must be set free from her bondage to reproduction and from any maternal impulses that would exclude her from her economic role. She must be set free from all gender-based stereotypes and all culturally inscribed understandings of "femininity," positive or negative, so as to be free to engage, unrestrained, in the world of wage labor. She is to be redefined as metaphysically unhindered, so that even if there remain socially embedded gender expectations, these remain exterior to herself and have nothing to do with who she in fact is. She is now self-made and self-defined, free from all past forms of "traditional womanhood" as embodied by her foremothers. While the culture continues to associate womanhood with a vast network of meanings and symbols, even while seeking to deconstruct the same, these are now to be curated by the self-conscious individual actor, with an end toward economic equality and psychological peace.[56]

In these ways, the modernization of work has led to newly fashioned sexual identities, and these newly shaped identities have come to be presupposed by the modern theologian. Human personhood is now redefined with woman and man as economic neuters, inhabiting the world of economic production and status attainment in the same ways and under the same conditions. As such, novel notions of human personhood have been swept into a set of unquestioned assumptions that determine in advance what the modern theologian can and cannot say concerning male-female identities and relations.

---

56. An important complement to my argument is Trueman, *Rise of Modern Self*. Trueman outlines some of the key components in the construction of the modern self, including whence we derive value and what is at stake in the contemporary politics of sexual identities.

In this way, in turn, the modern church has allowed its interpretations and applications concerning gender to be determined by a secular framework. In other words, the "theological anthropology" of the modern church is not so theological. Instead, our understanding of humanity as male and female has been determined a priori by alien claims. Humanity has been reduced to biology as interpreted by the social sciences. The criteria for truth in the church has thus seen a reversal. Traditionally, for Christians, as with every other major world religion, dogma has determined what is true and has set the parameters for what can be believed and practiced. Now, what is understood to be true (in accordance with the regnant secular plausibility structures) has come to determine dogma and set the parameters for what can be believed and practiced. The allotment of different identities and functions to woman and man according to their gender finds no place in modern belief or practice. Instead, in the realm of modern theology various forms of gender revisionism (as outlined above) have won the day.

The modernization of theology thus made space for new definitions of gendered personhood and sexual identities, which were themselves shaped by the modernization of work. The new "plausibility structures" that were established through these modernizing trends have rendered a robustly scriptural account of gender implausible, unacceptable. On the present foundations, the only theological account of gender that is acceptable is a thoroughly revisionist one which conceives of men and women as sexually distinct yet genderless beings whose chief aim is to overcome all sexism by achieving the interchangeability of the sexes. Inasmuch as Scripture offers an alternate account, Scripture must be revised.

But "the Scripture cannot be broken" (John 10:35).

What if the modern church were to engage human personhood from a radically theological perspective, where modern and secular accounts of gender are "revised" along scriptural lines, to reverse the modern trend? A response to this question, centering us on a theological account of sexual difference, will be the subject of the following chapters.

CONCLUSION

Contemporary evangelical engagements with male headship have produced two competing camps: loyalists who use the Scriptures to unwittingly justify a sexist economic regime, and revisionists who import contemporary de-gendered understandings of human personhood into the realm of Christian orthodoxy. In this chapter I have sought to demonstrate that the battleground of theological anthropology is indeed being fought largely on shaky structures alien to a robustly theological framework and have rendered a thoroughgoing scriptural account of gender incompatible with modern notions of the self and sexual identity. These new structures have been shaped significantly by the modernization of work, shaping in turn the new modernized sexual identities, which have themselves been made acceptable within the realm of Christian theological discourse by virtue of the modernizing of theological method.

Through industrialization, the domestic sphere became increasingly and unprecedentedly an impoverished sphere that could no longer offer its exponents a robust sense of self-worth and social value. With the economic sphere as the central locus of production and social esteem, the domestic sphere was now a consumptive sphere, socially demeaned. Following industrialization, then, as work became the prerogative of men, the man's novel identity as the sole wage earner served to bolster the male over the female identity in a newly unbalanced arrangement. In this setting, male headship could not but bolster the inherent sexism of the new economic regime.

The "loyalist" insistence that women embrace their historic domestic calling rings hollow as a vision for the reclamation of a dignified identity for women. At the same time, the revisionist trajectory leads toward a sublimation of the Christian story within a feminist story which uses Christian resources to its own ends, traversing beyond the bounds of Nicene orthodoxy. Conversely, I contend that Christian interpreters who are committed to historic orthodoxy as expressed in the Nicene tradition are bound to affirming a non-revisionist account of gender, in accordance with the Scriptures. This will necessarily involve, in some way, affirming the scriptural naming of the man as "head" in relation to the woman. We do not need better historical-critical exegetical practices or more innovative revisionist interpretations in order to make sense of such a claim. Rather, we stand in need of a different framework.

CHAPTER 5

Soteriological Heads
Headship in Canonical Perspective

Wherefore, dearly beloved, Catholic plants, Members of Christ, think What a Head ye have!

—AUGUSTINE OF HIPPO[1]

All forms of worldly order can be but pointers to the divine order.

—CHARLOTTE VON KIRSCHBAUM[2]

IN THE PREVIOUS CHAPTER I argued that modern theological engagements with gender and male headship have typically fallen short of offering a robustly theological account of each. The dominant approach has been to allow the data of contemporary social sciences to determine in advance what can be said theologically. In the present chapter I seek to establish more clearly a theological account of the head in order to (in the next chapter) set out the basic contours for a theology of gender that is both theologically rooted and practically instructive for Christian faith and practice.

Building on the arguments put forth in chapter 2, here we consider more fully the claim that, in canonical context, headship fundamentally means representation. More specifically, I will argue that in the context of

1. *WSA* 3.4:96.
2. Kirschbaum, *Question of Woman*, 63.

the Scriptures of Israel the head functions principally as a *soteriological representative*: i.e., the head is the one in whom the salvation or damnation of the body are mediated. To be clear, the "salvation" mediated by OT heads is always derivative, a salvation which is only finally accomplished in, with, and by the Lord.[3] More specifically, this salvation of heads to their household bodies is always given as a *sign* or *figure* of the salvation which is the prerogative of only "one head," namely Christ (see Hos 1:11). "Heads" are thus scripturally depicted as representatives in whom members find "salvation" in a way that figures the salvation of God. In this way, creaturely heads qua heads are not themselves "saviors" of their bodies, but *soteriological figures*, and as such signs and means by which the salvation of God is proclaimed in the world. In a Christian figural perspective, the status of the male as "head" is in this way limited, circumscribed by its typological relation to Christ, the true "head" and "Savior" of the body (Eph 5:23).[4]

In what follows we will explore the soteriological dimensions of the head in two stages: first, I will outline the ways in which the head functions as a *soteriological synecdoche* in the OT—or, more specifically, as a figure of synecdochal salvation;[5] second, I will trace the ways in which this soteriological figure takes shape in *redemptive history*, beginning with Adam and culminating in Christ. In the end we will see that the OT "head" figure, though not exclusively soteriological, functions principally to indicate *soteriological representation* (not "authority," as so often has been assumed and argued), and is picked up as such in the NT. In fact, we will see that the OT itself presents a broad and complex account of the head, offering in its own figural use of the term a guide to later NT christological readings. Moreover, I argue that only when the head is read figurally, taking in the full range of the OT figure, that NT usage of the term can be rightly apprehended.

---

3. E.g., Isa 45:14–25 speaks of the "everlasting salvation" of the Lord as the salvation of God alone. He alone is the Savior (vv. 21–25); see also Heb 5:9; 2 Tim 2:10.

4. For the OT head to bear a "figural" or typological relation to Christ is not merely a semiotic but an ontological claim. The male head of household does not merely "signify" Christ as head; rather, he *is* the head and as such signifies or figures Christ. For a discussion on the relation between figural, allegorical, and typological readings, see Young, *Biblical Exegesis*, 152–53. Young distinguishes between "ikonic" allegory (drawing on relations within the text) and "symbolic" allegory (drawing on relations between the text and something "extrinsic" to it) (209–12). Both are included under the term "figural" as I deploy it.

5. I use the term synecdoche throughout to denote a figure of speech in which a less inclusive term is used for a more inclusive term, as "a part for a whole."

In this chapter my "figural" methodological commitments are most clearly employed. Following the NT writers and church fathers, here I engage Scripture not to understand the texts primarily in their historical-cultural settings. Rather, the canon in its received form is the primary interpretive context, with each text to be engaged principally for its relation to the canonical center of Christian figural interpretation: namely, Christ and the good news of the kingdom proclaimed in his person and work. To this end, I have sought to engage texts broadly with attention to major themes and figures as they relate to the overarching storylines of Scripture which find their culmination in Christ.[6]

THE HEAD AS SOTERIOLOGICAL SYNECDOCHE

Throughout the OT the "head" consistently functions as a soteriological figure for blessing and cursing. Families, tribes, and peoples are subsumed within their heads to signal their vicarious attainment of salvation or damnation. In the cultural-linguistic imaginary of the OT, when the head is blessed, the whole body is blessed, when the head is cursed, so the whole body. We will consider these claims first in their literal-anatomical dimensions as applied to the individual, and then in their metaphorical-political dimensions as applied to the group. These soteriological dimensions will become all the more clear when considered through the lens of Christ's "headship."

A. The Head as Anatomical (or "Literal") Synecdoche

The soteriological significance of the anatomical head finds its roots in the opening chapters of Genesis, when God declares the defeat of the serpent's "head" through the woman's seed. "I will put enmity between you and the woman, and between your offspring and her offspring; he shall bruise your head, and you shall bruise his heel" (Gen 3:15). Some of the early church fathers refer to this pronouncement as the *protoevangelium*—that "first" (*proto*) proclamation of "good news" (*evangelium*) concerning God's salvation from sin, death and the devil.[7] There appears

---

6. See "Methodology" in the introduction. By "final form" I refer to the books of the Old and New Testaments as adopted by the church catholic and listed in various letters and confessions, e.g., WCF 1.1–10.

7. Justin Martyr and Irenaeus each explicitly interpret Gen 3:15 as a promise of

to be a double meaning in the Hebrew phrase: the serpent's *physical* head will be crushed, and so too the serpent's *metaphorical* head, the person of Satan. Central to both levels of meaning is that humans will triumph over Satan through the crushing of the serpent's head. The crushing of the head is the crushing of the whole person—in this case the entire demonic realm represented by and existing under Satan, the "head" of the serpent.[8]

Various OT writers pick up on this theme of the crushing of the enemy's anatomical head as "soteriological promise." In the book of Judges, the crushing of the head becomes a focal point of judgment: "[Jael] struck Sisera; she crushed his head" (Judg 5:26).[9] "And a certain woman threw an upper millstone on Abimelech's head and crushed his skull" (Judg 9:53; see also 9:57).[10] It is worth noting that in both of these examples, it

---

the gospel to be fulfilled in Christ. See Wenham, *Genesis 1-15*, 80–81. Here Wenham offers a brief overview of the rise and use of *protoeuangelion* as a descriptive term for Gen 3:15.

8. See Witherington, *Torah Old and New*, 51. This theme is taken up in Revelation, which identifies the "ancient serpent, who is called . . . the deceiver" as being at war with "the woman" and going off to "make war" with the woman's "seed" but is in the end "conquered" (Rev 12:1–17; 20:1–3, 10). The writer of Revelation presents his apocalyptic account of the devil's demise as the fulfillment of the Gen 3 promise concerning the crushing of the serpent's head. Moreover, the defeat of this "ancient serpent" is what ushers in the final judgment and the defeat of death and Hades (Rev 20:11–15). The defeat of the serpent's head is the defeat of the whole body. Taylor notes, "The concept of the wicked forming a kind of body of which the Devil is the head was familiar to Aug. from the *Liber regularum* of Tyconius, Donatist theologian of the late 4th century (ML 18.15–66). . . . Also found in Cyril of Alexandria, Hilary, Ambrose, and Ambrosiaster, as well as in certain later writers" (John Hammond Taylor, in Augustine, *Literal Meaning of Genesis*, 293).

9. Jael's "crushing" of Sisera's head results in praise from Deborah and Barak: "Most blessed of women be Jael." This same phrase is found on Elizabeth's lips concerning Mary (Luke 1:42). Medieval writers observing this parallel deemed Jael a forerunner to Mary, herself conceived as an antitype of Eve—specifically as the one who crushes the enemy's head. See Branson, *Judges*, 87. Ambrose makes much of the fact that it is a woman who defeats the enemy and sees Jael's victory as a type of the church's victory over Satan ("Concerning Widows," 8.47–8.50, in Franke, *Joshua, Judges*). Origen likewise sees in Jael a type of the church: "[Jael] killed [Sisera] with a stake, then, which is to say that she overthrew him by the power and cunning of the wood of the cross" (*Homilies on Judges*, 5.5.1). See also Walsh, "Jael's Story"; Wilson, "Pugnacious Precursors." Wilson points to several other early examples where Jael is seen as a type of Eve and forerunner of Mary in "crushing" the head of Satan.

10. See Jordan, *Judges*, 86, 175; Hamilton, "Skull Crushing Seed," esp. 35. Hamilton notes that the term for "skull" here, *gulĕggōlet*, is rendered into Greek as *Golgotha*, the place of the skull where Christ is crucified, drawing the reader's mind to the Abimelech story (53).

is a woman who enacts the crushing of the enemy's head, echoing God's promise to Eve (Gen 3:15).[11] These stories thus recall the soteriological promise of head crushing as a synecdochic figure of God's salvation and are, moreover, consistent with the chief theme of Judges and its structural framework: namely, that the salvation of God is wrought through various judges, or "heads" (e.g., Judg 10:18; 11:8–11) over Israel, most poignantly depicted in the crushing of the enemy's "head."

Following the time of the Judges, the anatomical head comes into view in David's striking with a stone and cutting off Goliath's head (1 Sam 15:45–51), the bruising of his head signaling the victory of God over the enemy.[12] This head-bruising motif is likewise present in the fall of the Philistine god, Dagon ("and the head of Dagon . . . [was] lying cut off" [1 Sam 5:4]), and the defeat of the dissenter and rebel, Sheba ("they cut off the head of Sheba the son of Bichri and threw it out to Joab" [2 Sam 20:22]). Various psalms refer to the head in this way as well: "But God will strike the heads of his enemies" (Ps 68:21); "you broke the heads of the sea monsters on the waters" (Ps 74:13); "You crushed the heads of Leviathan" (Ps 74:14).[13] Habakkuk explicitly connects the salvation of Israel with the crushing of the enemy's head: "You went out for the salvation of your people. . . . You crushed the head of the house of the wicked" (Hab 3:13–14).[14]

---

11. The deuterocanonical book of Judith has a woman as conqueror of the enemy's "head" (13:18).

12. In the history of interpretation, Goliath's head becomes a figure of the devil's head, cut off by Christ (and Christians). See, e.g., Augustine, *WSA* 3.20:144.1; Josephus Maria de Turre, quoted in Lubac, *Medieval Exegesis*, 197–98; Bede, *In primam partem*, 161. In the early Reformed tradition the David-Goliath story was related to the victory of Christ over Satan. See Cooper and Lohrmann, *1–2 Samuel*, 79, 96. Verrett explains how Goliath is portrayed in snakelike terms (his armor is "scaly" [1 Sam 17:5]), before his head is smitten by a stone and cut off (1 Sam 17:46, 51) (*Serpent in Samuel*).

13. Augustine offers his own figural reading of this psalm. He quotes it as follows: "*You have broken in the head of the dragon.* Of what dragon? We understand by dragons all the demons that war under the devil: what single dragon then, whose head was broken, but the devil himself ought we to understand? . . . That head is the part which received the curse, to wit that the seed of Eve should mark the head of the serpent. . . . What is this but that the worshippers of the devil had become the body of the same?" (*WSA* 3.18:74.13).

14. Robert Haak notes that this phrase—"you shatter the head"—"has a long history in the ancient Near East" and can be understood in both its literal and metaphorical dimensions (*Habakkuk*, 99). David Baker likewise understands the phrase "striking the head" as an idiom denoting the defeat of the enemy army as a whole" (*Nahum, Habakkuk, Zephaniah*, 74). He continues, "This could also be an allusion to the 'head' being the ruler, the Babylonian king who would be struck and completely defeated (cf. 2 Sam

The head also comes into view as the focal point of judgment in Israel's sacrificial system, where Israel's sins are laid on the head of the sacrifice through a "sin offering," whether goat, ram, or bull. "Aaron and his sons laid their hands on the head of the bull of the sin offering. And he killed it" (Lev 8:14–15). The head of the bull comes into focus as the locus of judgment for Israel's sin and guilt, their guilt transferred to the bull. As the guilt of the nation symbolically falls upon the bull's head in these rites via the priestly representative, the whole bull is lost and the whole people atoned for (Lev 9:7). This is dramatized before the people over and again in ancient Israel's liturgically shaped life.[15] Perhaps it is with these rites in mind that the saying develops in Israel: "His blood shall be on his own head"—an oft-used metaphor for judgment of the whole person.[16]

Not only is the anatomical head the locus of judgment but also of blessing and salvation. "A blessing is on the head" of the one who does what is right (Prov 11:26). "May [blessings] be on the head of Joseph" (Gen 49:26). Such a blessing of course is for Joseph's whole person and, by extension, to all those "in" him (i.e., his lineage). In Lev 13–14, a diseased head represents the uncleanness of the whole body, and when the diseased person becomes clean again his head is to be anointed with oil, signaling the cleansing of the whole person. Similarly, in Ps 133 the goodness and unity of Zion is depicted by the pouring of oil on Aaron's head.[17] In the anointing of Saul's head, as "prince over [the] people Israel," the salvation of all of Israel is proclaimed (1 Sam 10:1).

In the Psalms, David refers to God as "the lifter of my head" (e.g., Pss 3:3; 27:6; 110:7), as the one who accomplishes salvation—in this case,

---

22:39; Job 26:12; Pss 18:38; 89:10). This contrasts the head which is struck in defeat with the head which is anointed in victory."

15. The priests were to take sacrifices to the Lord on behalf of the twelve tribes, lay their hands on the head of the sacrifice, and slay it, so standing in the place of Israel as the offending party of the covenant. See Exod 29:10, 15; Lev 1:4; 3:2, 8, 13; 4:4, 15, 24, 29, 33; 8:14–15; 16:21.

16. See Josh 2:19; 2 Sam 1:16; 1 Kgs 2:9, 32–37; Ezra 33:4; Acts 18:6. The phrase is first used in the Rahab story. According to Cyprian, Rahab is here a type not of the "head" (Christ) but of the "body" (the church): "Rahab . . . was a type of the church. . . . This figure [of Rahab] declares that all who are to live and escape the destruction of the world must be gathered into one house alone, the church, while if any of the gathered goes outside . . . his blood will be upon his head, that is, he will have himself to blame for his damnation" (Cyprian, *Ep.* 14, quoted in Franke, *Joshua, Judges*, 14).

17. Augustine sees Aaron here as a type of Christ, and the anointing of Christ's head as the anointing of his body, the church. "The ointment is on his head, because Christ is one whole with the Church, but the ointment comes from the head. Our Head is Christ crucified and buried" (*WSA* 3.20:133.6).

for the king, and thus, through him, for the nation.[18] In Ps 140 David prays, "O Lord, my Lord, the strength of my salvation, you have covered my head in the day of battle" (v. 7). Here the protection of the head is the "strength" of David's "salvation." This link between the protection of one's head and the attainment of salvation is likewise made in Isa 59:17: "He put on righteousness as a breastplate, and a helmet of salvation on his head" (see also Eph 6:17). In each case, the head comes into view as the locus of salvation for the whole person. When the head is saved, the whole body is saved; when the head is crushed, so the whole body.

B. The Head as Political (or "Metaphorical") Synecdoche

In the above passages, the anatomical head functions as a soteriological synecdoche for the whole person, whether anointed and protected unto salvation, or crushed (bruised, cut off) unto destruction. In each case, the condition of the head is representative of the whole person. Moreover, as we have noted, the person whose head is crushed or lifted/anointed is often representative of more than his own individuated body, representing the crushing or saving of a people "in" or "under" him. It is to this corporate dimension of the head to which we now turn—again, in its soteriological dimension.

Returning to the book of Judges, we find God's salvation is wrought for Israel through various "heads" raised up to crush enemy "heads."[19] "Who is the man who will begin to fight against the Ammonites?" the leaders of Gilead ask. "He shall be head over all the inhabitants of Gilead" (Judg 10:18). They later turn to Jephthah to make him head (11:8–9)—on the condition that he in fact saves Israel. Here, the head *is* savior of the people; the savior of the people *is* the head. And under the head, all Gilead is saved.[20]

---

18. Augustine offers christological readings of these psalms along these lines in *WSA* 3.15:3.10; 3.19:110.14. The "lifting" of the head also comes into view in Gen 40, where Pharaoh "lifted up the head" of one to be restored and "lift[ed]" the "head" of another to be hanged (vv. 13, 18, 20–22).

19. The titles "judge" and "head" are at times interchangeable. See, e.g., Exod 18:25; Deut 1:12–15.

20. So Augustine: "They had said: You [Jephthah] will be our head (Jc 11,8); because the head of the male is Christ (cf 1 Co 11,3), and Christ is the head of the body of the Church (Cf Ef 5,23). Finally, after Jephthah freed them from all enemies, they did not make him king, so that we understand that what was said referred more to the prophecy about Christ than to Jephthah himself" (*WSA* 2.3:49).

Samuel, in appointing Saul as Israel's first king, says to Saul, "Though you are little in your own eyes, are you not the head of the tribes of Israel? . . . And the Lord sent you on a mission and said, 'Go, devote to destruction the sinners, the Amalekites, and fight against them until they are consumed'" (1 Sam 15:17–18). Here Saul's identity as "head" over Israel is linked to his saving mission. And so it is with his successor, David, who prays: "You delivered me from strife with the people; you made me the head of the nations. . . . Great salvation [the Lord] brings . . . to David and his offspring forever" (Ps 18:43, 50).[21]

The salvation wrought by heads in Israel does not represent military victory only, but also redemption from sin through the priestly ministry of atonement. Aaron stands as the primal "head priest," at the beginning of Israel's high priestly line (Ezra 7:5). As such Aaron functions as the representative of all of Israel in their liturgical rites, "bearing" the names of the twelve tribes on his own body before the Lord "on the shoulder pieces of the ephod" (Exod 28:12). On the Day of Atonement, Aaron is "to lay both his hands on the head of the live goat, and confess over it all the iniquities of the people of Israel, and all their transgressions, all their sins. And he [is to] put them on the head of the goat and send it away into the wilderness" (Lev 16:21). In this way, Israel's sin is symbolically transferred from Aaron, as "head" priest over Israel, onto the head of the goat: head for head, execution for expiation. Standing in Aaron's place, all subsequent "head priests" would likewise stand in the place of Israel, representing Israel before the Lord in the same sacrificial rites.[22]

This role of the "head" (as a soteriological figure) is not only for judges, kings, and priests, but also for fathers, or "household heads." In macro perspective, the blessing of the "head" (e.g., Adam, Noah, Abraham, Israel, Joseph, etc.) is given for his entire household and all of his descendants afterward.[23] In micro perspective, within Israel, the father of

---

21. For Augustine it is Christ who speaks the words of this psalm, although, "whatever things are spoken in this Psalm which cannot apply to the Lord Himself personally, that is to the Head of the Church, must be referred to the Church. For the whole Christ speaks here, in whom are all His members" (*WSA* 3.15:18.2, 18.45, 18.51).

22. For examples of the OT "head priest," see 2 Kgs 25:18; 1 Chr 27:5; 2 Chr 19:11; 24:11; 26:20; 31:10; Ezra 7:5; 8:29; Jer 52:24. Moreover, the Levites as a whole (from whom Aaron and the priestly line are chosen) serve a representative function before the Lord on behalf of Israel, to "guard over the people of Israel" (Num 3:8) and to serve in a mediating role for all the tribes, as stand-ins for the firstborn sons of Israel (Num 3). As Edmund Clowney notes, "The firstfruit of the harvest and the firstborn of the stock was viewed as representative of all the rest" (*Unfolding Mystery*, 101).

23. See, e.g., Jer 31:7 where Israel is identified as "head" of all the redeemed nations.

each household serves as covenant representative, making sacrifices of atonement (Num 7:1–3; see also Job 1:4–7) and covenant promises (Josh 24:1–28) on behalf of the household. It is the household head's covenant status—marked out as a circumcised descendant of Abraham—that functions as the chief indicator and necessary sign of the entire family's covenant status (Deut 7:3–4). Accordingly, when a foreign woman is married to a "head" in Israel, she too is of Israel (e.g., Ruth; Rahab).[24]

The function of the household head as covenant representative is illuminated further in Moses's instructions concerning heads with respect to their daughters and wives:

> If a woman vows a vow to the LORD and binds herself by a pledge, while within her father's house in her youth . . . if her father opposes her on the day that he hears of it, no vow of hers, no pledge by which she has bound herself shall stand. And the LORD will forgive her, because her father opposed her. (Num 30:3–5)

Once she is married, her husband functions as her new "head," under which the same conditions apply (Num 30:6–8). Household heads thus represent and, under certain conditions, can "stand in for" their members in covenant before God, even to mitigate their offences and subsume their wrongs.

The story of Achan illuminates this further. When Achan sins (Josh 7:1), the Lord states that "*Israel* has sinned; *they* have transgressed my covenant that I commanded them; *they* have taken some of the devoted things; *they* have stolen and lied and put them among their own belongings" (Josh 7:11). And it is because of "Israel's" (viz. Achan's) sin that "the people of Israel cannot stand before their enemies . . . [and] have become devoted for destruction" (Josh 7:12). The sin of one member in Israel thus becomes the sin of the whole people. Further, this is not merely a formal (in name only) attribution of one man's sin to the whole people; rather,

---

24. See Friel, "Mutuality and Male Headship." Friel explains, "Even *kiddushin* [betrothal] . . . conveys the idea that men are covenanted directly by circumcision, whereas women are covenanted only vicariously through their fathers or husbands" (254). See also Hoffman, "Jewish Wedding Ceremony," 134–35. Two gentile women, Ruth and Rahab, feature in Jesus's genealogy in Matt 1:5 and are included in Christ's lineage by virtue of their heads, Boaz and Salmon, respectively. Origen makes this connection, noting Salmon's relation to Rahab as "head" and comparing her inclusion in Israel to the inclusion of "the nations" in Christ, "who is head of all" (*Homilies on Joshua*, 79–80).

this one man's sin in fact renders the entire people guilty. *All* are to be "devoted to destruction."[25]

What must Israel do, then, to be at peace and make amends for the sin of its member, Achan? Correspondingly, the consequence is not simply the destruction of the individual, Achan, but of the entire household over which he stands—"his sons and daughters and his oxen and donkeys and sheep and his tent and all that he had" (7:24). All is to be devoted to destruction. "And all Israel stoned him with stones. They burned them with fire and stoned them with stones" (7:25). Here again the head (Achan) and household members cannot be separated, even as the head (Israel) and members (Achan and his household) cannot be separated. The judgment of the individual (Achan) is inescapably the judgment of the head (Israel), and the judgment of the head (Achan) is the judgment of his members (Achan's household).[26]

There is a significant difference in this example, however, between the consequences for the erring head and those for the erring member. Where the member (Achan in relation to Israel) is in the wrong, Israel is to cut off from among them the erring member. Where the head (Achan in relation to his household) is in the wrong, his body is subsumed with him in judgment. In other words, here bodily members under the judgment of God are to be cut off from the head (and the rest of the body) lest the whole body suffer, while the head's demise necessitates the demise of the whole body.

The "head" in these examples thus functions as the representative member in whom salvation or damnation is realized, and in this way functions as a figure of God's salvation. Where the head is blessed, so is the whole body. Where the head is judged, so is the body. In each of the aforementioned cases the head's actions, decisions, honors, or disgraces, in fact become those of his members.[27] In short, the OT presents

25. Note that this unity in judgment between individuals and collectives by no means suggests that the Scriptures have no place for judgment upon individuals qua individuals (e.g., Lev 10; Ezra 18; Jer 31). Still, where individuals do wrong, such wrongdoing is necessarily understood in relation to the collective. See Berman, "Sin of Achan"; Mol, *Collective and Individual Responsibility*, 190-95.

26. "The soul who sins shall die. . . . If [a righteous man] fathers a son who is violent . . . [the son] shall surely die; his blood shall be upon his own head" (Ezek 18:4, 13; see also Jer 31). As Mol has argued, the OT evinces a complex picture which develops the notion of personal responsibility, yet within a strongly collectivist framework (*Collective and Individual Responsibility*, 262).

27. It is in this light that we can begin to understand the phenomena of the exile of entire families due to the sins of their "heads" (e.g., 1 Chr 5:23-26).

a world where the head and the body are consistently presented as a single unit—bound together such that all that belongs to the members belongs also to the head, and all that belongs to the head belongs to the members.[28]

Moreover, it is of significance that in the context of covenant promises and blessings, that which belongs to the head often outweighs or overcomes that which belongs to the members. The father, as head, can overcome the folly of his children, saving them from the consequences of foolish oaths. Israel is permitted to cut out the sin of Achan from among them, and so be saved. This same dynamic continues in the scriptural story where David's descendants cannot altogether avoid his blessing, nor Joab's descendants his curse.[29] The blessings of the head thus consistently overpower the weaknesses of its members, and though the weaknesses of the members affect the head, under a righteous head their force is mitigated and at times expiated.

In sum, the "head" figure is often deployed in the OT as a soteriological figure, where an individual's identity is altogether wrapped up with the identity of his or her "head," and likewise the head's identity with the actions of his members. When the head is blessed or cursed, so the whole body. The head is thus presented in various instances as a figure of corporal and corporate salvation, as the soteriological representative of the body.[30]

---

28. One material example of this is that if a woman inherited land from her deceased father, that land would become the property of her "head" (viz. husband) upon marriage (see Num 36:1–4).

29. E.g., 1 Kgs 2:33. Accordingly, while Jehoram does evil in God's sight, "Yet the LORD was not willing to destroy Judah, for the sake of David his servant, since he promised to give a lamp to him and to his sons forever" (2 Kgs 8:19). See also Exod 12:15, 19; 30:33, 38; 31:14; Lev 7:20–27; 17:4–14; etc.

30. Headship as such has significant figural implications concerning the headship of Christ, to be explored further below. Admittedly, the head as soteriological representative is a difficult concept to square with the regnant individualist values of the West and its emphasis on autonomy, personal rights, and the freedom of the individual to choose and construct his or her own identity. To identify so closely with one's family so as to share in its guilt is all but foreign to Western social understandings. For the "sins of the father," for instance, to fall on his children—affecting and even corrupting his children—strikes most as unjust, even if we cannot help but acknowledge the unruly reach of familial dysfunction in patterns of generational sin, systemic abuse, and poverty. Nonetheless, presented to us in Scripture is a collectivist (not an individualist) social world wherein individuals cannot be pulled apart from their origins and broad familial networks; this includes the nefarious consequences of erring heads and members on the entire family-collective.

SALVATION HISTORY: A TALE OF HEADS

Every body's salvation is bound up with its head. As the head goes, so goes the body. As we have seen, this is true at the anatomical level, speaking of the life and salvation of the individual; and this is true at the political level, speaking of the life and salvation of the collective. We should expect that the Bible's redemptive narrative will reflect this.

Indeed, the head figure does frame all of redemptive history. This is evident in the various OT genealogies, tracing Israel's history through heads of household, following the line of God's promised seed. In this section we will focus on three examples of covenantal head representatives: Adam, Noah, and Abraham.[31] Each of these functions distinctly as a head, each in his own way figuring the saving headship of Christ.

What is to be emphasized here, again, is that the representative head is a *soteriological* representative: one in whom salvation and damnation are mediated, ultimately standing in typological relation to the "one mediator between God and men, the man Christ Jesus" (1 Tim 2:5). Again, this is not to suggest that any of these exemplars in fact offers salvation to his members; rather, each is a *figure* or sign of the ultimate salvation which is accomplished in and by the Lord Jesus alone as "head above all" (1 Chr 29:11).

Before outlining how these three function as key exemplars of the "head" figure in redemptive history, it is important to note that nowhere in Scripture is any one of them referred to explicitly as a "head." Yet each clearly fits the description of what a "head" is according to the Bible's own definitions (e.g., Num 1:4; Isa 9:14–15). Moreover, as I will argue, each embodies the meaning of the scriptural figure as *the soteriological representative of a body*. In a Christian figural reading, each is identified as a "head" because each stands in typological relation to Christ as "head" of a "body" and, as such, as a type of "savior" (see Eph 5:23).[32]

---

31. David Wenkel argues that these three, along with Moses, feature as the chief "covenant heads" in the background for Paul's scriptural imagination ("Noah as New Adam," 75, 78). For Augustine, they are the first three representatives of the world's "seven ages": infancy (Adam), childhood (Noah), and adolescence (Abraham), leading to Christ, the fully mature human. See *WSA* 1.19:1.23.35–1.23.41.

32. Such claims are basic to "federal theology" (or "covenant theology"), which came to understand the scope of the canon covenantally, with various "heads" framing the entire "history of redemption." The beginnings of this theological tradition are often traced back to the seventeenth-century Reformed theologian Johannes Cocceius (or, at times with Patrick Gillespie or Francis Turretin); see, e.g., Willem J. van Asselt's *Federal Theology of Cocceius*. Some have argued, however, that federal theology is

One of the suppositions underlying this claim, to be further developed below, is that NT Christology is informed and established on the basis of the scriptural claims of Israel. When Paul pens, for instance, that Christ is "the head... the Savior" of the body (Eph 5:23), the apostle is not offering a creative christology de novo; rather, this is an exegetical claim, as with Paul's general teaching concerning Christ "in accordance with the Scriptures" (1 Cor 15:3). In other words, Paul can proclaim Christ as "head" only because the Scriptures of Israel figurally depict him as such.

A. Adam

Adam, the sinner: At his fall
Death like a conqueror seiz'd us all;
A thousand new-born babes are dead
By fatal union to their head.

...

We sing thine everlasting Son,
Who join'd our nature to his own;
Adam the second, from the dust
Raises the ruins of the first.

—Isaac Watts[33]

Standing at the genesis of humanity, Adam is scripturally depicted as the "fountainhead" (Calvin), the singular source of the human race.[34] As Augustine put it: "No one was born except through Adam."[35] From a purely

---

established earlier with Calvin and Zwingli, who themselves continue a tradition from the patristics which gains momentum among medieval scholastics. For this argument, see Lillback, *Binding of God*; see also Muller, *After Calvin*.

33. "The First and Second Adam," in Watts, *Hymns and Spiritual Songs*, bk. 1, hymn 124.

34. While Adam is nowhere explicitly referred to in Scripture as "head," he functions as such, as is picked up in the early church (e.g., Ephrem the Syrian, John Chrysostom, Theodore of Mopsuestia, Cyril of Alexandria). Adam's "headship" is later developed by Reformed theologians such as Paul Bayne, Francis Turretin, Charles Hodge, and William Shedd.

35. *WSA* 1.12:3.12.

literary perspective, it is difficult to get around this point.[36] Genesis begins with the creation of *adam* (mankind [1:26–31]): the man from the dust, the woman from the rib of the man (2:5–25), these alone created in God's image (1:26).[37] This status of "imaging" God is given uniquely to Adam and to all those of his flesh and bone. This is confirmed through the various genealogies which link all of life back to Adam (e.g., Gen 5:1–32; Luke 3:23–38), and in the Lukan retelling of the canonical narrative: "And he made from one man every nation of mankind to live on all the face of the earth" (Acts 17:26; see also 1 Cor 5:21–22).

Adam thus stands as the head of the human household in its scriptural depiction—its progenitor and primal representative. In the second creation account of Gen 2, it is indeed Adam with whom God makes his original covenant, prior to Eve's creation (Gen 2:16–17).[38] Adam is promised "death" for transgressing God's commands, or life for obedience. Nevertheless, we find this promise is not for Adam only but for all those in and from him—for Eve (3:2–3) and all their progeny (3:14–24). All are implicated in God's covenant with Adam by virtue of their relation to him. With Adam thus standing as the "head" of God's covenant dealings with humanity, it is not surprising that although it is the woman who first disobeys God's command, he is the one with whom God begins and ends his words of judgment (3:9–19), "the man" whom God casts out of the garden lest he "taste of the tree of life" (3:22–24).

Adam thus stands as the representative figure in whom the entire human family might find itself blessed or cursed. His status as the

---

36. In the history of interpretation, the chief internal literary challenge to this claim was the presence of "Cain's wife" (Gen 5:17), who perhaps indicates human existence prior to or apart from Adam. The traditional line of interpretation, following Augustine, held that Cain married one of his sisters not mentioned in the story. See Augustine, *Questions on the Heptateuch*, 1.1. There is debate as to whether Origen and/or Julian the Apostate held to a view that humans existed prior to and/or concurrent with Adam; however, this view was generally dismissed throughout church history and was only substantively developed in the seventeenth century by the French intellectual Isaac de la Peyrere (1594–1676). See Livingstone, "Preadamites."

37. Note that the Hebrew *adam* can stand both for the individuated man, Adam (Gen 2:20; 3:17), or as shorthand for Adam and Eve (Gen 1:26–27; 3:22–24), or for mankind as a collective (Gen 6:1–7; 9:5–6). Adam thus functions as synecdochal head, principally for Adam and Eve, and later for all those in and from him.

38. I use "covenant" here to refer to an agreement involving God's promises and warnings that, if transgressed, involves God's judgment. The Reformed tradition has emphasized the importance of God's first "covenant" with Adam as one of several covenants and part of a larger "federal" or "covenant theology." See Karlberg, *Federalism and Westminster Tradition*.

fountainhead of the human race implicates all those "in" him. In this way the genealogical "headship" of Adam involves a soteriological dimension. As the head and beginning of the race, Adam's fall implicates all those in, with, and after him. This understanding is expressed later in the OT where Adam alone is identified as the one who "transgressed the covenant" (Hos 6:7).[39]

All of this is picked up, moreover, in Paul's own exegetical reflections on the Genesis creation accounts, where the sin of Eve is conceived fundamentally as Adam's sin, and Adam's death as the death of the entire human family (Rom 5:12–21; 1 Cor 15:22). Although Eve's sin is prior to Adam's (Gen 3:1–6; 2 Cor 11:3; 1 Tim 2:13), Paul's affirmation remains that it is in "the one man," Adam, that death comes to reign (Rom 5:12). This affirmation concerning "the one man" is brought into relation with "the one man, Jesus Christ" (5:15) who is the Second Adam, the beginning of a renewed humanity.[40]

Not only does Adam stand as the representative of humanity in general but of Eve in particular. Paul draws specifically on the relation of Adam to Eve as her "head" in identifying the man as "head of the woman" (1 Cor 11:3): "For man was not made from woman, but woman from man. Neither was man created for woman, but woman for man" (11:8–9; see Gen 2:18–22). This entire pericope (1 Cor 11:2–16) is midrash on the opening chapters of Genesis, with Adam conceptualized by Paul as the primordial human "head."[41] Adam is the head representative of Eve and of the entire human race. As such, Adam bears a representative responsibility for the one-flesh union of which he is head. While their disobedience was shared, it was in Adam that all died.

---

39. So Calvin: "Here, then, is the relationship between the two: Adam, implicating us in his ruin, destroyed us with himself; but Christ restores us to salvation by His grace" (*Institutes*, 2.1.6). For Bonhoeffer, Gen 1–3 is an account not of Adam and Eve only, but of all humanity in their wake (*Creation and Fall*, 100).

40. Notions of Christ as the "beginning" of humanity are closely tied to identifications of Christ as "head" (viz. "representative") both in the NT (e.g., Col 1:15–23; 2:19; Eph 1:22; 4:15) and among the fathers. For Hilary, "the Head, which is the beginning of all things, is the Son; but the Head or beginning of Christ is God" ("On the Councils," §26). For Cyril, "the Father is *the head of the Son*; the beginning is One" (*Catechetical Lectures*, 11.14; emphasis added). For Augustine, "the beginning of His ways is the Head of the Church, which is Christ" (*principium et caput Ecclesiæ est Christus*) ("Treatise on Faith," 4.6; see also 9.18).

41. See Ciampa and Rosner, "1 Corinthians"; Neusner, *Genesis Rabbah*; *Gen. Rab.* 8:9; 22:2. Augustine, too, sees Paul's writing in 1 Cor 11:2–16 and Eph 5:21–33 as figural readings of Gen 2–3 (*On Genesis*, 115, 132–37).

Paul thus draws out the implications of Adam's "headship" in two ways, chiefly: first, as the head of Eve, Adam functions as a type of *Christ in relation to the church* (1 Cor 11; Eph 5); second, as the head of the human race, Adam functions as a type of *Christ in relation to humanity* (Rom 5; 1 Cor 15).[42] While Adam's headship is developed along these distinct lines, in each case we find Adam identified as covenant representative, whose covenant status implicates all "in" him.

Following Paul, this notion of Adam as "head" (viz. representative), both of Eve in particular and of all their progeny in general, is likewise taken up by the church fathers. Theodore of Mopsuestia (392–428) juxtaposes Adam with Christ "as the head and beginning of [human] existence."[43] He likewise titles Adam the "head" in relation to Eve as the prefigurement of Christ and the church.[44] John Chrysostom (349–407) deems Adam both head of humanity generally and of Eve specifically;[45] and Augustine says much the same.[46] Adam's identity as head is taken up in similar ways by theologians into the modern era, to be most fully developed in later Reformation and post-Reformation traditions.[47]

Admittedly, each interpreter (including Paul and the church fathers after him) who identifies Adam as "head" deploys the term in his or her

---

42. Luke 3:38 presents Adam as the first "son of God." With earthly flesh formed from the dust (Gen 2:7), God alone was his Father. He was sent into a garden (2:8) and commissioned to live in covenant faithfulness (2:16–17). Out of his side would come a bride who would be brought to him (2:22). She was his body, his own flesh and blood (2:23). He would become "one flesh" with her (2:24). As such, his fate would be the fate of his bride (3:22–24). And because they and their offspring would be consigned to death, a Second Adam would come and recapitulate all these elements of Adam's life. The true son of God would be formed from human flesh, but with God alone as his Father. He would be sent into a garden, commissioned to undo the curse through covenant faithfulness, even through death on a cross. From his own body his bride would find life, united in him as one flesh. As such, his bride would share in his fate—life and salvation in him.

43. Theodore of Mopsuestia, *Commentary on John*, 98, 148. See also Theodore of Mopsuestia, *Pauluskommentare*, 187; McLeod, *Theodore of Mopsuestia*, 119.

44. Theodore of Mopsuestia, *Commentary on John*, 37–38. See Augustine, "Reply to Faustus," 12.8; J. Edwards, *Images or Shadows*, 60–61; Ridderbos, *Paul*, 379.

45. See Chrysostom: *Homilies on Corinthians*, 220; *Homilies on Genesis*, homilies 14, 17; *On Marriage and Family*, 44.

46. At one point he calls Adam the (apostate) "head" of "the whole human race" (Augustine, "Treatise on Faith," 25.99). Augustine also draws Adam and Eve into typological relation with Christ and the church (*WSA* 1.19:2.133).

47. See, e.g., Ephrem the Syrian, *Nisibene Hymns*, hymn 18, line 189; *Hymns on the Nativity*, hymn 1; Theodoret, *Dialogues*, 3.225; Irenaeus, *Against Heresies*, 1.18. See also Wilken, "Exegesis and the History of Theology"; McFarland, *In Adam's Fall*, esp. 51–52.

own distinctive way. One emphasizes Adam's "beginning" role, another his "saving" role; one emphasizes his relation to all of humanity, another his relation to Eve. But a major current running through the history of interpretation is that Adam's "headship" connotes his *representative responsibility in relation to his own flesh*. In this way, Adam stands in typological relation to Christ as "head" specifically in terms of his *representative responsibility* in relation to his "body."[48]

Following Adam and Eve, all would walk in the fallenness of their first parents. Their sons would be murderers (e.g., Gen 4:8, 23), and in due time the fallen members of Adam would spread across the earth, until God saw that "the wickedness of man was great in the earth, and that every intention of the thoughts of his heart was only evil continually" (6:5; see also 8:21).

B. Noah

"But," we are told, "Noah found favor in the eyes of the Lord" (Gen 6:8). Although God "determined to make an end of all flesh" for the prevailing violence in the earth (6:13), he instructed Noah to build an ark. "I will bring a flood of waters upon the earth to destroy all flesh.... But I will establish my covenant with you, and you shall come into the ark, you, your sons, your wife, and your sons' wives with you" (6:17–18). It is with Noah, on behalf of his family, and in turn on behalf of the whole human family, that God thus establishes his covenant. It is by virtue of Noah's righteousness that Noah's entire household shares in this blessing. In this way we find Noah as another "household head" under whom all "with" him would be saved. All other flesh would die. "Only Noah was left, and those who were with him in the ark" (7:24).

After the flood subsides, we are told, "God remembered Noah and all the beasts and all the livestock that were with him in the ark" (8:1). It is interesting that, while failing to mention his family, the writer mentions "the beasts and all the livestock." Evidently the naming of Noah is the naming of his whole family with him—*Noah* the one whom "God remembered"—*Noah* the one in whom his members are saved.

Not surprisingly, as the story continues Noah persists in his representative mediating role in the renewed world, presenting an offering to

---

48. So Daniélou: "As in the first instance... Adam was the head; so with the coming of Christ in the flesh a new Kingdom is founded... of which Christ is the head" (*From Shadows to Reality*, 37).

the Lord as priest on behalf of the people. By virtue of his offering God promises his blessing to all of Noah's offspring forever, even to all of the earth, thereby renewing with Noah and his sons the creational mandate given to Adam (compare Gen 9:1–3 with 1:28–30).[49] In these ways Noah too is depicted as a mediating head on behalf of his family, even as a new Adam, father of a new beginning, and the one in and under whom all peoples would be blessed.[50]

Once again, as with Adam, Noah's genealogical and household headship is laden with soteriological implications. Whereas in Adam all die, in Noah all are given a new beginning. The story continues, "Then God said to Noah and to his sons with him, 'Behold, I establish my covenant with you and your offspring after you, and with every living creature that is with you . . . that never again shall all flesh be cut off by the waters of the flood, and never again shall there be a flood to destroy the earth" (9:8–11; see also 6:18). Here, the pattern of covenant making with the male representative—"to Noah and to his sons"—continues, with the blessing given to the head for the whole body. In and through Noah and his sons and their offspring after them, every living creature is given a promise—even the whole earth—that they will be exempt from destruction by flood. What is more, as covenant representative Noah demonstrates that he himself has the authority to bless or to curse those under him (9:24–27). In these ways, Noah is clearly marked out as a covenant "head" in whom all those "with him" experience a kind of salvation.

Admittedly, Noah is nowhere explicitly developed in the apostolic writings as a "head." Still, the figure is implied in the Petrine Epistles, where the salvation of the "eight persons" of Noah's house are said to have been "saved through water," which "now prefigures saving baptism" (*antitypon nyn sozei baptisma*) (1 Pet 3:18–21).[51] Christian "baptism," conceived here as "antitype" (*antitypon*), implies a number of associative typological relations, including, for example, the floodwaters as type of

---

49. Genesis 8:20—9:17 details God's response to Noah's covenant faithfulness wherein God's covenant promises are extended to "all flesh" and "all future generations," and even to the earth (9:11–13).

50. See Wenkel, "Noah as New Adam." Jean Daniélou shows that this Adam-Noah-Christ typology is picked up by the fathers (*From Shadows to Reality*, 76). See also Schreiner, *Covenant and God's Purpose*.

51. See 2 Pet 2:4–9 where Noah's faith comes in view "for the salvation of his household" (*eis soterian tou oikou autou*).

the baptismal waters, the ark as type of the church, and Noah as type of Christ.[52]

All of this is discerned and developed by the fathers, who find in Noah a type of Christ precisely as the soteriological "head." For instance, in his reflection on the Petrine passage Justin writes, "In the flood was implicit the mystery of man's salvation.... Now Christ, the first-born of every creature, is become the head of a new race."[53] Augustine, too, draws on this typological relation, saying, "At one time the Church was in the house of Noah alone." And later, "[Christ] is our Head; His Ark is His Church."[54] Others have perceived the same.[55] Noah stands as the "head" in whom humanity is saved from the deluge and given a new beginning. As such he stands, along with Adam, as a type of Christ, the beginning of a new humanity, whose salvation is the salvation of all who are in him.

C. Abraham

How large the promise! how divine,
To Abra'am and his seed!
"I'll be a God to thee and thine,
"Supplying all their need."

Jesus the ancient faith confirms
To our great fathers given;
He takes young children to his arms,
And calls them heirs of heaven.

—Isaac Watts[56]

---

52. See Daniélou, *From Shadows to Reality*, 79, 83, 101.

53. Justin, *Dial.* 138.2–138.3. Or, later, in comparison with Noah: "Christ, through his resurrection, becomes the Head of a new race" (quoted in Daniélou, *From Shadows to Reality*, 91–92). See also Augustine, "Reply to Faustus," 12.15, 12.19.

54. *WSA* 3.20:129.5, 132.8; see also Augustine, "Reply to Faustus," 12.23.

55. E.g., Tertullian, *De Baptismo*, 8 (PL 1:1209B); Cyril of Jerusalem, PG 33:982A (quoted in Daniélou, *From Shadows to Reality*, 98); Hugh of Saint-Victor, "De Noe Arca Morali," 1.14; Lubac, *Medieval Exegesis*, 23; Zinn, "Hugh of St. Victor."

56. "Abraham's Blessings on the Gentiles," in Watts, *Hymns and Spiritual Songs*, bk. 1, hymn 113.

As the descendants of Noah repopulate the earth and disperse after the building of Babel, the Lord then makes a covenant with one man from all the families of the earth:

> Now the Lord said to Abram, "Go from your country and your kindred and your father's house to the land that I will show you. And I will make of you a great nation, and I will bless you and make your name great, so that you will be a blessing. I will bless those who bless you, and him who dishonors you I will curse, and in you all the families of the earth shall be blessed." (Gen 12:1–3)

Abram's story begins with leaving his father's house (Gen 12:1) and taking Sarai his wife (12:5) to an unknown land, reflecting the primal call of Adam (2:24). The promise given Abram in 12:1–3 is for his entire household (see also 15:5–6; 17:1–8); it is "in" Abram that "all the families of the earth shall be blessed" (12:3). In this way, Abram's genealogical headship, as with Adam and Noah, bears a soteriological dimension. As the beginning of a new people and a renewed humanity, Abram stands as the one through whom "all the families of the earth shall be blessed."[57]

As head of this renewed humanity, God gives Abram and his offspring through him a sign of this covenant promise, at which time his name is changed to Abraham:

> As for you, you shall keep my covenant, you and your offspring after you throughout their generations. . . . Every male among you shall be circumcised. . . . Every male throughout your generations, whether born in your house or bought with your money from any foreigner who is not your offspring, both he who is born in your house and he who is bought with your money, shall surely be circumcised. So shall my covenant be in your flesh an everlasting covenant. (Gen 17:9–13)

The covenant made with Abraham has great ramifications for all those "in" and "after" him, for women, men, daughters, sons, and servants—all are included in their father's blessing.

Although all share in the blessing of their head, it is the sons—as prospective household heads—who bear the mark of this covenant. And it is this mark made in the male's flesh that distinguishes those within from those without God's covenant: "Any uncircumcised male who is not circumcised in the flesh of his foreskin shall be cut off from his people;

---

57. Hahn, *Kinship by Covenant*, 200; see also Rad, *Genesis*, 160.

he has broken my covenant" (Gen 17:14). The woman who marries a sign-bearing covenant head under this dispensation thus finds a share in the covenant blessing, while she who marries an uncircumcised man apparently jeopardizes her status.[58]

Abraham thus stands as the head representative of God's people, Israel. As the primal bearer of the covenant sign of circumcision, the one set apart by God "in" (*bekh*) whom "all the families of the earth" would be blessed, he prefigures Christ's covenant headship.

The apostolic writings bear witness to Abraham's identity as covenant head in typological relation to Christ. In the Gospels he is presented as the "father" over the household of faith (Matt 3:9; 8:11; Luke 3:8; John 8:39). According to Paul, the only hope for salvation among the nations is to be "grafted in" to Abraham (Rom 11:11–31; Gal 3:29). It is "in" Abraham, "the father of us all" (Rom 4:16), that the nations find blessing.[59] In fact, Abraham's identity as a covenant "head" is assumed in Gal 4, where Paul says of Abraham's two wives, Sarah and Hagar, "these women are two covenants" (v. 24). To fill out Paul's "allegory," if these women are "covenants" it is by virtue of their relation to Abraham, the head of each (Gen 17:19–21).[60] And it is in these ways that Abraham,

---

58. See J. M. Cohen, "Hatan damim"; Heger, "Patrilineal or Matrilineal Genealogy," 245–46. It is important to note that following the apostolic era the determining mark or "sign" of participation in the new covenant in Christ, for Jews and gentiles, becomes baptism, not circumcision. According to the early fathers, circumcision was a sign that found its end in Christ (R. Williams, "Bunsen's Biblical Researches," 64). That circumcision corresponded to, and was replaced by, baptism was a notion suggested by several of the church fathers, but only explicitly developed as a matter of sacramental consequence by Bede. See C. O'Brien, "Bede's Theology of Circumcision."

Whereas under the OT dispensation, a woman might have been included among Israel by virtue of her one-flesh relation to her circumcised husband, under the new covenant it is through Christ, the final household head, and "by the circumcision of Christ" (Col 2:11–12), that all, both male and female, are included in the promises of God given to Israel. Only by baptism *into* the circumcised Christ—being "buried with him in baptism" (Col 2:12)—can men and women alike participate in this "everlasting" covenant marked by circumcision (Gen 17:13). In this way, we might say that under the Abrahamic covenant, the household head in Israel was a figure of Christ, specifically as a mediator of the covenant to his household. In and after Christ, all such "head" figures are revealed for what they are: namely, shadows and types of Christ's covenant mediation. Whereas OT household heads prefigured Christ by mediating a covenant status to their families, NT heads post-figure Christ, who is finally revealed as the one who *alone* mediates salvation.

59. See P. O'Brien, *Letter to the Ephesians*, 98n49.

60. As the head of these dual covenants Chrysostom speaks of Abraham as "head of all" (*Homilies on Romans*, homily 8). See also Augustine, *Lectures or Tractates*, tractate 11.13.

too, stands in typological relation to Christ. What was given "in" Abraham (Gal 3:8) "through faith" (3:14) as "promise" (3:18) is now given "in Christ . . . through faith" (3:26) in "the fullness of time" (4:4). "And if you are Christ's, then you are Abraham's seed, heirs according to promise" (3:29).

The Abraham-Christ typology is also discerned by the church fathers.[61] Augustine asks, for instance, "Who in Abraham leaves his country and kindred that he may become rich and prosperous among strangers, but He who, leaving the land and country of the Jews, of whom He was born in the flesh, is now extending His power, as we see, among the Gentiles?"[62] In this way, Augustine highlights the Abraham-church and Christ-church typology—a typology that continued to be developed by such figures as Theodore, through Thomas, Luther, Pascal, and most meticulously with Jonathan Edwards.[63]

Admittedly, the more frequently noted Abrahamic typology among the fathers appears to bring Abraham into typological relation with God the Father, and Isaac with Christ the Son. In each case, the "beloved son" is offered by the father as an atoning sacrifice, each willingly, each bearing the wood, each for the blessing of the nations.[64] Still, arguably, the Abraham-Christ relation offers a far more extensive typology—a typology which centers on Abraham's faithfulness, obedience and sacrifice, with "the divine testing of Abraham . . . recapitulated and extended in Jesus."[65] In any case, for our purposes it is as the household head and

61. Daniélou cites Irenaeus, *Against Heresies*, 4.25.1; and Origen, *Homilies on Genesis*, 3.4–3.7; but he observes that Abraham is "only rarely considered as a type" in rabbinic and early church tradition (*From Shadows to Reality*, 117).

62. Augustine, "Reply to Faustus," 12.25. Elsewhere he notes, "At one time the Church was in Abraham alone," suggesting Abraham is the household representative of the old covenant church (*WSA* 3.20:125.5, quoted in Daniélou, *From Shadows to Reality*, 186; see also *WSA* 3.1:4.11).

63. See, e.g., Gregory, "Theodore of Mopsuestia's Commentary," 36, 129, 138; Aquinas, *Summa Theologica*, q. 56, art. 2–5; Luther, *Lectures on Galatians*, 114; Pascal, *Pensées*, 10.643, 10.680; "Misc. no. 1069," in J. Edwards, *Typological Writings*, 208–9.

64. See Schoeps, "Sacrifice of Isaac." Schoeps identifies this type in Clement of Alexandria, Irenaeus, Tertullian, Origen, and Augustine. Another oft-explored Abrahamic typology is Abraham as a type of Israel (Moberly, *Bible, Theology, and Faith*, 83, 112; see Exod 20:20) and/or of the Christian/church (Moberly, *Bible, Theology, and Faith*, 134, 147; Rom 4:16).

65. Moberly, *Bible, Theology, and Faith*, 229. Building on Rad, Moberly argues that "the primary analogy or typology" in Gen 22, as picked up by NT writers, is not that of Isaac with Christ but "that of Abraham with Christ." Moberly specifically links "the two Abraham narratives [in Gen 18 and 22] with the narrative construal of Jesus as Son of God in Matthew's Gospel" (160).

representative of the people of God that we find Abraham standing as a "head" in typological relation to Christ, as the one "in" whom the nations are finally "blessed" (Eph 1:3), the "everlasting father" (Isa 9:6) in whom God "gathers" his children (Matt 23:37; Heb 2:13).[66] Just as "in Abraham" all are welcomed as children of God through faith, so now "in Christ Jesus you are all children of God, through faith" (Gal 3:26; see also John 8:39–41). Abraham is the great household head who points us to the great Father of all, just as Christ is the greater household head and true revelation of the Father (John 14:9).

Once again, as with Adam and Noah the "headship" of Abraham is genealogical; Abraham stands as the beginning of a new people, and as such (again, as with Adam and Noah), he stands as one "in" whom salvation is found. Abraham is the head of a new humanity being restored, and thus serves as a figure of Christ, the true head, "bringing salvation for all people" (Titus 2:11).

We have thus examined three OT figures who stand as representative "heads" of God's people, each in typological relation to Christ as figures of *soteriological representation*, each established as such in the NT, and discerned and developed as such by the fathers. With these examples I have not sought to offer a comprehensive account of any one of these head figures in their functions as "heads," but simply to demonstrate the ways in which each one is scripturally depicted as a mediator of covenant status and salvation to its "body," and as such stands as a figure of Christ, the true and final head.[67]

D. Christ

Up to this point we have considered the head figure as it has been employed in the OT, noting ways in which the apostolic and patristic writers engaged with these OT texts and figures in their christological and soteriological dimensions. As we have seen, early Christian writers discerned

---

66. Hebrews 2:11–16 likewise depicts Jesus as the one in whom God gathers his children: "Behold, I and the children God has given me" (see Isa 8:18). This is followed by "he helps the offspring of Abraham" (Heb 2:16). As with Abraham, Jesus and his offspring "are all of one" (2:11).

67. As Daniélou remarks (referring to Adam and Noah as redemptive "types" of Christ as "head"), "Each of the types of Christ in the Old Testament brings out some aspect of the redemption [of Christ]" (*From Shadows to Reality*, 91–92).

a connection between *OT heads* as representatives and mediators of the covenant and *Christ* as head. We now turn to engage directly with NT namings of Christ as "head" in order to more fully "discern the head" in its christological dimension, and so too to "discern the body" (to adapt Paul's phrase in 1 Cor 11:29). Our objective is to establish more clearly the meaning of headship, christologically understood, in order to be in a position in the final chapter to apply "headship" to a contemporary theology of gender.

As will become clear, the NT use of the head figure, while transfigured in light of the person and work of Christ, corresponds to its OT soteriological use, where the head is a synecdoche for the whole body and denotes soteriological representation. We will consider these claims in light of three texts which deploy three interrelated images: (1) Christ as head of the body (Eph 1:22–23), (2) Christ as head of the bride (Eph 5:22–33), and (3) Christ as "head of every man" (1 Cor 11:3).

(1) Christ, the Head of His Body

And he put all things under his feet and gave him as head over all things to the church, which is his body, the fullness of him who fills all in all. (Eph 1:22 23)

From the early church onward, many have argued, and more have assumed, that wherever the Greek term *kephale* is used as a descriptor of Christ or man in the NT it is to be understood as a synonym for "rule" or "authority." Beginning as early as the 1950s, however, biblical scholars began to build an alternate case that NT uses of *kephale*, at least in some places, means "source." This interpretation has been largely overturned by more recent scholarship, with a return to the former understanding.[68] Not only is *kephale* rarely if ever used to denote "source" in ancient Greek, but as Peter O'Brien puts it, such a translation renders Paul's message in Ephesians "inexplicable," at least in the context of Eph 1:22-23. Here, "The term 'head' expresses [Christ's] ruling authority."[69]

However, the *kephale* as authority tradition, represented more recently by O'Brien and others, detaches Paul's notion of *kephale* from the scriptural-theological notion of the head as it is narratively given in the Hebrew Scriptures. As I have been arguing, to understand *kephale*

---

68. E.g., Fitzmyer, "*Kephalē* in 1 Corinthians"; Lakey, *Image and Glory*, 31. For a history of this debate, see Wolters, "Head as Metaphor," 138–39.

69. P. O'Brien, *Letter to the Ephesians*, 145–46. See also Hoehner, *Ephesians*, 185–87.

as "ruler" or "authority" is to conflate the scriptural term with notions of rule (*arche*). But in classical Greek *kephale* was rarely if ever used to denote the title of "ruler" or "chieftain." Instead, the NT use of *kephale* as a title is clearly an adaptation of the OT title *rosh*, now deployed in the Greek language.[70]

As demonstrated in chapter 2, *rosh* (and therefore *kephalē* as a translation of it) is best understood not in terms of rulership but of representation.[71] The next question to consider is the extent to which our OT understanding of *rosh* as "soteriological representative" fits with and so illuminates Paul's use of *kephale* in Eph 1:22–23.

In this passage, at the beginning of Paul's letter, Jesus is proclaimed as "head over all things," and "far above all rule and authority and power and dominion" (1:21), the one for whom God "put all things under his feet" (1:22). Clearly Paul associates Christ's identity as head with his rule and power. For this reason many have understood the use of *kephale* here to be coincident with "rule" and/or "authority." However, we should note that an *association* between words is not the same as an *identity of meaning*. As an alternate approach, we will consider Paul's use of *kephale* as soteriological representative of a corpus.

If *kephale* is understood as "authority" in this passage, it does little to elucidate the soteriological and unitive dynamics of the text. That God gave Christ as head *authority* "to the church, which is his body" makes some sense. But that God gave Christ as head *representative* "to the church, which is his body" fits better the context of the passage. Unless the

---

70. See Bedale, "Meaning of κεΦαλή," 211. As already established in ch. 2, it is only as a translation of *rosh* that *kephale* takes on a meaning beyond its classical anatomical use. Accordingly, when it is taken up in Greek scriptural discourse—*specifically as a translation of* rosh—the metaphorical use of *kephale* is to be discerned in accordance with its Hebrew scriptural use. Bedale notes the same: "Now on any interpretation of these passages [Col 1:18; 2:19; Eph 1:22; 4:15] it seems clear that we shall have to invoke ראש as determining the sense of κεΦαλή" (212). He goes on to say, "It seems a fair inference that St. Paul, when using κεΦαλή in any but its literal sense, would have in mind the enlarged and metaphorical uses of the term 'head' familiar to him from the Old Testament" (213).

71. The Hebrew anatomical head is a synecdoche for the whole person: head and body, body and soul. As such, when used metaphorically (e.g., to denote the "head" of a mountain or the "head" of a family/clan) it is functioning as an extension of its basic anatomical meaning—namely, the "head" is that person (member, object) that represents the whole. This notion of representation carries into temporal contexts as well—e.g., where *rosh* denotes the "head" of the year or the "head" of the harvest. In such contexts, the term connotes primacy in order, with the head serving as a representative portion (whether of time or of harvested goods).

saints are one body with Christ, as his own members and *represented* by him as their "head," the claims of this passage are in fact unintelligible—namely, that the saints are blessed "in Christ with every spiritual blessing in the heavenly places" (1:3), chosen "in him" (1:4), have redemption "in him" (1:7), are united "in him" (1:10). Because Christ is the *representative member* of his body, of which the saints are a part "through faith" (2:8), they can be "seated" with him at God's "right hand in the heavenly places" (1:20; see also 2:6). It is as the synecdochal representative of the body that Christ reigns with *authority,* to be sure, but to suggest that his "headship" *means* authority ignores the very meaning of the head in its broader scriptural context.

The "rule" of Christ that is explicitly pictured here is not that of the head "over" his body, but of Christ *with* his body "over all things"—over the rest of creation. Paul alludes in Eph 1:22 to Ps 8:6, where the psalmist says "you [God] have put all things under his [man's] feet," proclaiming humanity's "dominion" over all of creation. In context, the "all things" of the psalmist denotes the "all" of creation *which is subject to man.* Understood christologically, "all things under his feet" does *not* mean that Christ's *body* is in subjection to Christ but rather that *all of creation* is in subjection to Christ and his body.[72] Here Christ is not deemed "head *of* all things." Rather, he is here said to be "head *over* all things" (*kephalen huper panta*) and is as such given as "head . . . to the church [*te ekklesia*], which is his body" (Eph 1:23). In short, it is as the corporeal head that Christ rules over all of creation *with his body.*

It should be pointed out that the suggestion to understand Paul's use of *kephale* in terms of representation is not altogether novel among Pauline interpreters, even if it is rarely offered as a definition of *kephale's* fundamental meaning. Even those like O'Brien who have argued that *kephale* for Paul means "ruling authority" make recourse to the language of representation in describing Christ's function as "head."[73] The twentieth-century biblical scholar Herman Ridderbos likewise uses the notion of representation for his exegesis concerning the Pauline meaning of *kephale.* For instance, commenting on Eph 1:22 he concludes that

---

72. See P. O'Brien, *Letter to the Ephesians,* 145.

73. E.g., P. O'Brien writes, "The idea of the incorporation of many into a representative head . . . appears in the LXX . . . as well as in Paul" (*Letter to the Ephesians,* 98). "[The people of Christ] have been united in him, the inclusive representative of the new order, as members of his body" (200). O'Brien later explains Christ's headship in terms of his being the "inclusive representative of the new order" (331).

kephale here denotes "the containment and *representation* of the one in and through the other." For him, "In this inclusive and *representative* sense Christ is Head of the church."[74] V. Norskov Olsen takes a similar approach, describing the head "as a prominent or honored *representative* of the whole, rather than authority or source."[75] In each of these cases, the notion of "representation" is used to describe headship, even if the "head" title is itself defined in other ways.

As I have argued, however, the Hebrew *rosh* is best defined as the representative member of a body, with a characteristic soteriological function in relation to that body. (The head is the one in whom the body finds salvation or damnation.) This is precisely how Paul picks up the figure as applied to Christ in Eph 1:22–23. Here Christ as "head" is not fundamentally the *authority over* the body, not its overlord, but the *representative member* in whom the whole body is saved, involving the body in his authority "over all things."

(2) Christ, the Head of His Bride

Wives, submit to your own husbands, as to the Lord. For the husband is the head of the wife even as Christ is the head of the church, his body, and is himself its Savior. . . . Husbands, love your wives, as Christ loved the church and gave himself up for her, that he might sanctify her. . . . In the same way husbands should love their wives as their own bodies. He who loves his wife loves himself. . . . "Therefore a man shall leave his father and mother and hold fast to his wife, and the two shall become one flesh." This mystery is profound, and I am saying that it refers to Christ and the church. (Eph 5:22–32)

Modern headship controversies have spent much time contending whether the "head" figure in this passage denotes "source" or "authority." We will consider whether a definition of *kephale* in its modified OT sense—as soteriological representative—might better elucidate this text. Certainly, this passage would seem to agree with the meaning of *kephale* as "authority." To start with, the passage begins with a call for wives to

---

74. Ridderbos, *Paul*, 382; emphasis added. See also p. 85.

75. Olsen, *New Relatedness*, 108. He goes on: The head "is not 'the first' or 'the top' of a hierarchical structure, but of an organic unity and is therefore representative. . . . It is in the strength of the representative nature that headship has a certain 'authority,' but in the form of a caring and loving responsibility which represents the will and purpose of a common oneness, equality, and action" (109–10).

"submit" to their own husbands, "as to the Lord." *Why?* "For the husband is the head of the wife even as Christ is the head of the church, his body." Clearly Paul sees as implicit in the "head" identity a kind of authority in relation to the "body," which demands a certain "subjection" and "respect" from the body toward the head (Eph 5:22, 33).

This is not surprising since the head, as representative of the body, implies a certain kind of authority in relation to the body. Whatever this authority entails, however, it is not the authority of an overlord to a subordinate, but of one member whose identity and interests are altogether bound up with those of the rest of the body. Further, Paul makes clear in this passage that whatever authority is proffered here is circumscribed and defined by the figure of Christ, who, as head, "gave himself up for [the church]" (Eph 5:25). As Christ comes to his church as a servant head (John 13; Eph 5:25–27; Phil 2; 1 Pet 2), this servanthood indicates what the authority of the head is for. Christ is indeed the head who subjects himself, willingly, as a servant, and in this way reframes the relations of Christian "authority" to every "subject."

To be clear, saying that Christ has a certain authority as "head" of the body is *not* to say that *kephale* here *means* authority. The OT meaning of the head as soteriological representative of a body remains illuminative for understanding *kephale*, even here.

"For the husband is the head of the wife even as Christ is head of the church, himself Savior of the body" (Eph 5:23 AT). We might say, by parallel, that just as "the husband is [the representative] of the wife" in his one-flesh union with her, so "Christ is [the representative] of the church" in her one-flesh union with him. It is as the church's one-flesh *representative* (not *authority*) that Christ "gave himself up for her" (5:25); it is as her *representative* that he promises to "present the church ... holy and without blemish" (5:27); it is as her one-flesh *representative* that the head is to love his wife as his own body (5:28); as her *representative* that the church must "see that she respects her [head]" (5:33). To remove the word "representative" and replace it with "authority" in any of the aforementioned clauses only obscures the bound relation of head to body in each phrase. By retaining the OT sense of head as representative for understanding *kephale*, the entire text is held together by the matrimonial substructure of a one-flesh unitive love. With the head as representative of the body, in contrast to "authority over" the body, all notions of authority and subjection are qualified according to the unitive love of the head as representative member of the body.

Where the OT head has been a soteriological figure, so we see the same in Paul's teaching here. The head of the body *is* the "Savior," he says (5:23), sanctifying and cleansing the body (5:26), even presenting it "holy and without blemish" (5:27).[76] The soteriological dynamic of this passage comes through even clearer with its strong allusions to the OT figure of God's people as his bride.[77] In this figure, the notion of God as husband and head of his bride is understood best not in terms of his "authority over," but rather, again, as corporeal representative. As Bedale concludes in reference to this passage: "Finally, when κεΦαλή is seen as signifying not mere 'overlordship', but rather a certain relationship of one to the *being* of another, it is possible to do full justice to the great passage in Eph. 5:22–33 in which the Church is presented to us as the Bride of Christ."[78]

(3) Christ, the Head of Every Man

But I want you to understand that the head of every man is Christ, the head of a woman is man, and the head of Christ is God. (1 Cor 11:3)

First Corinthians 11:2–16 is an extremely challenging text for a variety of reasons that go beyond the grammatical. Its historical and cultural contexts and seemingly ad hoc arguments involve complex issues of ancient anthropologies and cosmologies.[79] Here, however, we are simply engaging this passage for what it says directly about Christ's identity as "head," and whether the OT sense of *kephale* as soteriological representative helps to make sense of Paul's assertions in this context.

As a whole, 1 Cor 11:2–16 concerns orderly worship and centers on gendered propriety. Commending to the Corinthians "the traditions" that had been delivered to them (11:2), Paul begins by setting out a theological principle for ordered worship, specifically through the use of head coverings: "But I want you to understand that the head of every man

---

76. None of this is to suggest that husbands are "saviors" of their wives in the way that Christ is Savior of his body. Rather, the husband as "head of the wife" is to figure, point to, and proclaim the saving headship of Christ, the only Savior. "That Christ is also savior of the body signals that there are limitations to the analogy" (Foulks, *Ephesians*, 244).

77. See Foulks, *Ephesians*, 243; also 64.

78. Bedale, "Meaning of κεΦαλή," 215. Although Bedale rightly argues that *kephale* here, following the OT *rosh*, is not a matter of "overlordship," he sees its basic meaning as "top" or "priority."

79. See Murphy-O'Connor, *Keys to First Corinthians*, 150.

is Christ, the head of a woman is man, and the head of Christ is God" (11:3). This order serves as the guiding principle for most of what follows in vv. 4–16. If one understands head to mean "authority" in each of these statements, it makes some sense of the passage but leads to apparent theological contradictions when it comes to God's trinitarian relation as "authority" of Christ.[80]

Conversely, if one understands head to mean "representative," indicating an order of relations, this helps to make sense of all three clauses. The idea presented in this passage is one of a head and body relation—between God and Christ, Christ and man, man and woman—that is not a relation of superordinate to subordinate, but of a beginning to an end, a representative (first) to a represented (second); or, to use Paul's terms, it indicates a relation of the origin to its "glory."[81] In each case the former (God, Christ, man) is in some sense "prior" to the latter (Christ, man, woman), and the latter is the "glory" of its head. God (the Father) is the head of Christ, and Christ his glory; Christ is the head of man, and man his glory; man is the head of woman, and woman his glory.

In each of these three "heads" is contained a body. To say "God" is to say Father and Son; and the Son is his glory. To say "Christ" is to say Christ and the church; and the church is his glory. To say "man" is to say man and woman; and the woman is the glory of man.[82] With each, the former represents the latter; not as its "authority" but as its "beginning" and thus its representative member.

Admittedly, the head as *soteriological* representative is not at the fore in this passage, centered as it is on orderly worship. Still, we might ask

---

80. E.g., Bruce Waltke argues that *kephale* here means "authority," indicating a "hierarchy of social relationships." He qualifies this, saying that the hierarchy does not speak of a difference in dignity or worth but of "job relationships, responsibilities to each other and ultimately to God" ("1 Corinthians 11:2–16," 49). David Garland is likewise dissatisfied with interpreting *kephale* here as "authority." He argues, instead, for the meaning of "preeminence," as a play on the "anatomical and metaphorical meaning of 'head'" (*First Corinthians*, 508).

81. Waltke aptly notes on this point that Christ is the "head" of man because "we exist through him" (1 Cor 8:6; Col 1:16); man is the head of the woman because "man does not originate from woman, but woman from man" (1 Cor 11:8; cf. Eph 5:23); and God is the head of Christ because "all things originate from God" (1 Cor 11:12) ("1 Corinthians 11:2–16," 48–49).

82. Here I understand Paul to use the word *aner* (man) in its inclusive sense: i.e., *men* are not the glory of Christ but *mankind*, viz. humanity; and women are not the glory of *men* but of *mankind*. Kenneth E. Bailey argues that this approach makes the best sense of this passage (*Paul Through Mediterranean Eyes*, 307; see also Garland, *First Corinthians*, 523).

how an understanding of the head in its soteriological dimension might inform our understanding of the order of "heads" here presented. Obvious challenges are raised immediately with claiming God as the "head" of Christ in any soteriological sense. Surely God is not the "savior" of the divine Son.

Still, it is as *Savior* that Jesus is sent by God into the world, coming "from God" and returning "to God" as such—the Son "given all things" (John 13:3) in order to see "all things" finally return to the Father. It is in the Son that all things are reconciled to God (Rom 5:10; Eph 2:14–16). We might say, then, that it is God, as soteriological head of Christ, *to* whom all things are finally reconciled. By parallel, it is Christ, as soteriological head of mankind, *in* whom humanity is represented—and so reconciled—to God. Finally, man, as a head, is the one *by* whom humanity is represented to God.

The order of "heads" here corresponds to an order of "glory." Christ is the glory of God (John 14:13; 17:1; Eph 3:21), with God as his representative head. Humanity is the glory of Christ (John 17:10; 1 Cor 11:7), with Christ as our representative head. Woman is the glory of humanity (1 Cor 11:7), with man as her representative head. We will consider and develop these claims in the next chapter.

CONCLUSION

In the present chapter I have sought to demonstrate that the "head" figure, in both OT and NT perspectives, denotes soteriological representation. The OT *rosh* was representative of a corpus and a mediator of salvation to the rest of the body. As we have seen, this theme is picked up in the NT. In deeming Christ "head of the church" and "head of every man," Paul was not inventing a new concept or metaphor. Rather, he was taking a common Jewish OT figure—the "head"—and applying it to Christ, the head to whom "all things" are finally gathered. In this way, Paul insists that this most ancient and fundamental characteristic of human social life—namely, the ordered relations of household members to their head, as scripturally depicted—is fulfilled in Christ.[83]

---

83. The typological reading of, e.g., Jonathan Edwards seems to follow Paul and the earliest Christian interpreters in perceiving a close connection between the natural world, its scriptural depiction, and the revelation of God in Christ. For Edwards, "Very much of the wisdom of God in the creation appears in his so ordering things natural, that they livelily represent things divine and spiritual . . . in that the state of mankind is

For the average first-century Jew, attuned to the Scriptures of Israel—where the *rosh* was understood as representative and mediator of the household—the claim that Christ was the true and final *rosh* was pregnant with possibilities (Luke 24:25–45). Whatever headship meant in Israel's covenantal history, Paul's contention was that the "substance" of this "shadow" has arrived (Col 2:17); the promise is fulfilled; the reality is here, fully present in Christ. *Christ* is the "head of every man" (1 Cor 11:3). "*He* is the head of all rule and authority" (Col 2:10). *He* is "head of the church," himself "Savior" of the body (Eph 5:23; see also Col 1:18). And *he* is the one whom God gave "as head over *all things* to the church" (Eph 1:22). *Christ* is finally revealed as the "one head" that the children of Israel "appoint for themselves" in the messianic age (Hos 1:11).[84] *Christ* has become "the head corner stone" (Ps 118:22),[85] the Lord of whom David prophesied, "*Yours* is the kingdom, O Lord, and *you* are exalted as head above all" (1 Chr 29:10–13).

In sum, the head is that member who represents the whole body. As such, the head functions as a soteriological representative, with earthly heads pointing typologically to the true and final head and Savior, Jesus Christ. As head, Christ calls us his own and represents us to the Father. As head, he comes to us as a servant, washing our feet, loving us to the end (John 13:1–5), even laying down his life (Eph 5:25). As head he has become the object of our judgment, the final sin offering. As head he takes our disgrace to the place of the skull, and there his head is crowned with thorns that we might be given "a beautiful crown" (Prov 4:9; Rev 2:10; 14:14)."[86] "*Wherefore, dearly beloved, Catholic plants, Members of Christ, think What a Head ye have!*"[87]

The question now moves to what this all means for the church today. Is the man still to be understood as the "head" of the woman? If so, in

---

so ordered, that there are innumerable things in human affairs that are lively pictures of the things of the gospel, such as . . . marriage [and] family" ("Misc. no. 119," in *Miscellanies*, 284). Again, for Edwards, God has "from the beginning of the world to the end of the Old Testament history, . . . represent[ed] divine things by outward signs, types, and symbolical representations, and especially thus to typify and prefigure future events" (*Typological Writings*, 202).

84. "And the children of Judah and the children of Israel shall be gathered together, and they shall appoint for themselves one head. And they shall go up from the land, for great shall be the day of Jezreel."

85. See *WSA* 3.19:118.16–118.21.

86. See Cyril, *Catechetical Lectures*, 13.23.

87. *WSA* 3.18:96; emphasis added.

what sense? And how might this head and body figure, theologically understood, help to shape a theology of gender? These will be the questions for our engagement in the final chapter.

CHAPTER 6

Figural Heads

Toward a Constructive Theology of Gender

Every supposedly objective reasoning simply promotes its own difference, and disguises the power which is its sole support.

Theology [is] itself a social science, and the queen of the sciences for the inhabitants of the *altera civitas*, on pilgrimage through this temporary world.

—JOHN MILBANK[1]

AS I ARGUED IN chapter 4, modern theological approaches to gender have tended to presuppose and affirm characteristically modern accounts of human personhood, set on the stage of our postindustrial economic structure. The newly fashioned *homo economicus* has triumphed as the ideal type to which male and female alike are to conform, each shaped according to the needs of economic production and the value systems of the ascendant cash nexus. The modern theologian receives this newly understood self, genderless and at home in a secular age, as an anthropological given a priori to theological reflection.

For the modern discipline of theological anthropology, it is anthropology which determines theology. With the social sciences determining what can be said theologically, the result is a stunted, quasi-theological anthropology which marshals scientific and social-scientific findings to

---

1. Milbank, *Theology and Social Theory*, 5, 382.

bolster one of the contemporary anthropologies already on offer. What is more, such "theological" anthropologies (so called) are invariably put in service of modernist ideals, such as freedom, equality, and progress—themselves *Christian* ideals, to be sure, but each defined in accordance with secular and materialist understandings of "the good," unhinged from the Christian social and ontological foundations on which they were built in the first place.

Theology, in this system, becomes a useful tool in service of other disciplines, baptizing their results into its own name, offering nothing substantive to the discussion. This is perhaps especially true where gender is concerned, with contemporary theologies of gender all too often serving only to affirm one or the other side of an ideologically polarized debate, rather than offering a theologically substantive response which draws its own lines and calls all ideological accounts into conformity with the life and pattern of Christ.

In what follows, I propose that a Christian anthropology presupposes that the shape of the human life is substantively given in the Scriptures, and that the meaning of gender is to be discerned therein, if aided and informed by contemporary social-scientific claims and concerns. More specific to the aims of the present chapter, I propose that the "head" figure offers one way—*not the only way*—to approach such a scripturally delineated account of gender. Indeed, the scriptural naming of humanity as a corporeal unity—male and female, head and body—offers one point of departure for a robustly theological account of humanity in its gendered dimension, most fully illuminated in the transfigured glory of Christ and the church.

This approach should be distinguished from modern theological anthropologies which typically begin with reflections on the meaning and significance of the doctrine of the *imago Dei*—a doctrine established in creation (Gen 1:26) and teleologically linked to the person of Christ (Col 1:15). After having determined the meaning of the divine image, such approaches draw from this doctrine theological significance (or not) for gender relations.[2] In the present work, however, while assuming the creational and christotelic significance of the *imago Dei* as basic to a theology of gender, we begin by engaging the "divine image" from another angle—namely, from Christ, the image of God, revealed as *totus*

---

2. E.g., Roberts, *Body Parts*; Cortez, *Theological Anthropology*. As an exception to this, Beth Felker Jones begins with the *imago Dei* in its eschatological dimension (*Marks of His Wounds*).

Christus, head and body, in typological relation to the man and the woman.[3] In doing so, we follow the apostle Paul's figural reading of the creation accounts, where Adam and Eve are presented as the paradigmatic male "head" and female "body," which are in turn figures of Christ and the church. As we shall see, Adam and Eve together constitute a personified anthropology, and are received as such in the NT generally.[4]

To be clear, this is not to eschew those theological anthropologies that center on the *imago Dei*, christotelically understood. Rather, the present account is intended to complement such theologies. Following Karl Barth, I maintain that a uniquely Christian anthropology begins with the revelation of God given in Jesus Christ, who at the same time reveals the true nature of human personhood.[5] We ought not ask what it means to be human apart from engagement with the paradigmatic human, Jesus the Christ of Nazareth. But as we have seen, this Jesus is "head," together with a "body" (Eph 5:23-33; Col 1:15-20). Christ, then, as the paradigmatic human—*totus Christus*, head and body—is the one in whom we discover who we are as a head and body duality, male and female.

In order to explore a theology of gender from this standpoint, in the present chapter we will begin by considering what it means to say that the man is "head" in typological relation to Christ the head and that the woman is "body" in typological relation to Christ the body (i.e., the church). In the end, what we will find is that gender is by no means incidental to who and what we are in this sacramentally profuse universe, as creatures made by God for the purposes of God. Rather, humans—male and female—are created to proclaim in our very being the movement of the triune God toward us—from the Father, in the Son, and through the Holy Spirit. The God who made us to be united to him in "one-flesh" covenantal union (in the Son, by the Spirit), made us likewise to reflect this very union within our creaturely life together, as male and female. In this perspective, it is indeed the dynamic union of Christ with the church which illuminates for us the meaning of gender.

---

3. On the *totus Christus*, see Meconi, *One Christ*, 194-211; Lubac, *Medieval Exegesis*, 93-94.

4. See Katz, "Social Psychology of Adam," 545.

5. See *CD* 3/2:44. For a more recent christologically rooted approach, see Cortez, *ReSourcing Theological Anthropology*.

THE MAN AS A FIGURE OF CHRIST THE HEAD

> You are not a master, but a husband. You have not acquired perchance a handmaid, but a wife. . . . Be a sharer in her love.
> —AMBROSE OF MILAN[6]

In contemporary ecclesial debates concerning "male headship" the head is typically construed as either being the source or the leading/authoritative member of a body. However, I have argued that the OT head (*rosh*) is to be understood primarily as the body's *synecdochal representative*, where one member is singularly deemed the representative head in relation to the whole, as a spiritual, legal, and/or social designation (see ch. 1).

We have also seen that the notion of the head representative is developed in the OT as a *soteriological* figure, and is taken up as such by the apostle Paul, where headship is finally given its fullest and clearest definition in the "transfigural" revelation of Christ as "head." It is in Christ's identity as head representative of the church that we finally discern the meaning of the man's identity as head, as a figure of Christ (1 Cor 11:3; Eph 5:21–33).[7]

And what does it mean that the man as "head" is a figure of Christ? The designation denotes first and foremost (1) a *theological status* and (2) a *nuptial responsibility*.

A. Male Headship as Theological Status

The man's status as head representative is fundamentally a theological status, which is to say that it is a status which relates the man first and foremost *not* to the polis or even to the family or household, but to God, and to the angels and principalities in the heavenly places.[8] Granted, the

---

6. Ambrose, *Hexameron*, 174.

7. Ephesians 5:21–33 is where these multiple dynamics are explicitly drawn together. Christ is the soteriological head (*soter*) of his bride (v. 23), who is "one flesh" with his body (v. 31), all in the manner of a *self-giving* head who "gave himself up for her" (v. 25), that she might "stand with" (or "beside") (*parastese*) himself (v. 27).

8. For all its baffling logic to the contemporary world, the notion that the man as the representative "head" stands before an attentive cosmos—specifically before angels and heavenly principalities—is made explicit in 1 Cor 11:2–11, which corresponds to a plethora of similar passages where the angels and "rulers and principalities in the heavenly places" stand in awe of the mystery of Christ uniting himself with the church

man as representative head in Paul's day implied not only a theological status before God but also a legal and social status in relation to the polis. Still, for Paul, the social status of the head was rooted in something more fundamental—namely, in the ground of God's own being, with God as the head of Christ, Christ the head of man, and man the head of woman (1 Cor 11:3). Whatever status the man has as "head" relates him first to God, and more specifically to Christ in relation to the church (Eph 5:21-33).[9] Headship for Paul is thus first a theological status with secondary social manifestations, not the other way around.

As we have seen, the head is a synecdoche for the whole body. This claim finds expression in the OT identity and function of the household head, though its significance in the NT era changes in important respects. In the OT, the man's representative status involved a series of ritualized responsibilities—specifically his participation with and on behalf of his family in the liturgical and ceremonial rites of Israel, including circumcision, animal sacrifice, observance of holy days, and so on. In these ways, the OT household head served as a mediator of covenant membership for his household.

In the NT era, however, such covenant mediation through the male household head all but disappears. What becomes clear in this new dispensation is that the man as head is a *figure* of the true Mediator, Christ. Here the man qua head does not in fact mediate salvation to the body, but proclaims in his being the salvation mediated in Christ alone. The man is the head after the pattern of Christ; but Christ alone is head *and Savior* of the body (Eph 5:23). It is before God and a watching cosmos, then, that the man in Christ ultimately stands as representative of the one-flesh union, and is as such a figure (sign, proclamation) of Christ's mediating and self-giving love.

One significant implication of this change is that women are revealed as joint heirs with men, given the full covenant status as "sons" of

---

(1 Cor 4:10; Eph 1:22-23; 3:8-10; 6:12; Col 2:15; 1 Pet 3:22; Heb 1:14; 13:2). Paul explicitly relates the man's identity as "head" to head-covering practices in all "the churches of God" (1 Cor 11:16) and to the church's accountability before "the angels" (11:10). Angels revere "the glorious ones" (2 Pet 2:10-11; see also Jude 8-9). Christians are those who have come before "innumerable angels in festal gathering" (Heb 12:2, 22), with warnings of judgment (Heb 12:24-25). In Revelation it is the angels who watch over the churches and to whom the churches are accountable (Rev 1:20; 2:1, 8, 12, 18; 3:1; etc.).

9. Some have suggested that Paul here is taking up and Christianizing Greco-Roman household codes; but it seems he is rather doing the opposite: redefining household codes in accordance with Israel's Scripture.

God (Gal 3:26; 4:6). Whereas the covenant sign of the OT (circumcision) was given only to males, the NT applies the new covenant sign (baptism) to all. Accordingly, we find that the NT woman, too, functions in equal manner with the man as a kind of mediator of covenant blessing (1 Cor 7:14). She, too, enters into the "holy of holies," welcomed into the very presence of God in the person of Christ (Luke 10:39). She too prays and prophesies in the assembly (Luke 2:36; Acts 2:17; 1 Cor 11:5).

What remains consistent from OT to NT is that the head is presented as the *representative of the body*, by definition. The man as head represents his own "flesh" to God and to all of creation. For this reason we have identified the man's status as head to be fundamentally a *theological* status: a status by which he is related first and foremost to God in Christ. This becomes all the more clear when we consider the specific *responsibilities* of the head that are proper to his status.

B. Male Headship as Nuptial Responsibility

If headship signals the man's status as the body's representative member, and if this is fundamentally a *theological* status, what does his "headship" entail functionally? This question has driven much of the contemporary debate over "headship," centrally concerned with what headship entails practically for the husband-wife (and in some cases minister-church) relation. The centrally debated claim has been that headship entails the man's exercising authority through leadership and initiatory action.

According to Paul, however, the man's representative status is not explicitly linked to his "leadership" but instead to a set of *self-giving responsibilities*, chiefly his *responsibility for the purity and perfecting of the body*. Exhorting husbands as "heads," he says: "love your wives as Christ loved the church, and gave himself up for her, that he might sanctify he. . . . so that he might present the church to himself in splendor" (Eph 5:25–27). It is precisely as the head representative that the man is called to take final responsibility for pursuing and perfecting the sanctity of the one-flesh union of which he is a part—and all of this in order that he, after the pattern of Christ, might "present" his bride, with himself, to Christ "in splendor" (v. 27). As Christ takes final responsibility for the sanctification, wholeness, and flourishing of his bride, so the man with his wife (vv. 27–28).[10]

---

10. See Kirschbaum, *Question of Woman*, 50, 75. In First Corinthians Paul makes

In these ways, Paul's NT "head" figure is simply a development of the OT figure, understood christologically. As we saw in chapter 2, the OT *rosh*, as household representative, was ultimately responsible, morally and covenantally, for the well-being of his household. Again, this did not mean that the woman/wife was any less involved in pursuing and perfecting the peace of the home than the man/husband. It meant, more modestly, that when the household as a whole was judged and held to account by Yahweh, it was the man who was held to account and judged in a primary manner. The man bore a certain final responsibility. In this Paul discerns a figure of Christ as head of the church, and the man/husband as a reflection of this figure.

In short, then, *to say that the man is the representative head of the woman is to say that the man bears a certain and final responsibility for the flourishing of that one-flesh union of which he is the head.*[11] Put differently, the head, as the body's representative member, bears a responsibility which centers on the flourishing of the whole body.[12]

Practically speaking, this suggests that the man/husband is to take full and final responsibility under God for the flourishing of his marriage, and will be held accountable for this. Where the nuptial relationship is stalled, stagnant, or at a stalemate, he is not permitted to take a passive role. In the midst of trouble and discord, he is to know himself to be finally responsible for sanctifying this one-flesh union and persist in his covenant responsibilities, unwilling to abdicate his pursuit of the good of the whole, all after the pattern and in the power of Christ.

In affirming such a gender-specific calling, it is worth considering at least one way in which such a calling is offered as a matter of counterbalance. The woman, as one who bears in her own body a relation of possibility to reproduction, bears a natural relation to a very literal "self-giving" for the sake of another. For the woman who renders this possibility a reality, in fact carrying and nurturing a child within her own

---

explicit that Christ indeed represents all those "in him" to the Father, explaining that the Son, whose head is God (1 Cor 11:3), returns all things to the Father (15:20–28) "that God may be all in all" (15:28).

11. For similar conclusions, see Sweeney and Trainor, *Politics of Conjugal Love*, 152–57; and Torrance, "Introductory Essay," 19, 36, 110.

12. So 1 Tim 3:4–5, where the overseer "must be one who manages his own household well" that he might prove worthy to manage "the household of God" (Titus 1; 1 Tim 2–3; specifically 1 Tim 3:15). It is worth noting that the wife is likewise to serve as household manager/ruler (*oikodespoteo*) with her husband (5:14), even if in a way that does not finally exert authority (*authentein*) over him (2:12).

body, the call to self-giving for the good of another takes its own unique, imposing shape as the woman's bodily life is encumbered, even debilitated for a time, in order that another might live and flourish. In some cases—gratefully far less now than ever before—in this process her life is demanded in its entirety, given completely, even unto death, for the sake of her own flesh and blood. What is demanded of the woman by nature is thus demanded of the man, as a kind of divine imposition, to offer what is not by nature required of him: to lay down his very life.

Moreover, it is important to note that any such distinctively gendered calling (such as the man's first-order responsibility) is immediately qualified by the unitive dimension of his shared identity with the woman as "one flesh." Whatever the man characteristically is or does in relation to the woman, the woman herself has a share in. The man can only be what he is, as head, through and with the woman as the body of which he is a part. Their union is in fact one of deeply mutual, if asymmetrical, submission (Eph 5:21), as the man gives *himself* for the good of the woman, and the woman responds by submitting to the man as her head in an act of free and loving service under God (Eph 5:22, 25).[13]

In this call, too (that the wife "submit" to her husband), it is clear that the man bears a certain responsibility for the whole body.[14] Inasmuch as the wife is called to submit to her husband as head, as her own willing self-offering for their mutual good, to that extent he will be held accountable for the ways he loves, leads, serves, and sanctifies—or fails to do so. And he will be judged accordingly.[15] Moreover, he will be judged not

---

13. See Kirschbaum, *Question of Woman*, 75. See also John Paul II, *Man and Woman*, 92.7.

14. The wife's call to "submit" in this passage must be understood in light of the believer's freedom in Christ (Rom 8:1–11; Gal 5:1–13) shared across all social divisions (Gal 3:28; Col 3:11), understood *not* as a "yoke of slavery" (Gal 5:1) but as a call to "faith working through love" (5:6). Such submission is not so much a matter of the wife's bending her will to her husband's in a battle of wills, but a call to "serve one another through love" (5:6, 13). With this blunt call for the woman's "submission in everything," even "as to the Lord," many have raised the concern that this will lead to women suffering silently under wicked, abusive men. See, e.g., Levitt and Ware, "Anything with Two Heads." For this reason, it is imperative that such a call is taught with equally urgent instructions: e.g., that submission does *not* entail silent suffering under abuse, that all authorities in Christ must stand against any and all forms of abuse, that any indications of abuse will be investigated, that men will be held to account (disciplined, reported) for any such abuse, etc. For one example of such instruction in a complementarian context, see Study Committee (of the Presbyterian Church in America), *Report on Domestic Abuse*.

15. See Col 3:19; 1 Tim 3:2–5; Jas 3:1–2; 1 Pet 3:7.

only for whether he promoted the moral actions of his wife or whether he did no active harm to her, but for whether he *sacrificially pursued her good*: "Husbands, love your wives, as Christ loved the church and gave himself up for her" (v. 25). The husband is thus created—purposed—to live after the pattern of Christ, namely to pursue the bride, move toward the bride, and even offer his life for the bride, ultimately presenting the bride together with himself as one flesh to Christ (vv. 26–27).[16]

The wife may do much the same, of course, reciprocally—pursuing her husband, sanctifying her one-flesh union with him, even offering her life for her husband. Indeed, such reciprocation is entirely appropriate as her shared responsibility under God. Still, it is the head whose identity as such binds him to take final responsibility for effecting in his marriage the pursuant and perfecting love of Christ.

This "representative responsibility" ascribed to the husband naturally raises the question of whether this status and responsibility entails a position of *authority over* the wife—a question which, as I have noted, has been at the center of modern headship debates. A certain kind of authority is indeed assumed to accompany the "head" status. This authority is implied in our central text of Eph 5:21–33 by the call for the wife's submission—a call which is based on the husband's relation to her as head: "Wives, submit to your own husbands. . . . *For* the husband is the head of the wife" (vv. 22–23).[17] Two things must be noted concerning the nature and extent of the man's authority in this passage.

First, the man's authority as head is necessarily circumscribed according to his nature and function as the head *of a body*, with its necessary conceptual limitations. The authority of a king differs from that of a mother, from that of a coach or tutor, from that of a team captain. Each might be said to have a certain kind of authority, but the authority of each is limited according to the nature of the relation. So it is with the head. In fact, the notion of the head as "authority *over* the body" marks a break with the corporeal metaphor. Members of a body are of such a unity that each member is by nature utterly bound together with and in the service of the rest of the members, such that it is nonsensical to speak of one member having authority "over" any other (see 1 Cor 12:21–26).

---

16. As Christ left his Father to hold fast to his bride—a movement ascribed to Adam in relation to Eve (Gen 2:24)—so the man is to "leave his father and mother and hold fast to his wife" (Eph 5:31). Here, too, we see Christ taking the active part in pursuing and perfecting his relation to the church.

17. See Olsen, *New Relatedness*, 110.

The NT accordingly distinguishes the husband's relation to the wife from any superior-inferior relations, never once describing the man as "ruler" (*archon*) of the wife but instead as her "head."[18] The word "ruler" (*archon*) is in fact predominantly used in the NT of demonic and governmental authorities, and those religious authorities allied with them. Moreover, not only is *archon* never used of the husband in relation to his wife, but, significantly, neither is it used of Jesus in relation to his disciples (or to the church, or to anyone else for that matter). Instead, Jesus is deemed *kephale* in a way juxtaposed with *archon* (Eph 1:22—2:2), and it is as head (*kephale*) of his body (*soma*) that Christ stands, with his body(!), over every rule (*arches*) and authority (*exousias*) (1:21).[19]

Neither is the man in the NT ever given the unidirectional role of having "authority over" (*exousiazo*) the woman. Rather, the only place where Paul uses the term with reference to the man-woman relation is in the context of husband-wife "sexual" relations (1 Cor 7:2), where Paul says the husband "has authority over" (*exousiazei*) the wife, and the wife "has authority over" (*exousiazei*) the husband (7:4), each in like manner.[20] For this reason, the authority of the head representative must not be construed as anything other than an authority *with and for the body*.[21]

---

18. It might be argued that 1 Pet 3:1–9 offers an exception here, upholding Sarah as an exemplar for calling Abraham "lord" (*kyrion*). Even here, however, the point is not to establish a ruler-ruled relation between husband and wife but to commend to wives an attitude of "respect" (1 Pet 3:2) toward their husbands—not demanded as law but invited as a disposition of tenderness and humility (3:8) in taking the attitude of a servant after the pattern of Christ (3:18–22), as is becoming of those shaped by the gospel. Even as she calls him lord, the husband is to "show honor" to the wife as a joint "heir" in "the grace of life" (1 Pet 3:7). In short, what is commended is an attitude of deference, not ontological subordination.

19. While the titular *archon* (ruler) is not used of Christ in relation to the church, *arche* (most often translated "beginning") is used of Christ at least once, in Col 1:18.

20. Later in the same passage, Paul speaks of the importance of one having "authority" *not* over his "maiden" but over his own "will" (v. 37). See Sweeney and Trainor, *Politics of Conjugal Love*, 162. Some might appeal to the passage in 1 Cor 11:10, which states that the woman ought to have a sign of authority (*exousian*) on her head; commentators often interpret this as a sign of her husband's *authority over her*. For a discussion concerning the complexities of this passage, see Waltke, "1 Corinthians 11:2–16."

21. Chrysostom makes this very point, insisting that the title of head does *not* denote a relation of ruler to ruled but is instead used specifically for the purpose of differentiating the man/Christ from other authorities and distinguishing the head title from notions of supremacy. "In order then that when you hear of the Head you may... behold Him not as supreme Ruler only, but as Head of a body" (*Homilies on Ephesians*, homily 3). Chrysostom speaks of the husband and wife as joint "rulers" of the home: "For where the head is in harmony with the body, . . . how shall not all the other members be at peace? For when the rulers are at peace, who is there to divide and break up

Second, not only is the head's authority circumscribed by these conceptual limitations, but the very notion of authority is itself redefined in the NT after the pattern of Christ as a *self-giving authority*—an authority in service of the other. This notion is clear not only from the NT headship passages we engaged in the last chapter (Eph 1:22–23; 5:21–33; 1 Cor 11:3) but follows a broad NT theme wherein the function of authority is redefined in terms of servitude. As Jesus says to his disciples,

> You know that the rulers [*archontes*] of the Gentiles lord it over [*katakyrieuousin*] them, and their great ones [*megaloi*] exercise authority over [*katexousiazousin*] them. *It shall not be so among you.* But whoever would be great [*megas*] among you must be your servant [*diakonos*], and whoever would be first [*protos*] among you must be your slave [*doulos*], even as the Son of Man came not to be served but to serve, and to give his life as a ransom for many. (Matt 20:25–28)[22]

Jesus could not have been clearer. Among his followers, positions of "priority" (*protos*; a notion closely associated with the place of the "head") are sharply contrasted with notions of rule and authority, and instead described in terms of "servanthood" and "slavery." All of this is ultimately exhibited, according to Paul, in Christ's own example:

> who, though he was in the form of God, did not count equality with God a thing to be grasped, but emptied himself, by taking the form of a servant [*doulon*], being born in the likeness of men. And being found in human form, he humbled himself by

---

concord? . . . This then is a point of the highest importance, and of more consequence than wealth, or rank, or power, or aught else" (*Homilies on Titus*, homily 4). Hugh of Saint-Victor likewise juxtaposes a "ruler of his kingdom" with a "head of the family in his own home" ("De Noe Arca Morali," 1.4). Ridderbos observes a similar distinction, where Christ as head denotes his identity as the representative, not ruler, of the body: "Head thus points . . . first of all to a relationship of beginning . . . the containment and representation of the one in and through the other. . . . In this inclusive and representative sense Christ is Head of the church" (*Paul*, 380–82). Such a distinction between the man as ruler and the man as head seems to capture the difference between the male-female relation prior to the fall (viz. man as head of, and joint ruler with, the woman) and the disordered relation of ruler-ruled thereafter (viz. man as ruler of the woman). Compare Gen 1:28 to 3:16.

22. See also Mark 10:42–45; Luke 22:24–30. In the Markan version Jesus says that the Gentiles "exercise lordship over" (*katakyrieuousin*) the people (10:42). This corresponds to the dynamics of the curse, where the man will "exercise lordship" (*kyrieusei*) over the woman (Gen 3:16 LXX). "But it shall not be so among you" (Mark 10:43). Here we find a reversal of the curse in Christ.

becoming obedient [*hypekoos*] to the point of death, even death on a cross. (Phil 2:6-8)[23]

In sum, whatever authority is being proffered here in Ephesians for the man is necessarily circumscribed and defined by the figure of Christ: specifically, by Christ's self-giving authority for the good of the bride. As Christ comes to his church as a servant head, such servitude marks the function of his "authority" as head (John 13; Eph 5:25-27; Phil 2).[24]

The husband, as head, is to follow Christ in his self-giving love for his own "body," offering himself for the sanctification, cleansing, splendor and holiness of his own flesh. Moreover, Paul makes it explicit that such self-giving love is not to be given from a place of superiority but from a place of reverence and regard—as one loves himself (Eph 5:28-30). In short, the man qua man, in his one-flesh union with the woman, is constituted the head of a body in a way that figures Christ in relation to the church.

There is an all too obvious problem with this claim, suggesting as it does that every man—even the delinquent, adulterer, abandoner, and abuser—simply by virtue of being married figures Christ as a "head" to his bride. Such a claim needs clarification. Indeed, to say that the man figures Christ is not to suggest that every man as head is de facto anything like Christ as head, or figures Christ's self-giving love simply by virtue of being a man. On the contrary, in his fallen state the man's natural likeness to Christ is "by nature" (Eph 2:3) utterly obscured.

Nevertheless, in Paul's Letter to the Ephesians we find that Christ names his people as they are "in him"—namely, as those who "in him ... have obtained an inheritance" (Eph 1:11): no longer "dead in [their] trespasses and sins" (2:3) but "alive together with Christ," "seated ... with him in the heavenly places" (2:5-6), "saints and members of the household of God" (2:19). It is by virtue of this new identity in Christ that we are named heirs, inheritors, saints and members of God's house; and it is as such that the man, too, is named "the head." The man is thus named a Christ-imaging "head" in the same manner in which the man or woman

---

23. The same word to denote the "obedience" undergone by Christ here is used by Paul to denote the "obedience" required by children to parents (Eph 6:1) and slaves to masters (6:5)—a more severe obedience than what is called for by wives to husbands (5:21: *hypotassomenoi*). See also 1 Pet 2:18-25.

24. So Chrysostom: "Thou art the head of the woman. . . . So let us rule the women . . . not by seeking greater honor from them, but by their being more benefited by us" ("Homilies on 2 Thessalonians," homily 5).

in Christ is named a Christ-imaging "saint." It is not because our lives are in full conformity to Christ that we are so named, but because of who we are *in Christ*—and, hence, who we are becoming in and through him. Christ thus calls the man to become what he has already made him to be.[25]

Christ names us as we are, restored and recreated in him. The question then is not *whether* the self-indulgent, absent, or even abusive man is a "head," but what kind of head he is. The man cannot forfeit his representative status and responsibility but is to be judged and held to account, first in the church (1 Pet 4:17), and ultimately by God and his angels, for his action, inaction, or mal-action as head.[26]

In sum, the man's status as head representative is fundamentally a theological status denoting a representative responsibility. As head of the male-female one-flesh union the man represents Christ to his household and his household to God and to the angels; and as such he is responsible for the flourishing of the one-flesh union under God—namely, to love and to cherish his bride, as Christ does his church, and to seek her good, as Christ does his church, so as to present their union to God pure and without blemish, as Christ does his church. In this way, the man figures (signifies, patterns, proclaims) Christ in relation to his bride.

Turning to our next section, we will find that, ultimately, the proof of a man's likeness to Christ as head will be measured by the woman's flourishing as the glory of their union.

THE WOMAN AS A FIGURE OF CHRIST THE BODY

Whereas the man is the head of the woman, the woman is the body of the man. As such she figures Christ the body, the church.[27] The primal scrip-

---

25. As Peter Leithart puts it, "In Christ, God has opened a future determined solely by his promises. . . . We are who God's word says we are. We are now who we will be" (*Baptism*, 6).

26. See n8 above.

27. Although the phrase "Christ the body" is not used explicitly in the NT, I use it here to make explicit the notion that "the body of Christ," the church, is in fact *Christ*—not as a second incarnation but as a body united in his own flesh (Col 1:24; Eph 1:22–23). That the church is at times referred to as "Christ" in the NT is noted and developed by Augustine in *WSA* 3.4:33.8 (here Augustine cites Matt 25:40; Acts 9:4; Eph 1:22). Following Augustine, I use the phrase "Christ the body" to keep in view that the body is not an inferior entity, separate from Christ, theologically speaking, but is one with Christ, identified with Christ.

tural identification of the woman as the body of the man is expressed by Adam at the woman's creation: "This at last is bone of my bones and flesh of my flesh" (Gen 2:23). The term "flesh" (*basar*) is the closest Hebrew equivalent to the Greek *soma* and the English equivalent, "body."[28] And it is this expression of Adam—that Eve is *basar* of his own *basar*—that comes to be understood by the apostle as a figure of the husband-wife relation which is in turn a figure of the Christ-church relation (1 Cor 11:2-16; Eph 5:21-33).[29] For Paul, the woman is the body of the man's own body, even as Eve is the body of Adam, and as the church is the body of Christ.[30]

The point that needs further engagement here, however, is not simply *that* the woman is the body of the man, as a figure of Christ's own body, but *what this figural relation entails*. What does it mean to say that the woman is the "body" of man—*body of his own body*—as a figure of the body of Christ? What we will find is that *to be the figural "body" of man is to be (1) the glory of man and, as such, (2) the center of man's affections*. Put differently, as the church is the glory of Christ, so woman is man's glory; and as the church is the center of Christ's affections, so woman is the center of man's affections, rightly ordered.

A. Woman as the Glory of Man

Where male headship is conceived in terms of male authority, the place of the body is conceived in terms of female submission. But where the head

---

28. *Basar* seems originally to have meant "skin," used as a metonym for "man" or "human." In this sense, it differs from the Greek (Platonic) *soma*, which indicates a body-soul dualism. The ontological distinction implicit in the Hebrew term is not so much between body and soul as it is between the carnal and the spiritual person, the body animated by the divine breath and the body that is not. The meaning of the term *soma* as used in the NT is much determined by its Hebrew cognate. See M. Baumgärtel, *TDNT* 7:1045-48; Eduard Schweizer, "σάρξ," *TDNT* 7:105-23; J. Harding and Dawes, "Body."

29. See M. Baumgärtel, *TDNT* 7:1079. Junia Pokrifka describes 1 Cor 11 as "a rabbinic-style interpretative conclusion based on Genesis 2:20-23" ("Redeeming Women," 19). The woman as the body/flesh—the *idia sarx*—of man is likewise found in Sir 25:26.

30. For Paul, the woman is the *soma* of the man in a manner that corresponds to OT conceptions of human flesh. One implication is that the female *basar* is to be understood as an ensouled flesh, a totality in itself. Likewise, the male *rosh* is a synecdochal head—a totality that assumes a body with it. The union of head and body then cannot be conceived as two incomplete and competing parts that together constitute a whole. Rather, each is a synecdochal whole—and yet, in union with the other sex, is joined into a renewed and reconstituted one-flesh union.

is conceived in terms of bodily representation, what of the body? The man as representative of the one-flesh union corresponds to the woman as *the glory of that union*.[31] The term "glory" in Hebrew (*kavod*) literally means "heaviness," the weight or substance of a thing. As the man figures Christ as the *representative member* of the church, so the woman figures the church as the *glory* of Christ. The head is the representative of the body. The body is the glory of the head.

The OT begins with the woman identified as the body (*basar*) of man; and the body throughout the OT is associated with glory. In the opening chapters of Genesis, the body of Adam, made from the dust, is created in the divine image (Gen 1:26–27), displaying God's likeness in all the earth (2:7; see also 5:3; 9:6). As such, the human body is fashioned to reflect the divine glory (Pss 21:5; 24:7–10; Isa 43:7), or as the psalmist puts it, is "crowned with glory" (*vattechasserehu . . . vekavod*) (Ps 8:5). Although the glory of the body is "like the flower of grass" (Isa 40:6 LXX; 1 Pet 1:24), impermanent and fading away, it is glory nonetheless—a glory from dust returning to dust (Pss 7:5; 16:9–10; 49:16–17; Eccl 3:20). Though humans are created principally to reflect the divine glory (Isa 43:7), such glory is obscured and lost through human rebellion. Still, God will reward with "glory" those who fear him (Prov 22:2–4), and is restoring embodied humanity with glory through the anointed Son and King (Pss 8; 21:5; 24:7–10).[32]

---

31. Gordon, "Glory"; Strong et al., *Exhaustive Concordance*, H3519. Applied to persons metaphorically, it refers to a person's honor or worth, often referring by extension to a person's wealth.

32. Paul develops this theme of an original human glory lost and recovered. He explains that humans "exchanged the glory of the immortal God for images" (Rom 1:23). This exchange leads to the degradation of "their bodies" (1:24), with Jews and gentiles alike set to "seek for glory" (2:6), having "fall[en] short of the glory of God" (3:23; see also *Gen. Rab.* 12:6). The good news, however, is that Jesus is restoring "the glory of the children of God" (Rom 8:21; 9:4, 23), which entails "the redemption of our bodies" (8:23), bodies to be "glorified" through conformity "to the image of [God's] Son" (8:29–30), "through the body of Christ" (7:4). As Paul puts it elsewhere, it is in Christ that we "are being transformed into the same image from one degree of glory to another" (2 Cor 3:18). It is only in Christ that the glory of the *imago Dei* is restored, through "the glory of Christ, who is the image of God" (2 Cor 4:4). The writer of Hebrews makes this explicit also, perceiving in Christ the restoration of human glory: "He is the radiance of the glory of God" (Heb 1:3); "you have crowned him with glory and honor" (2:7; see also Ps 8:5). Here it is no longer *enowsh* (mankind) in general or *ben aḏam* (the son of mankind) who is crowned with glory (as in Ps 8), but Jesus specifically is in view (Heb 2:7) as the center and progenitor of a new humanity. In "bringing many sons to glory" (2:10), human flesh is again made glorious, sharing in the "one source" of Christ (2:11), with the fleshly *soma* of the church now revealed as "the glory

The creation accounts of Gen 1 and 2 each culminate, in turn, with human body formation as the climax of creaturely glory, first with humanity conceived as a totality, second with an ordered humanity of man from the dust and woman from the man. Mankind, in the first account, is presented as the *glory of God* in all creation; the woman, in the second, as the *glory of man*. In the first, the making of the body of *adam* receives the Creator's acclamation, "very good" (Gen 1:31). In the second, it is the fashioning of the woman which elicits man's adoration, his joy and praise (2:23; 1 Cor 11:7).

Paul apparently follows this scriptural-creational logic when he identifies the man as the glory of God, and the woman of his flesh as the glory of man (1 Cor 11:7; 15:40–41).[33] While the man and woman together are the image and glory of God, it is the man, as the head of the male-female union, who principally represents *God's* glory in the earth; and it is the woman, as the completion of humanity, who principally manifests *human* glory in the earth.[34] In Paul's words, "The man is the head of the woman. . . . Man is the glory of God . . . . woman is the glory of man. For man is not from woman, but woman from man" (1 Cor 11:3, 7–8 AT).[35]

---

of Christ" (2 Cor 8:23; Eph 3:21). The OT theme of a lost and fading human glory (Pss 7:5; 16:9–10; 49:16–17; Jer 2:11), which finds its restoration in the messianic Son and King (Pss 8; 21:5; 24:7–10), thus finds its fulfillment in Jesus. For a similar argument, see Gregory of Nyssa, *Life of Moses*, 2.26–2.30.

33. See Pokrifka, "Redeeming Women," 19.

34. When Paul deems the woman "the glory of man" it is unclear whether his phrase is best understood as "the glory of man viz. males (only)" or "the glory of man viz. mankind." The matter centers on the lexical range of the Greek word *aner*, here translated "man." Some argue that this word always designates an adult male or males, and others that it is at times used as a synonym for *anthropos*, and thus can designate a male or female (see, e.g., Acts 17:34 where *andres* clearly has a woman as one of its referents; Jas 1:20; Rom 4:8). For the latter position, see Blomberg, "Today's New International Version"; Bock, "Do Gender-Sensitive Translations Distort?" For a rebuttal to this position, see Poythress and Grudem, *Gender-Neutral Bible Controversy*. In what follows, I argue that in this context Paul's use of *aner* designates the male specifically, yet *in a manner that is representative* of the male-female relation. Hence, to be the glory of the male *is* to be the preeminent glory of *humanity*.

35. Some have seen Paul's reflections here as subordinationist, stating that Paul is making the man out to be the image of God, and woman the image of man, leaving the woman as an image of the image instead of an image of God. Pokrifka responds by insisting that, for Paul, "the 'not good' state of the man being alone is gloriously rectified by the formation of the woman, which is met with the man's joyful praise of the woman. In other words, Paul suppresses the more obvious truths about the woman as the image and glory of God and highlights the more subtle point about her relation to the man" ("Redeeming Women," 19).

As Paul here makes explicit, the logic of his claim that woman is "the glory of man" is grounded in the order of creation, where Eve, as the "body of [Adam's] body" (Gen 2:23), is welcomed by *adam* (mankind) as the crowning glory of creation. Further, the figural reach of Paul's claim extends from creation to the new creation, where the church, as a new Eve, is welcomed by the Second Adam, Jesus Christ, as his glorious "body" and bride (Eph 5:23). With such claims Paul is discerning and developing a figure where Eve—and all women in her likeness—figures the church in relation to Christ. Eve is the glory of Adam, woman the glory of man, the church the glory of Christ.[36]

For Paul, the church is the glory of Christ and the preeminent locus of Christ's glory in the world. It is where the "mystery hidden for ages in God" is on display for all to see, "so that *through the church* the manifold wisdom of God might be made known to the rulers and authorities in the heavenly places" (Eph 3:9–10); "to him be glory in the church" (3:21)! It is *in the church*, says Paul elsewhere, that the "glory of Christ" has shone (2 Cor 4:4–6); "*we* have this treasure in jars of clay" (4:7). The shining glory of Christ is thus the treasure of the clay-formed church. The "churches" in Christ in fact *are* "the glory of Christ" (Rom 15:7; 2 Cor 8:23; Eph 1:12). In sum, Christ's body is his glory.

And Paul sees the woman as a figure of Christ's body (Eph 5:23). The bridal imagery of the woman purified and presented "in splendor" (5:27) announces the woman as one who is "cleansed," made "holy and without blemish" (Eph 5:26–27). In this way, the woman indicates the eschatological nature *not* of women only but of *all* the human members of Christ's body. In this way, the woman is here revealed as the paradigmatic human form and telos—each member, male and female, to be purified in Christ and presented in splendor through him.

Likewise, Paul sees in the woman a sign of the whole church's call, for both women and men, to reciprocate steadfast love toward her nuptial head in humility and respect (5:24, 33; see also 1 Pet 3:1–4). In this way the woman again is a figure of the fully human life lived in faithfulness to God. It is as the form of the woman's life bears a similitude to the form of Christ the body that she most poignantly images God and manifests

---

36. While it is beyond the scope of this chapter to engage the Marian dimensions of this figure, Mary, too, has been conceived as a figure of the church, in typological relation to Eve. From as early as the second century, Mariology and ecclesiology have been woven together through the tradition, continuing into contemporary, especially Roman Catholic, contexts. See Balthasar and Ratzinger, *Mary*, esp. 138–44.

human glory before God and the attentive and marveling angels (1 Cor 11:7-11; Eph 3:10-13; 1 Pet 1:12).

In sum, as the church manifests the glory of Christ in the world, so woman manifests the glory of mankind. As the church is where Christ's beauty and splendor are preeminently manifest in the world, so the woman is the preeminent manifestation of human glory. As we will explore in the conclusion, this is a claim concerning the woman in her totality—her being, words, and deeds. Following the figure of Eve and the church we might conclude that *the woman is the glory of man as one who manifests the glorious splendor of humanity to all of creation, before God and the entire cosmos.* We now move to considering one implication of this theological claim.

B. Woman as the Center of Man's Affections

The church is the glory of Christ and, as such, the central object of his affections. We see this typified in OT nuptial imagery, where Yahweh is proclaimed the bridegroom of Israel and Israel his bride. God is passionately, even jealously, committed to redeeming a people—a bride made for the glory of his name (Hos 1-2; see also Exod 20; Ezra 39:25; Isa 43:7). God thus pursues glory by restoring glory to his people. This is made most clear in the incarnation, where in Christ God accomplishes more than a mere recovery of past glory. Whereas Israel *reflected* the divine glory, in Christ the divine glory is made *manifest* in human flesh. With the glory of God now manifest in the human flesh of Christ, all those "in Christ" are made partakers of his glory (Eph 3:21). They are "the glorious ones" (2 Pet 2:10-11; Jude 8-9; see also Isa 11:10; Dan 12:3), and so revealed as the central objects of Christ's affection (Eph 5:23; Rev 19-22). The glory which is Christ's is in this way shared with his body such that the glory of his body is inseparable from Christ's own glory, which is the glory of God (2 Cor 4:6).

To name the woman as man's glory is likewise to name the woman as the central object of man's affections, rightly ordered.[37] This seems to be the very point Paul is making in 1 Cor 11:2-16. When Paul says that "the woman is the glory of man" he is naming her as the focal point of

---

37. To use the bridal language of Ezekiel, it is the woman in her totality who is the "glory," the "joy," and the "desire" of her bridegroom (Ezek 24:16-25).

the man's "love, joy and devotion."[38] And it is precisely because she is the center of man's affections that the woman is to cover her head.[39]

Francis Watson interprets the purpose of Paul's head-covering injunctions as a fending off of the "male erotic gaze."[40] While Watson's argument makes sense in light of the gender norms and stereotypes in historical context, his approach is reductionist in at least one respect. Although the covering of woman's "glory" presumably serves to curtail the "male erotic gaze" in worship contexts as Watson says, such a curtailment is not the primary reason for the covering according to Paul's own stated logic.

As we have seen, the woman's status as the "glory of man" is a theological claim for Paul, following the order of creation: after the pattern of Adam and Eve, the woman is the glory of the man. Further, this theological claim finds its culmination in the first advent of the Second Adam, whose glory is his bride, the church (Eph 3:21).[41] Accordingly, Paul's identifying the woman as man's glory concerns far more than male erotic desire, even if *eros* is ingredient to man's multifaceted "love, joy and devotion."[42] Paul's reasoning is more fundamentally aimed at concealing *human glory* (and not simply concealing a sexual distraction) so that the

---

38. See Watson, "Authority of the Voice," 531.

39. Before God and the watching angels (1 Cor 11:10) the male represents *God's* glory manifested in humanity—glory to be on full display in worship; and, before the same audience, the woman manifests *human* glory—to be concealed as that which draws attention to itself rather than to the true object of worship (14:40). Watson makes the point that these arrangements do not indicate female subjugation but are made precisely for the purpose of *equality* in worship—that women may have freedom to pray and prophesy as the men ("Authority of the Voice").

40. For Watson, again, woman is the glory of man as the object of his love, joy, and devotion; and, as such, the woman ought not to be displaying her glory in this context (for Paul, a "glory" manifested most centrally in her hair [v. 15]), and so distract from the worship—and glory(!)—of God ("Authority of the Voice").

41. For Paul, that the woman-bride is the glory of the man-husband is ultimately a claim that concerns God's relation to his people (Eph 5:21–33).

42. As C. S. Lewis explains, eros is often reduced to "mere sexual appetite" when instead it should be understood as "a delighted pre-occupation with the Beloved—a general, unspecified pre-occupation with her in her totality." A man taken with eros, he says, "hasn't leisure to think of sex. He is too busy thinking of a person." He continues, "Sexual desire, without Eros, wants it, the thing in itself; Eros wants the Beloved" (*Four Loves*, 137). The Song of Songs proclaims the same, as the man is captivated by the woman (Song 4:9), and as the woman, in her totality, is conceived as the man's great desire (7:10). Early and medieval Christian readers (e.g., Origen and Bernard) understood the Song as presenting a type of Christ and the church. See King, *Origen on the Song*; Engh, *Gendered Identities*.

divine glory may appropriately be paramount in worship. In other words, the woman, for Paul, is not simply a sexual object (which needs covering), but she is the appropriate center of man's rightly ordered desire. For this reason, since the glory of God, and not human glory, is to be the gathered church's sole object of praise, the woman is to cover her head.

To summarize and conclude this section, we have seen that the nuptial union of male and female is a head and body union, and is a figure of the head and body union of Christ and the church. The man in relation to his wife is a figure of Christ, the head. This "headship" is fundamentally a *theological status* involving a *nuptial responsibility*. In short, the man is to live in relation to his wife after the pattern of Christ's self-giving love for the church, as the one finally responsible for pursuing and perfecting the one-flesh union and presenting it to Christ.

The woman, in relation to her husband, is a figure of Christ the body. As one flesh with the man, she is his glory and the teleological center of his affections. As such, the rightly ordered life of the woman manifests human majesty and splendor, defined not primarily in terms of "external" appearances but by the "imperishable beauty" of the heart (1 Pet 3:3–4). The human disposition of devotion toward God is revealed in the woman's sanctified life in relation to the man. She reveals to man what man is in relation to God. In short, this means that the woman is to live in relation to her husband after the pattern of the church's love for Christ, laying aside any and all ambitions for self-glorification for the one who has already laid down his life for her—not as a relinquishing of agency but as an agential act of self-giving love. As such she is, in her totality, the principal manifestation of human glory.

CONCLUSION

I have argued that the modern church is in need of a more robustly theological account of gender, and that the scriptural affirmation of the man and woman as a head and body corporeal unity is one way of pursuing it. Here, the man is the head of the one-flesh body—the representative of the male-female union under God. As such he figures (proclaims, signifies) Christ's representative status in relation to the church, taking full and final responsibility for the flourishing of the body, presenting the whole to God, after the pattern of Christ the head. The woman, correspondingly, is the body of the one-flesh union—its glory—and so the principal manifestation of human splendor in the earth, and the rightly ordered center of the man's love, joy, and devotion, after the pattern of the body of Christ.

I have insisted throughout that a Christian theological account of gender, if it is to be truly theological, must discern the shape of the human life as it is offered in the Scriptures, and apprehended centrally in the form of Christ's life for us—as head and body. Here, the man is the head of the woman as Christ is the head of the church, her representative member. The woman is the body of the man as the church is the body of Christ, his glory.

"And these two shall become one flesh" (Eph 5:31).

Returning to Eph 5, we find there is a teleological ordering of the genders toward *one another* in unitive love—a union which creates a new singularity, where two are more aptly described as "one flesh": head and body. It is in this head and body unity where the meaning and mystery of the genders is finally given: namely, the genders are figures of something else, pointing beyond themselves, to another unity of differences—to a God and his people; to a bridegroom and his glorious bride; to a man, Christ Jesus, and his ecclesial body, the church—the two become one.

Conclusion

Transfiguring Headship

According to Heidegger, each age has one issue to think through, and one only. Sexual difference is probably the issue in our time which could be our salvation if we thought it through.

—Luce Irigaray[1]

SEXUAL DIFFERENCE IS ONE of the most pressing philosophical and political issues of our time. At the heart of debates over sexual difference is the question of sexual equality. More specifically, the question of women's equality with men as a matter of human rights emerged with unprecedented force in the UK and North America in the 1950s and 1960s and has been a matter of widespread global concern for the last fifty years.[2]

The scriptural figure of the male "head" can be seen as an affront to such pan-global pursuits of sexual equality, a commendation of male privilege in the face of a world working to deconstruct the old order of

---

1. Irigaray, *Ethics of Sexual Difference*, 5.
2. The pursuit of women's equality in the context of global male dominance became a central concern of the United Nations. The equality of the sexes has been deemed a basic human right, articulated in the 1995 Beijing Declaration and Platform for Action, and adopted by 189 nations. Prior to this, in 1979 the UN General Assembly had adopted the Convention on the Elimination of All Forms of Discrimination against Women (CEDAW), often described as an International Bill of Rights for women's equality (United Nations, "Gender Equality"). See also "Globalization and Its Impact," in Ishay, *History of Human Rights*, 296–301. The concern for women's equality is part of a larger discourse concerning human rights which became clearly articulated as a matter of universal human interest in the Enlightenment era. See "Human Rights and the Enlightenment," in Ishay, *History of Human Rights*, 63–116.

patriarchy. In the preceding chapters I have sought to engage this tension between scriptural and contemporary notions of sexuality and the relation of each to notions of sexual equality and justice. Rather than assuring the contemporary reader of a safe and certain path toward sexual equality, we have found that the gendered "head and body" figure has problematized contemporary understandings of sexuality and equality, even calling into question some of the definitions and goals which have become basic to our egalitarian and secular age.

And yet, that a scriptural account of gender would problematize contemporary definitions and goals is precisely what one should expect, as the scriptural witness calls into question human valuations of every kind. Where justice is described in a manner that excludes a scripturally delineated justice we must ask, *Whose justice? Which rationality?* And where sexuality is described in a manner that excludes a scripturally delineated vision of sexuality we must ask, *Whose sexuality? Which vision of sexual equality?*[3] To be clear, the pertinent question is not *whether* each gender should enjoy justice and equality but *how* gender justice and equality are to be conceived and sought.[4]

Admittedly, a biblical account of gender where the man is named the head of the woman and the woman the body/flesh of the man will remain objectionable to many. It is the objectionable nature of these claims that I wish to engage more fully in what follows.

HEADSHIP IN A SECULAR AGE?

I have argued that the Scriptures offer us an image—a figural depiction—toward a lived theology of gender. The figure is that of a head and a body: "The man is the head of his wife, even as Christ is the head of the church, his body" (Eph 5:23). Here there is no "one plus one, creating a coupling of exactly the same kind" but rather a "duality of two parts that make a

---

3. See MacIntyre, *Whose Justice? Which Rationality?* Among feminist theoreticians there are several distinct visions of sexual equality. E.g., the "difference feminists" emphasize the distinct needs, desires, and goals of each sex, whereas the "equality feminists" posit that the desires and needs of the sexes are understood as fundamentally the same, so that a more generic equality might be pursued. Each of these positions can be further complicated by their identification with selected goals of broader feminist movements such as liberal, reformist, or radical feminisms. See Maynard, "Beyond the 'Big Three.'"

4. See Achtemeier, "Impossible Possibility."

whole which is unique, novel, nonduplicable."[5] Here we are speaking of a head with its body, and a body with its head; each one alive in itself yet ordered toward the other so as to find a new kind of wholeness in and with the other (see Rom 12; 1 Cor 12; Eph 4). Such a starkly gender-differentiated proposal involving a male "head of the woman" strikes the modern reader as problematic. And understandably so.

As we have seen, rapid social changes in the modern West led to a widespread sense of dispossession among women. This process, which we traced back to the rise of capitalism and industrialization, culminated in the twentieth century in the rise of powerful feminist ideologies which sought to restore balance to an increasingly imbalanced gendered arrangement. To affirm in the present context that the man is the head, with whatever power, influence, or authority this designation might entail, will arguably only perpetuate the dynamics of a gender imbalance in favor of male privilege. Moreover, the title "head" as a male designation is all the more offensive considering that the "head" has come to denote the authoritative position in a structured hierarchy, and is linked with modern anatomical conclusions that the head (or brain) is the intelligent control center of the body, and therefore the superior and commanding member.[6]

Accordingly, contemporary responses to commendations of "male headship" have typically sought to comprehensively deconstruct male power. This includes an excision of "male headship," not only in terms of secular and religious nomenclature, but as a working category altogether. By the twentieth century, notions of the male-headed home had come to be understood in terms of authority, breadwinning, provision, protection, honor, and representation. With the rise of feminism's second wave, however, all of this came to be challenged as strong cultural and intellectual forces sought to divest men of the inordinate power that had been handed them through the course of the postindustrial era. Gender equality after the second wave would now *require* that all of the distinctions which had to that point come to be ascribed to men qua men—including a prominent or distinguished place in the family—be overthrown, or at least shared with women.

---

5. Illich, "Sad Loss of Gender," 4. Prudence Allen improves upon Illich's notion of the man and woman as "two parts," emphasizing instead that the male-female duality is a complementarity of two wholes, that each is a complete person in an "ontologically important sense" ("Man-Woman Complementarity," 95).

6. For an outline of the historical development of the "head" title, see ch. 2.

Or so it was thought.

I have argued that a corrective was certainly needed in response to the newly imbalanced arrangement of male dominance in the wake of industrialization. I have also argued that the scriptural account of gender, as I have laid it out, puts certain constraints on how such a corrective might be pursued. Centrally, the pursuit of gendered balance will not entail a denigration of the man's identity and function as head; rather, it will involve a recovery and redefinition of the head status.

The man is the head after the pattern of Christ. This is a descriptive claim, following the scriptural witness. Any prescriptions attached to the man's head identity are limited, then, by this description. Framed this way, the matter for concern is not *whether or not* the man is the head (or *should be* the head), but *what it means* for the man to be the head—including how this claim might shape our reading of history and of the male identity in his contemporary cultural setting.

In this perspective, a Christian response to historic and contemporary forms of male dominance is not to deny or denigrate the man as head representative, with whatever power or prominence this entails; rather, following the scriptural naming of the man as head, a Christian response will likewise name things as they are and call them into conformity to the pattern of Christ. This will involve evaluating all forms of male power/prominence in light of the Scriptures' own definitions.

Should one find that the man, in the dynamic of his one-flesh union with the woman, has indeed characteristically exercised a certain kind of power vis-à-vis the woman, the response will not be to deny or deconstruct man's power but to identify the nature of that power and call it into the service of Christ. In this way, the Scriptures press us to consider that the solution to any variety of male delinquencies is not to deny the male identity as head (again, with whatever power, prominence, influence it entails), but to name the man as he is and call him to repentance and conformity to Christ. Far from denying or decrying the male identity as "head" (or "representative"), this path will lead to an honest appraisal of man's historically instantiated cultural identities—his tendencies, strengths, weaknesses, and predilections—with a related call to use his power and position in service of others, to the glory of God.

The woman's status as the glory of mankind will likewise be upheld in an honest appraisal of woman's historically instantiated being. Should one find that the woman, in her dynamic one-flesh union with the man, is indeed one who uniquely manifests human glory in her deeds and being, including her life-giving capacities, the appropriate response will be to acknowledge and celebrate her as such and, more than that, to collaborate for her freedom and flourishing. If the woman is the glory of man, all of humanity should indeed have an interest in seeing women encouraged and empowered to fulfill her various vocations, including of course that of producing, nurturing, and raising new life in our world.

It is not incidental that she, the glory of man, is likewise the giver of life, fashioned after the likeness of Eve, "the mother of all living" (Gen 3:20). Her status as "mother," whether as a potentiality or actuality, is itself a glory to be beheld. It is in fact a mark of shame on our world where the vocation of the mother has been rendered inglorious, substandard, second rate.

Central as the glorious vocation of the mother will be to many women, this will not be the calling of all. If she is man's glory, humanity should be further invested in encouraging and empowering women's vocational callings of other kinds—intellectual, artistic, scientific, literary, and so on. Such a proposal stands in stark contrast to the ways that women have so often been limited and silenced, as though *men* were man's glory. A scriptural account of gender says otherwise. Far from denying her unique status as the "glory of man," the call is thus to *discern* this status as a lived reality, with the woman called to use her glory-status and potentiality in service of others, ultimately to the glory of God.

In the course of this work we have thus set out and developed two central theological affirmations: that the man is the representative head of the one-flesh union, and the woman is the glory of that union. In what follows, we will consider some implications for what such a vision might entail today. As we do so, it will become clear that some of the implications of this theological vision will have most concrete ramifications for the man and the woman in their one-flesh union.

A. Implications for Men

To review: I have argued that male headship entails most basically that a man, in one-flesh union with a woman, is to take responsibility for pursuing and perfecting the flourishing of the body of which he is head. He is to *lay down his life for the body*, which will involve his loving and self-giving pursuit of the woman's flourishing. The woman is his glory, after all, and as such he is to have the woman of his own flesh as the center of his love, joy, and devotion. Here we will develop some of the implications of these claims.

First, the male "head" prioritizes the flourishing of his body. For the married man, his wife's flourishing is to be prioritized above all other priorities. He is explicitly to love her "as his own body" (Eph 5:28), even "as Christ loved the church" (5:25). For this reason, the man cannot use his love or devotion to anything—even to God—as an excuse *not* to love, pursue, or serve the interests of his wife. The man who "devotes" himself to God and so escapes his nuptial responsibility has rejected the commandment of God (Mark 7:9-13) and abandoned his call to live as a head after the pattern of Christ.

Second, the male as "head" is to encourage the woman to develop and put to use her capacities, talents, and gifts. She is his glory, after all. Rather than stifling or silencing the woman, the man is to be an agent of encouragement and empowerment. As Christ restores, revitalizes and catalyzes his body for work and ministry of all kinds in the world, so the man is to be a catalyst for the woman. For this reason, where male headship has been invoked to limit or silence the woman in her calling to serve and to glorify the church, this stands in contradiction to the headship of Christ. Whatever limits or silences are to be enacted in the head and body relation are to be freely given, as a woman's willing offering, not as the result of a man's coercion or domineering rule. The Lord delights in sacrifices freely given (Ps 51:16-19).

Moreover, where male headship has been used to justify male dominance over the woman, Christ's headship stands in judgment over all such forms of counterfeit enactments of headship. The head, after the pattern of Christ, does not seek his own interests or insist on his own way but bears, believes, hopes, and endures all things (1 Cor 13:4-7). Headship as such cannot be used to justify any manipulation toward its own ends. If anything, it will entail the sharing of authority with the woman, after the pattern of the Father with the Son, and Christ with the church (Matt 28:18-20; 1 Cor 11:3).[7]

In all of these ways, male headship involves the pursuit of the woman's freedom and flourishing to do and to be in accordance with the fullness of her nature and calling. This is at least in part why, in debates

---

7. To be clear, such "sharing of authority" does not entail the blurring of gender differences or contradicting God's law by any means. Rather, it entails the full participation of women with men in ways that are appropriate to their distinct identities and callings.

over women's ordination, it is so dissonant when "male headship" is invoked as a reason to restrict and shut women down, as a matter of male "authority over" the woman. Where male heads invoke their authority *as* heads to limit the body, we might ask, *Does Christ use his authority as head to limit or suppress his body the church?* Or, does he instead call his church to be sharers in his authority, messengers and ministers of his presence to the ends of the earth? Contrary to certain uses of the head figure in modern headship debates, male headship, after the pattern of Christ, entails that men are to encourage, commend, and uphold women in their gifts and callings *to manifest glory, to make glorious things, and to make things glorious*—including productive works of the intellect, music, art, literature, etc. Where male headship has been used to stifle women's contributions and productivity, here we find that male headship, rightly understood, serves the opposite end: namely the woman's flourishing as the glory of man. If man is the head, with whatever power, prestige, and authority it entails, he is what he is for the benefit and flourishing of the body. She is his glory; and he is to receive and regard her as such.[8]

B. Implications for Women

I have argued that the woman, as the glory of man, is the preeminent manifestation of *human* glory in the earth. What this means is that we should expect that women will characteristically and uniquely display human splendor and majesty, not only in her very being but in her doing, her contributions in any number of spheres. Indeed, such glorious productivity should not be limited to one particular sphere, but should be expected and encouraged in every sphere, with human glory shining most brilliantly not only in the uniquely female capacities to generate and sustain human life, but in works of care and intellect, performative arts and science, and indeed as man's co-heir, co-laborer, and helper in all of creation (Gen 1–2). Indeed, if the woman is in fact the glory of man, we should expect that her being in the world will naturally glorify all aspects

---

8. To be clear, nothing of what I have said here necessarily serves as an argument in favor of women's ordination. To say, e.g., that a husband shares his authority with his wife is not to say that the wife should *become* a husband, much less take on the vocation of a father (literal or priestly!). The husband and wife each has a distinct identity, and therefore, even where their authority is shared, each has a distinct way of carrying out this shared authority under God. The question of whether or not a woman might take on the particular vocation of an ordained elder/priest/bishop is beyond the scope of the present chapter.

of the world we inhabit in a manner that regularly elicits man's wonder and praise.

As an aside, it is for this reason that it is all the more disgraceful that men throughout history have so regularly used positions of power to limit, silence, and denigrate women's productive contributions, rather than to encourage, commend, and uphold women in their gifts and callings. If the woman is the man's glory, rightly ordered, then to exclude or overlook women's creative contributions to the life of the family, church, and world is to be lamented where it has happened and opposed where it persists. Moreover, this is why the denial of women's contributions to the life and ministry of the church, specifically—including in areas of teaching, worship, discipleship, praying, and prophesying—has been so disconcerting. While the head is to cherish and uplift the body, he has instead too often restricted and inhibited her. Conversely, Jesus invites his whole body, men and women, to have a share in his ministerial authority. He even praises women as exceptional in ministry. It is a woman, after all, who is to be remembered "wherever" the gospel is preached—"what she has done will also be told in memory of her" (Matt 26:6–13).[9]

Further, as the preeminent manifestation of human glory, the woman embodies in her rightly ordered life the disposition of every human in relation to God—namely, in faithfulness responding to God's initiating love. As the church is the glory of Christ and so seeks to honor and love Christ, so the woman as man's glory will seek to honor and love the man. Such self-giving love is often spoken of in the Scriptures in terms of the voluntary offering of oneself, one's "subjection," unto another. In the words of First Peter, "Wives, be subject to your own husbands" (1 Pet 3:1). In a world that foolishly prizes "external adorning," true "beauty" is instead marked by "a gentle and quiet spirit, which in God's sight is very precious" (3:3–4). It turns out that in God's kingdom, glory shines not in

---

9. None of this suggests that women should necessarily be ordained to the ministry of word and sacrament within any or every denominational branch of the church catholic. But in any branch where women are systematically barred or inhibited from taking on meaningful leadership in general—including in areas of worship, discipleship, and teaching—we must conclude that such convictions have more to do with a culture of male dominance, little to do with a Christ-patterned headship, and are out of step with NT teaching and practice concerning the full inclusion of women with men as joint heirs, disciples, and servants in God's house, many of whom may be gifted and called to serve in areas of evangelism, teaching, and leading in any number of ways (e.g., Luke 2:38; John 20:18; Acts 18:26; Rom 16:3–7; 1 Cor 14; Phil 4:2–3; Titus 2:3–5; see also Prov 31).

external but in internal beauty, not in forcefulness but in gentleness, not in many words but in few.

In spite of all the ways such a text might be used against women (1 Pet 3:1; see also Eph 5:22; Col 3:18), any such use misses the point. There is no command here (or anywhere else in the Scriptures, for that matter) for men to subjugate women. Moreover, in relation to other Jewish and Greco-Roman texts of the same era, it is striking that the NT never once roots the call for the woman's "submission" in her inferiority. Rather, the NT everywhere presumes women's equal status with men as joint heirs in the heavenly kingdom. In every place where a woman is called to submit, then, it is always a call to discipleship—to lay aside what is hers by right and, as an act of her own agency, to submit herself in loving self-sacrifice for the good of another.

It should also be noted that what Peter speaks of here is not women's subjection for the purpose of male privilege, but a subjection which *adorns the woman with glory* after the pattern of Christ and his kingdom. It calls the wife to pursue that beauty which is most precious to God—not in the external "adorning" (braided hair, jewelry) but in the inner person of the heart—the *kardias anthropos* (3:4). This holistic and enduring "beauty" is related to the woman's respectful and pure conduct, her gentleness and quietness, and even her "subjection" to her own husband.[10]

Being "in subjection" is perhaps the last thing any contemporary woman—any person—would want to hear as an "implication" of a theological doctrine. It sounds little different than the invitation to "come and die." In fact, these are one and the same. The woman in subjection to the man is in this way a figure of the church in relation to Christ, calling man into a life not of greatness but of servitude, not of claiming his rights but of laying them down. The woman in a place of subjection in fact indicates what it means to be great and glorious in Christ's kingdom—"and whoever would be first among you must be slave of all," Jesus says (Mark

---

10. Lest any of these traits be wrongly attributed to the woman as uniquely "feminine" traits, we should point out that each of these behavioral traits is likewise explicitly given as *man's* prerogative. Men and women alike are to be respectful (Rom 13:7), pure (2 Cor 11:2), gentle (Matt 5:5), even "quiet" in certain respects (1 Tim 2:2), in subjection to God and to one another (Eph 5:21; 1 Cor 16:16). As Jesus says, the "blessed" in God's kingdom are marked by such humble dispositions as these—including poverty of spirit, meekness, purity of heart, and persecution (Matt 5:2–11). In these ways it is the woman who is called to instantiate in herself, most poignantly in relation to her husband, the paradigmatic *human* form in all its richness and beauty.

10:44). And Paul follows suit: "For though I am free from all, I have made myself a servant to all, that I might win more of them" (1 Cor 9:19).

Ultimately, such matters of "authority" and "subjection" are to be specifically enacted within the male-female one-flesh union after the pattern of Christ and the church. Here, the man as head-representative, and the woman as flesh-glory, are from and for each other in ways that enact and lead to their mutual flourishing in unitive love. It is this context which, as a "profound mystery" (Eph 5:32), presses each to an ever more faithful embodiment of the Christian virtues which are common to men and women both.

In sum, the man is a figure of Christ the head, and the woman in a corresponding manner a figure of Christ the body (viz. the church). The man represents the glory of God in his marriage and the woman the glory of man. He is her head; she is his body. He is her representative; she is his glory. Following the logic of the apostle Paul, we might say: *While she is primordially from him and for him, he is, in the course of redemption, from her and for her;* "in the Lord woman is not independent of man nor man of woman; for as woman was made from man, so man is now born of woman. And all things are from God" (1 Cor 11:11–12).

In the final section we will connect these claims to a broader cosmological context. What we will find is that, theologically speaking, gender is by no means incidental to who and what we are in this sacramentally profuse universe as creatures made by God for the purposes of God. In this world, such as it is, given by God, it is the dynamic union of Christ with the church that determines the meaning of gender.[11]

Admittedly, such lofty claims call for greater engagement than can be offered in the space of these final pages. I nevertheless seek to offer here concise points of connection between the theologically framed point of departure from which this work began, in order to show how the "theology of gender" articulated in these chapters fits within the created order, theologically conceived.

---

11. Such an approach to a topic as fraught as "male headship" simply follows the figural impulses of Augustine: "But if there is no way in which we can understand what has been written in a manner that is pious and worthy of God without believing that these things have been set before us in figures and in enigmas, we have the apostolic authority by which so many enigmas from the books of the Old Testament are solved"—namely, in discerning such "enigmas" as figures of Christ (*WSA* 1.19:2.2.3).

HEADSHIP IN A SACRAMENTAL COSMOS (CONCLUDING REMARKS)

The gendered claims of the Scriptures with which we have been engaging are necessarily and inextricably tethered to the sacramental cosmos that coheres with and corresponds to these Scriptures.[12] In such a sacramental world, ordered as it is in accordance with the Scriptures, human beings are figured as a head and body duality. Like the rest of creaturely artifacts, human beings share in the sacramental reality which encompasses all things created from and for God.[13] Such claims have been basic to Christian conceptions of the world throughout the history of the church, having come under the weight of serious criticism only as the sacramentalism of the so-called "pre-enlightened" age gave way to a new materialism which occludes the possibility of transcendence having any significant bearing on our perceptions of the world.[14]

In the world as given in the Scriptures, however, all of created reality is a *sacramentum*, a "mystery" which serves as a sign and symbol of who God is and who we are in relation to him. God has given us all of creation so that through creation our eyes might be lifted to him. The sun, moon and stars; the pluriformity of peoples; vast and beautiful landscapes; languages; music; thunder, waves, and all manner of nature's varied displays of power—all of these are "words" about God's glory and "speech" that extends "to the end of the world" (Ps 19:3–4).[15]

It is no surprise then that in such a world the most basic unit for ordering our social and civilizational structures—the normatively male-headed home—is also given to us by God to instruct and form creatures

---

12. By "sacramental cosmos" I mean that all of creation is a *sacramentum*—literally, a sacred "mystery" that reflects something of the divine (God, God's ways, God's glory, etc.) by virtue of its relation to God as God's handiwork. For a fuller definition and explanation, see the introduction.

13. See Radner, *Time and the Word*, 89.

14. See also J. Smith, *How (Not) to Be Secular*, especially 47–59. Boersma traces this modern "loss of transcendence" back to Scotus and Ockham (*Heavenly Participation*, ch. 4).

15. All of this is complicated by the effects of human sin in all of creation. However, as Calvin explains, the problem is not that the created order ceases to reflect the divine glory; rather, the problem is that fallen humanity is rendered unable to perceive such revelation on our own. As Calvin puts it, "It is therefore in vain that so many burning lamps shine for us in the workmanship of the universe to show forth the glory of its Author. . . . [Although] the invisible divinity is made manifest in [creation], . . . we have not the eyes to see this unless they be illumined by the inner revelation of God through faith" (*Institutes*, 1.5.14).

in wisdom. This, too, is sacred space. The husband, as head of the family, is given as a sign to his family and to the world of the way that Christ loves the church and gives himself up for her. The wife, in a corresponding way, is a sign to her family and to the world of the way that the church loves Christ—the way she responds to God in self-giving love.

In this sense, sexual difference from a theological perspective is part of God's sacramentally profuse world, its significance enmeshed within this vast network of ordered meaning which participates in the divine life. In this view, the kind of gendered ordering of life that we find in the Scriptures is not hopelessly sexist, but is in fact sacred, life giving, reality defining; and it is in reclaiming such a scripturally ordered vision that women and men alike will find a living source for becoming more fully human, more fully what we are.

Admittedly, such a head and body figure appears to favor the head *over* the body, the man *over* the woman. Such seemingly straightforward conclusions, however, are overturned by the Scripture's own upending of typical human valuations. "If anyone would be first, he must be last of all and servant of all," Jesus says (Mark 9:35). And our Lord is indeed the one who washes his disciples' feet (John 13:1–20).

Indeed, the human propensity to favor the head *over* the body—the top *over* the bottom, the first *over* the second—is challenged in terms of God's own priorities and valuations. "To the Jew first and then to the Gentile." This is not God's preference of one over the other—Jew over gentile—since it is the Jews who are chosen to be God's bearers of blessing to the nations (Gen 12:1–3), even through suffering (Isa 45:14–5; 1 Tim 4:10). In a world that esteems the first, this God surprisingly and consistently chooses the second—Isaac over Ishmael, Jacob over Esau, Joseph over Reuben. The "least" is greater than the highest, greater than the "great ones" and the lords. And the second is chosen to bring blessing to the first, and indeed to the whole world. In this world servitude is thus redefined as greatness, leadership as servitude, and "headship" as the laying down of one's life (Eph 5:25).

Moreover, in this world "the heart is the wellspring of life" (Prov 4:23)—not the head.

Some will still insist that however one defines headship—and especially where headship is conceived in Greek patriarchal terms (viz. "rulership")—to envision man as head in relation to woman remains unjust, as it continues to offer power to male hands only. In a world centered on relations of power and economically centered notions of freedom and equality, such a critique is both inevitable and pertinent. However, it is important to point out that in order to criticize a scriptural account of sexuality as such, one must inevitably do so from the vantage point of another story. The crucial question is not whether Scripture can be criticized according to the goals and valuations of a secular state—of course, it can—but whether Scripture might actually have something truer and more beautiful to offer than the competing narratives which have become prevalent in large part through the secularization of the West.

In sum, a gendered complemental ordering of households is given in the scriptural figure of the head. This ordering categorically has nothing to do with domineering or oppressive leadership, but everything to do with one member representing and serving the interests of the body. And actually, as we have seen, in a Christian perspective, headship is not really about the man/husband but about Jesus, the true head.

Jesus, in the Christian story, is the true head whose headship is enacted through sacrificial self-giving love and service. *He gives his life.* This is how the authority of the representative head is radically redefined, and thus contemporary notions of "authority as dominance" are subverted, even obliterated. *Headship means life for the other—for the "all" that constitutes the body.* It means serving, washing, bearing with, and preferring the other, all after the pattern of Christ. *And who is this Christ?* He is the high and exalted one who stoops down low, taking on our humanity; then lower still, being born under the law; then lower still, undergoing the miseries of this life; then lower still, "undergoing the wrath of God, and the cursed death of the cross, and continuing under death for a time"—and all this for the sake of the church.[16]

The man is thus made, and is being remade, after the pattern of Christ the head. The woman is made, and is being remade, after the form of Christ the body. He is the representative of the one-flesh union, finally accountable for pursuing and perfecting that union. She is the glory of the one-flesh union and the rightly ordered center of the man's affections.

"This mystery is profound, and I am saying that it refers to Christ and the church" (Eph 5:32).

The biblical concept of the male as "head" of the male-female relation is admittedly a difficult one to reconcile with life in our secular age. Yet, as I have argued, it has served as one of the ways that God orders creaturely life under his care and for our good. Through a male-female

---

16. This paragraph summarizes and quotes from the *Westminster Shorter Catechism*, q. 27 (Westminster Assembly, *Westminster Shorter Catechism*).

head and body duality, God has figured the entire story of salvation, and through it has heralded good news to every creature. All of this has been done with little regard for our prior assent to these realities. The Scriptures do not so much tell us who we ought to be as tell us who we in fact are. Headship, too, is not so much about what we are to do (law) as it is about who Christ is and what he has done (gospel). Headship is thus not a vacuous term to be dispensed with but a sign of the gospel. This should be no surprise. In the history of figural interpretation, Christ is the determinative lens by which everything in the OT is to be understood anew and by which the NT is ordered, since he is the fulfillment and substance of the law (Matt 5:17; John 5:39), and the revelation of the Father (John 14:9). As man and woman, male and female, it turns out that we ourselves are figures of the only eternal bridegroom and the only eternal bride; the two made one flesh, a head and a body, most glorious.

Bibliography

Abbott, Lyman. "Why Women Do Not Wish the Suffrage." *Atlantic Monthly* 92 (1903) 289–96.
Achtemeier, Elizabeth. "The Impossible Possibility: Evaluating the Feminist Approach to Bible and Theology." *Interpretation* 42 (1988) 45–57.
Agassi, Judith Buber. "Theories of Gender Equality: Lessons from the Israeli Kibbutz." *Gender & Society* 3 (1989) 160–86.
Alcoff, Linda. "Cultural Feminism Versus Post-Structuralism: The Identity Crisis in Feminist Theory." *Signs* 13 (1988) 405–36.
———. *Visible Identities: Race, Gender, and the Self*. New York: Oxford University Press, 2006.
Allen, Prudence. *The Aristotelian Revolution, 750 B.C.—A.D. 1250*. Vol. 1 of *The Concept of Woman*. 2nd ed. Grand Rapids: Eerdmans, 1997.
———. "Man-Woman Complementarity: The Catholic Inspiration." *Logos* 9 (2006) 87–108.
Ambrose of Milan. *Hexameron. Paradise. Cain and Abel*. Translated by John J. Savage. FC 42. Washington, DC: Catholic University of America Press, 2004.
Amussen, Susan D. "The Contradictions of Patriarchy in Early Modern England." *Gender & History* 30 (2018) 343–53.
Aquinas, Thomas. *The "Summa Theologica" of St. Thomas Aquinas*. Translated by Fathers of the English Dominican Province. London: Washbourne, Burns, 1912.
Aristotle. *Aristotle's History of Animals in Ten Books*. Translated by Richard Cresswell. London: Bell and Sons, 1902.
———. *The Politics*. Edited and translated by Carnes Lord. Chicago: University of Chicago Press, 1984.
Auerbach, Erich. *Mimesis: The Representation of Reality in Western Literature*. Translated by Willard R. Trask. Princeton, NJ: Princeton University Press, 1953.
Augustine. *The Literal Meaning of Genesis*. Edited by John Hammond Taylor. New York: Newman, 1982.
———. *On Genesis: "Two Books on Genesis Against the Manichees" and "On the Literal Interpretation of Genesis: An Unfinished Book."* Translated by Ronald J. Teske. FC 84. Washington, DC: Catholic University of America Press, 2001.
———. "Reply to Faustus the Manichaean." Translated by R. A. B. Mynors. In *NPNF*[1], edited by Philip Schaff, 4:155–345. Buffalo, NY: Christian Literature Co., 1887.
———. "A Treatise on Faith, Hope, and Love." Translated by J. F. Shaw. In *NPNF*[1], edited by Philip Schaff, 3:237–76. Buffalo, NY: Christian Literature Co., 1887.

Bachiochi, Erika, et al. "Can Contemporary Feminism Come to Grips with Reality? Four Responses to Abigail Favale." *Public Discourse*, July 18, 2021. https://www.thepublicdiscourse.com/2021/07/76816/.

Bailey, Kenneth E. *Paul Through Mediterranean Eyes*. Downers Grove, IL: IVP Academic, 2011.

Baker, David W. *Nahum, Habakkuk, Zephaniah: An Introduction and Commentary*. Edited by Donald J. Wiseman. TOTC. Downers Grove, IL: IVP Academic, 2009.

Balthasar, Hans Urs von, and Joseph Cardinal Ratzinger [Pope Benedict XVI]. *Mary: The Church at Its Source*. San Francisco: Ignatius, 2005.

Barr, Beth Allison. *The Making of Biblical Womanhood: How the Subjugation of Women Became Gospel Truth*. Grand Rapids: Brazos, 2021.

Barth, Karl. "The Strange New World Within the Bible." In *The Word of God and the Word of Man*, translated by Douglas Horton, 28–50. Boston: Pilgrim, 1928.

Bartlett, J. R. "The Use of the Word *ROSH* as a Title in the Old Testament." *VT* 19 (1969) 1–10.

Baulant, Micheline. "The Scattered Family, Another Aspect of Seventeenth-Century Demography." In *Family and Society: Selections from the "Annales"; Economies, Sociétés, Civilisations*, edited by Robert Forster and Orest Ranum, translated by Elborg Forster and Patricia M. Ranum, 104–16. Baltimore: John Hopkins University Press, 1976.

Baumgärtel, F. "καρδία." *TDNT* 3:606–8.

Baumgärtel, Michael. "σῶμα." *TDNT* 7:1024–94.

Beauvoir, Simone de. *The Second Sex*. New York: Vintage, 1973.

Beck, Ulrich. *The Brave New World of Work*. Cambridge, UK: Polity, 2000.

Bedale, Stephen. "The Meaning of κεΦαλή in the Pauline Epistles." *JTS* 5 (1954) 211–15.

———. "The Theology of the Church." In *Studies in Ephesians*, edited by F. L. Cross, 64–75. London: Mowbray, 1956.

Bede. *In primam partem*. Edited by Bruno Krusch. CCSL 119. Turnhout, Belg.: Brepols, 1969.

Behm, Johannes. "νοῦς." *TDNT* 4:954–56.

Behr-Sigel, Elisabeth, and Kallistos Ware. *The Ordination of Women in the Orthodox Church*. Geneva: WCC, 2000.

Bem, Sandra. *The Lenses of Gender: Transforming the Debate on Sexual Inequality*. New Haven, CT: Yale University Press, 1993.

Bennett, Judith M. "Feminism and History." *Gender & History* 1 (1989) 251–72.

Berman, Joshua. "The Making of the Sin of Achan (Joshua 7)." *BibInt* 22 (2014) 115–31.

Billings, J. Todd. "United to God Through Christ: Assessing Calvin on the Question of Deification." *HTR* 98 (2005) 315–34.

Bishop, Kelly Ladd. "I'm Tired of Churches Teaching Male Headship." *HuffPost*, Sept. 15, 2015; updated Sept. 15, 2016. https://www.huffpost.com/entry/im-tired-of-churches-teac_b_8125900.

Blackburn, Simon. *The Oxford Dictionary of Philosophy*. 2nd ed. Oxford: Oxford University Press, 2008. Ebook.

Blaising, Craig A., and Carmen S. Hardin, eds. *Psalms 1–50*. ACCS OT 7. Downers Grove, IL: IVP Academic, 2008.

Blankenhorn, David, et al. *Does Christianity Teach Male Headship? The Equal-Regard Marriage and Its Critics*. Grand Rapids: Eerdmans, 2004.

Blau, Francine D., and Lawrence M. Kahn. "The Gender Wage Gap: Extent, Trends, and Explanations." *Journal of Economic Literature* 55 (2017) 789–865.
Block, Daniel I. "Marriage and Family in Ancient Israel." In *Marriage and Family in the Biblical World*, edited by Ken M. Campbell, 33–102. Downers Grove, IL: InterVarsity, 2003.
Blomberg, Craig L. "Today's New International Version: The Untold Story of a Good Translation." *Bible Translator* 56 (July 2005) 187–211.
Bock, Darrell L. "Do Gender-Sensitive Translations Distort Scripture? Not Necessarily." *JETS* 45 (2002) 651–69.
Boersma, Hans. *Heavenly Participation: The Weaving of a Sacramental Tapestry*. Grand Rapids: Eerdmans, 2011.
Bonhoeffer, Dietrich. *Creation and Fall: A Theological Exposition of Genesis 1–3*. Edited by John W. De Gruchy. Vol. 3 of *Dietrich Bonhoeffer Works*. Translated by Douglas Stephen Bax. Minneapolis: Fortress, 2004.
Bould, Sally. "Development and the Family: Third World Women and Inequality." *International Journal of Sociology and Social Policy* 4 (1984) 38–51.
Bourguignon, Erika. "Sex Bias, Ethnocentrism, and Myth Building in Anthropology: The Case of Universal Male Dominance." *Central Issues in Anthropology* 5 (1983) 59–79.
Boydston, Jeanne. "Gender as a Question of Historical Analysis." *Gender & History* 20 (2008) 558–83.
Braaten, Carl E., and Robert W. Jenson, eds. *A Map of Twentieth-Century Theology: Readings from Karl Barth to Radical Pluralism*. Minneapolis: Fortress, 1995.
Brachet, Auguste. *An Etymological Dictionary of the French Language*. Translated by G. W. Kitchin. Oxford: Clarendon, 1878.
Bradley, Keith R. *Discovering the Roman Family: Studies in Roman Social History*. New York: Oxford University Press, 1991.
Branson, Robert D. *Judges: A Commentary in the Wesleyan Tradition*. Kansas City, MO: Foundry, 2009.
Bruno-Jofré, Rosa, and Jon Igelmo Zaldívar. "Ivan Illich's Late Critique of Deschooling Society: 'I Was Largely Barking Up the Wrong Tree.'" *Educational Theory* 62 (2012) 573–92.
Budziszewski, J. *On the Meaning of Sex*. Wilmington, DE: ISI, 2014.
Bultmann, Rudolf. "Demythologizing: Controversial Slogan and Theological Focus." In *Rudolf Bultmann: Interpreting Faith for the Modern Era*, edited by Roger A. Johnson, 288–326. Minneapolis: Fortress, 1991.
Butler, Judith. *Gender Trouble: Feminism and the Subversion of Identity*. Routledge Classics. New York: Routledge, 1990.
Byrd, Aimee. *Recovering from Biblical Manhood and Womanhood: How the Church Needs to Rediscover Her Purpose*. Grand Rapids: Zondervan, 2020.
Calvin, Jean. *Institutes of the Christian Religion*. Edited by John T. McNeill. Translated by Ford Lewis Battles. 2 vols. Philadelphia: Westminster, 1960.
Cantarella, Eva. "Greek Law and the Family." In *A Companion to Families in the Greek and Roman Worlds*, edited by Beryl Rawson, 331–45. Blackwell Companions to the Ancient World. Oxford: Wiley-Blackwell, 2010.
Catalyst. "Women in the Workforce—Canada: Quick Take." Catalyst, n.d. https://www.catalyst.org/research/women-in-the-workforce-canada/. Accessed Jan. 2020; link discontinued.

———. "Women in the Workforce—United States: Quick Take." Catalyst, n.d. https://www.catalyst.org/research/women-in-theworkforce-united-states/. Accessed Jan. 2020; link discontinued.

Cere, Daniel Mark. "Marriage, Subordination, and the Development of Christian Doctrine." In *Does Christianity Teach Male Headship? The Equal-Regard Marriage and Its Critics*, edited by David Blankenhorn et al., 92–110. Grand Rapids: Eerdmans, 2004.

Cervin, R. S. "Does *Kephale* Mean Source or Authority over in Greek Literature? A Rebuttal." *TJ* 10 (1989) 85–112.

Chrysostom, John. *The Homilies of S. John Chrysostom, Archbishop of Constantinople, on the Epistle of S. Paul the Apostle to the Romans*. Edited by Philip Schaff. Vol. 7 of *A Library of Fathers of the Holy Catholic Church*. Oxford: Parker, 1848.

———. *The Homilies of S. John Chrysostom, Archbishop of Constantinople, on the Epistle of S. Paul to Timothy, Titus, and Philemon*. Edited by Philip Schaff. Vol. 12 of *A Library of Fathers of the Holy Catholic Church*. Oxford: Parker, 1848.

———. "Homilies on 2 Thessalonians." Translated by John A. Broadus. In *NPNF*[1], edited by Philip Schaff, 13:377–98. Buffalo, NY: Christian Literature Co., 1889.

———. *Homilies on Genesis, 1–17*. Translated by Robert C. Hill. Washington, DC: Catholic University of America Press, 1986.

———. *Homilies on the Epistle to the Ephesians*. Translated by Philip S. Schaff. Oxford: Frowde, 1898.

———. *Homilies on the Epistles of Paul to the Corinthians*. New York: Christian Literature Co., 1889.

———. *On Marriage and Family Life*. Translated by Catharine P. Roth and David Anderson. Crestwood, NY: St. Vladimir's Seminary Press, 1986.

Ciampa, Roy E., and Brian S. Rosner. "1 Corinthians." In *Commentary on the New Testament Use of the Old Testament*, edited by G. K. Beale and D. A. Carson, 695–752. Grand Rapids: Baker Academic, 2007.

Clowney, Edmund P. *The Unfolding Mystery: Discovering Christ in the Old Testament*. Phillipsburg, NJ: P&R, 2013.

Cohen, J. M. "'Hatan damim'—the Bridegroom of Blood." *JBQ* 33 (2005) 120–26.

Cohen, Ronald. "The Political System." In *Handbook of Method in Cultural Anthropology*, edited by Raoul Narroll and Ronald Cohen, 484–99. Garden City, NY: Natural History, 1970.

Connor, Rachel A., et al. "Ambivalent Sexism in the Twenty-First Century." In *The Cambridge Handbook of the Psychology of Prejudice*, edited by Chris G. Sibley and Fiona Kate Barlow, 295–320. Cambridge Handbooks in Psychology. Cambridge: Cambridge University Press, 2016.

Cooper, Derek, and Martin J. Lohrmann, eds. *1–2 Samuel, 1–2 Kings, 1–2 Chronicles*. Reformation Commentary on Scripture OT 5. Downers Grove, IL: IVP Academic, 2016.

Cortez, Marc. *ReSourcing Theological Anthropology: A Constructive Account of Humanity in the Light of Christ*. Grand Rapids: Zondervan Academic, 2017.

———. *Theological Anthropology: A Guide for the Perplexed*. Guides for the Perplexed. London: T&T Clark, 2010.

Crivellato, Enrico, and Domenico Ribatti. "Soul, Mind, Brain: Greek Philosophy and the Birth of Neuroscience." *Brain Research Bulletin* 71 (2007) 327–36.

Crook, John A. "Patria Potestas." *Classical Quarterly* 17 (1967) 113–22.

Cyprian. *Epistulae*. Edited by G. F. Diercks. 2 vols. CCSL 3B, 3C. Turnhout, Belg.: Brepols, 1994–96.
Cyril. *The Catechetical Lectures of S. Cyril, Archbishop of Jerusalem*. Translated by John Henry Newman. Oxford: Parker, 1838.
Daly, Mary. *Beyond God the Father*. Boston: Beacon, 1973.
———. *The Church and the Second Sex*. London: Chapman, 1968.
Daniélou, Jean. *From Shadows to Reality: Studies in the Biblical Typology of the Fathers*. Translated by Wulstan Hibberd. London: Burns & Oates, 1960.
Davidoff, Leonore, and Catherine Hall. *Family Fortunes: Men and Women of the English Middle Class, 1780–1850*. Chicago: University of Chicago Press, 1987.
Davidson, James. "Bodymaps: Sexing Space and Zoning Gender in Ancient Athens." *Gender & History* 23 (2011) 597–614.
Dawson, John David. *Christian Figural Reading and the Fashioning of Identity*. Berkeley: University of California Press, 2001.
Desray, Fabienne. "A Holistic Society Examined by Gender-Based Analysis, Focusing on a Wodaabe Family in East-Central Niger." *Nomadic Peoples* 19 (2015) 53–72.
Dialeti, Androniki. "Patriarchy as a Category of Historical Analysis and the Dynamics of Power: The Example of Early Modern Italy." *Gender & History* 30 (2018) 331–42.
Dickens, Bernard M. "Transsexuality: Legal and Ethical Challenges." *International Journal of Gynecology and Obstetrics* 151 (2020) 163–67.
Dihle, A. "ψυχή." *TDNT* 9:626–44.
Dixon, Suzanne. *The Roman Family*. Baltimore: John Hopkins University Press, 1992.
Doak, Bob. "Hollywood, Popular Culture, and the Follow-Your-Heart Theme." *Studies in Popular Culture* 26 (2003) 65–75.
Douglass, Jane Dempsey. *Women, Freedom, and Calvin*. Philadelphia: Westminster, 1985.
Du Mez, Kristin Kobes. *Jesus and John Wayne: How White Evangelicals Corrupted a Faith and Fractured a Nation*. New York: Liveright, 2020.
Dunn, James D. G. *The Theology of Paul the Apostle*. Grand Rapids: Eerdmans, 1998.
Edwards, Cyril. *The Beginnings of German Literature: Comparative and Interdisciplinary Approaches to Old High German*. Rochester, NY: Camden, 2002.
Edwards, Jonathan. *Images or Shadows of Divine Things*. Edited by Perry Miller. New Haven, CT: Yale University Press, 1948.
———. *The "Miscellanies," a–500*. Edited by Thomas A. Schafer. Works of Jonathan Edwards 13. New Haven, CT: Yale University Press, 1994.
———. *Types of the Messiah*. Vol. 9 of *The Works of President Edwards: With a Memoir of His Life* [by Sereno Edwards Dwight]. New York: Converse, 1830.
———. *The Typological Writings*. Edited by Wallace E. Anderson et al. Works of Jonathan Edwards 11. New Haven, CT: Yale University Press, 1993.
Eggebroten, Anne. "The Persistence of Patriarchy: Hard to Believe, but Some Churches Are Still Talking About Male Headship." *Sojourners Magazine* 39 (2010) 22–24.
Elliot, Elisabeth. *Let Me Be a Woman: Notes to My Daughter on the Meaning of Womanhood*. Carol Stream, IL: Tyndale, 1977.
Engeroff, Karl Wilhelm. *An English-German Dictionary of Idioms*. Munich: Hueber, 1960.
Engh, Line Cecilie. *Gendered Identities in Bernard of Clairvaux's Sermons on the Song of Songs: Performing the Bride*. Turnhout, Belg.: Brepols, 2014.

Epstein, Cynthia Fuchs. "Reflections on Women and the Law in the USA." *International Social Science Journal* 59 (2009) 17–26.
Ertman, Martha M. "Exchange as a Cornerstone of Families." *Western New England Law Review* 34 (2012) 405–44.
Ferguson, Everett. *The Rule of Faith: A Guide*. Cascade Companions. Eugene, OR: Cascade, 2015.
Feuerbach, Ludwig. *The Essence of Christianity*. Translated by Marian Evans. 2nd ed. London: Trübner & Co., 1881.
Fitzmyer, Joseph A. "Another Look at *Kephalē* in 1 Corinthians 11:3." *NTS* 35 (1989) 503–11.
Flax, Jane. "Postmodernism and Gender Relations in Feminist Theory." *Signs: Journal of Women and Culture in Society* 12 (1987) 621–43.
Fleming, Donald. "Charles Darwin, the Anaesthetic Man." *Victorian Studies* 4 (1961) 219–36.
Foucault, Michel. "Nietzsche, Genealogy, History." In *The Foucault Reader*, edited by Paul Rabinow, 76–100. New York: Pantheon, 1984.
———. "On the Genealogy of Ethics: An Overview of Work in Progress." In *The Foucault Reader*, edited by Paul Rabinow, 340–72. New York: Pantheon, 1984.
Foulks, Francis. *The Epistle of Paul to the Ephesians: An Introduction and Commentary*. TNTC. Grand Rapids: Eerdmans, 1989.
Fox-Genovese, Elizabeth. Review of *Women and History, Vol. 1: The Creation of Patriarchy*, by Gerda Lerner. *JAAR* 55 (1987) 608–13.
Foxe, John. *The Acts and Monuments of John Foxe* ["Foxe's Book of Martyrs"]. Edited by Stephen Reed Cattley and George Townsend. 8 vols. London: Seeley & Burnside, 1837–41.
Foxhall, Lin. "Household, Greek." In *The Oxford Classical Dictionary*, edited by Sander M. Goldberg and Tim Whitmarsh. 5th ed. Oxford: Oxford University Press, 2016. Ebook.
Franke, John R., ed. *Joshua, Judges, Ruth, 1–2 Samuel*. ACCS OT 4. Downers Grove, IL: IVP Academic, 2005.
Frei, Hans W. *The Eclipse of Biblical Narrative: A Study in Eighteenth and Nineteenth Century Hermeneutics*. New Haven, CT: Yale University Press, 1974.
Friedan, Betty. *The Feminine Mystique*. New York: Norton, 1963.
Friedl, Ernestine. "The Position of Women: Appearance and Reality." *Anthropological Quarterly* 40 (1967) 97–108.
Friel, David M. "Mutuality and Male Headship: Liturgical Evidence from Marriage Rituals Throughout History." *Antiphon: A Journal for Liturgical Renewal* 21 (2017) 252–89.
Frova, Giulia. "Five Decades of Development Debate on Sustainability." *Development* 54 (2011) 271–81.
Gallagher, Maggie. "Reflections on Headship." In *Does Christianity Teach Male Headship? The Equal-Regard Marriage and Its Critics*, edited by David Blankenhorn et al., 111–25. Grand Rapids: Eerdmans, 2004.
Garland, David A. *First Corinthians*. BECNT. Grand Rapids: Baker Academic, 2003.
Glick, Peter, and Susan T. Fiske. "The Ambivalent Sexism Inventory: Differentiating Hostile and Benevolent Sexism." *Journal of Personality and Social Psychology* 70 (1996) 491–512.

Goettner-Abendroth, Heide. "Re-Thinking 'Matriarchy' in Modern Matriarchal Studies Using Two Examples: The Khasi and the Mosuo." *Asian Journal of Women's Studies* 24 (2018) 3–27.

Goldberg, Steven. *Why Men Rule: A Theory of Male Dominance*. Chicago: Open Court, 1999.

Goodman, Robin. *Gender Work: Feminism After Neoliberalism*. New York: Palgrave Macmillan, 2013.

Gordon, M. R. "Glory." In *Zondervan Pictorial Encyclopedia of the Bible*, edited by Merrill C. Tenney, 2:730–35. Grand Rapids: Zondervan, 1982.

Grant, Jonathan. *Divine Sex: A Compelling Vision for Christian Relationships in a Hypersexualized Age*. Grand Rapids: Brazos, 2015.

Greene-McCreight, Kathryn. *Feminist Reconstructions of Christian Doctrine: Narrative Analysis and Appraisal*. Oxford: Oxford University Press, 2000.

Greenough, K. M. "Women, Men, Children and Livestock: Partnerships and Gendered Negotiations in the Ful'be Household Livestock Enterprise." Center for Gender in Global Context, Dec. 2012. WP301. https://gencen.isp.msu.edu/files/1615/6294/0235/WP301.pdf.

Gregory, Charles David. "Theodore of Mopsuestia's Commentary on Romans: An Annotated Translation." PhD diss., Southern Baptist Theological Seminary, 1992.

Grubbs, Judith Evans. "Promoting *Pietas* Through Roman Law." In *A Companion to Families in the Greek and Roman Worlds*, edited by Beryl Rawson, 377–92. Blackwell Companions to the Ancient World. Malden, MA: Wiley-Blackwell, 2011.

Grudem, Wayne A. "Does κεφαλή ('Head') Mean 'Source' or 'Authority over' in Greek Literature? A Survey of 2,336 Examples." *TJ* 6 (1985) 38–59.

———. *The Gender-Neutral Bible Controversy: Muting the Masculinity of God's Words*. Nashville: Broadman and Holman, 2000.

———. "The Meaning of κεφαλή ("Head") An Evaluation of New Evidence, Real and Alleged." *JETS* 44 (2001) 25–65.

———. "The Meaning of *Kephale* ('Head'): A Response to Recent Studies." *TJ* 11 (1990) 3–72.

Haak, Robert D. *Habakkuk*. VTSup 44. Leiden: Brill, 1992.

Hahn, Scott W. *Kinship by Covenant: A Canonical Approach to the Fulfillment of God's Saving Promises*. New Haven, CT: Yale University Press, 2009.

Hamilton, James. "The Skull Crushing Seed of the Woman: Inner-Biblical Interpretation of Genesis 3:15." *Southern Baptist Journal of Theology* 10 (2006) 30–54.

Hanawalt, Barbara A. *"Of Good and Ill Repute": Gender and Social Control in Medieval England*. New York: Oxford University Press, 1998.

Harding, James E., and Gregory W. Dawes. "Body." Oxford Reference, 2015. From *The Oxford Encyclopedia of the Bible and Theology*, edited by Samuel E. Ballentine. https://10.1093/acref:obso/9780199858699.001.0001.

Harding, Thomas. *A Confutation of a Booke Intituled "An Apologie of the Church of England."* Antwerp: Hans de Laet, 1565.

Harris, Katie, et al. "Socio-Economic Disparities in Access to Assisted Reproductive Technologies in Australia." *Reproductive Biomedicine Online* 33 (2016) 575–84.

Hartley, L. P. *The Go-Between*. New York: Penguin, 1953.

Harvey, A. D. *Body Politic: Political Metaphor and Political Violence*. Newcastle, UK: Cambridge Scholars, 2007.

Hays, Richard B. *The Moral Vision of the New Testament.* San Francisco: HarperSanFrancisco, 1996.

———. *Reading Backwards: Figural Christology and the Fourfold Gospel Witness.* Waco: Baylor University Press, 2014.

Healey, Antonette diPaolo. "The Importance of Old English Head." In *Mapping English Metaphor Through Time*, edited by Wendy Anderson et al., 165–84. Oxford Linguistics. Oxford: Oxford University Press, 2016.

Heger, Paul. "Patrilineal or Matrilineal Genealogy in Israel After Ezra." *JSJ* 43 (2012) 215–48.

———. *Women in the Bible, Qumran and Early Rabbinic Literature: Their Status and Roles.* STSJ 110. Leiden: Brill, 2014.

Hegewisch, Ariane. "The Gender Wage Gap: 2017." Institute for Women's Policy Research, Sept. 2018. IWPR #C473. https://www.jstor.org/stable/resrep27246.

Held, Virginia. "Gender Identity and the Ethics of Care in Globalized Society." In *Global Feminist Ethics and Social Theory*, edited by Rebecca Whisnant and Peggy DesAutels, 43–58. Feminist Constructions. Lanham, MD: Rowman & Littlefield, 2008.

Hendrix, Lewellyn. "What Is Sexual Inequality? On the Definition and Range of Variation." *Cross-Cultural Research* 28 (1994) 287–307.

Herophilus. *The Art of Medicine in Early Alexandria.* Edited and translated by Heinrich von Staden. Cambridge: Cambridge University Press, 1989.

Hilary of Poitiers. "On the Councils." Translated by E. W. Watson. In *NPNF*[1], edited by Philip Schaff, 9:140–85. Buffalo, NY: Christian Literature Co., 1889.

Hocking, C. "The Way We Were: Thinking Rationally." *British Journal of Occupational Therapy* 71 (2008) 185–95.

Hoehner, Harold W. *Ephesians: An Exegetical Commentary.* Grand Rapids: Baker Academic, 2002.

Hoffman, Lawrence A. "The Jewish Wedding Ceremony." In *Life Cycles in Jewish and Christian Worship*, edited by Paul F. Bradshaw and Lawrence A. Hoffman, 129–53. Two Liturgical Traditions. Notre Dame, IN: Notre Dame University Press, 1996.

Hoinacki, Lee. "The Trajectory of Ivan Illich." *Bulletin of Science, Technology & Society* 23 (2003) 382–89.

Hoinacki, Lee, and Carl Mitcham, eds. *The Challenges of Ivan Illich: A Collective Reflection.* Albany: State University of New York Press, 2002.

Hugh of Saint-Victor. "De Arca Noe Morali." In *Selected Spiritual Writings*, translated by a Religious of CSMV, 45–156. London: Faber, 1962.

Huws, Ursula. "The Hassle of Housework: Digitalisation and the Commodification of Domestic Labour." *Feminist Review* 123 (2019) 8–23.

Illich, Ivan. *Gender.* New York: Pantheon, 1982.

———. "The Sad Loss of Gender." *New Perspectives Quarterly* 15 (1998) 4–8.

———. "Shadow Work." *Social Alternatives* 2 (1981) 37–47.

Irenaeus. *Against Heresies: Book III.* Translated by Henry Deane. Oxford: Clarendon, 1880.

Irigaray, Luce. *An Ethics of Sexual Difference.* Translated by Carolyn Burke and Gillian C. Gill. London: Athlone, 1993.

Ishay, Micheline. *The History of Human Rights: From Ancient Times to the Globalization Era.* Berkeley: University of California Press, 2008.

Jansen, Sharon L. *The Monstrous Regiment of Women: Female Rulers in Early Modern Europe*. New York: Palgrave Macmillan, 2002.

Jewel, John. *The Apology of the Church of England (1562)*. Edited by Henry Morley. London: Cassell, 1888.

———. *A defence of the Apologie of the Churche of Englande conteininge an answeare to a certaine booke lately set foorthe by M. Hardinge*. London: Wykes, 1567.

John Paul II. *Man and Woman He Created Them: A Theology of the Body*. Translated by Michael Waldstein. Boston: Pauline, 2006.

———. "*Ordinatio Sacerdotalis*: On Reserving Priestly Ordination to Men Alone." Vatican, May 22, 1994. https://www.vatican.va/content/john-paul-ii/en/apost_letters/1994/documents/hf_jp-ii_apl_19940522_ordinatio-sacerdotalis.html.

Jones, Beth Felker. *Marks of His Wounds: Gender Politics and Bodily Resurrection*. Oxford: Oxford University Press, 2007.

Jones, Ian, et al. *Women and Ordination in the Christian Churches: International Perspectives*. T&T Clark Theology. London: T&T Clark, 2008.

Jordan, James B. *Judges: A Practical and Theological Commentary*. Eugene, OR: Wipf & Stock, 1985.

Josberger, Rebekah L. "Between Rule and Responsibility: The Role of the 'AB as Agent of Righteousness in Deuteronomy's Domestic Ideology." PhD diss., Southern Baptist Theological Seminary, 2007.

———. "For Your Good Always: Restraining the Rights of the Victor for the Well-Being of the Vulnerable (Deut 21:10–14)." In *For Our Good Always: Studies on the Message and Influence of Deuteronomy in Honor of Daniel I. Block*, edited by Jason S. DeRouchie et al., 165–87. University Park: Pennsylvania State University Press, 2013.

Kantorowicz, Ernst. *The King's Two Bodies: A Study in Medieval Political Theology*. Princeton Classics. Princeton, NJ: Princeton University Press, 2016.

Karlberg, Mark W. *Federalism and the Westminster Tradition*. Eugene, OR: Wipf & Stock, 2006.

Kassian, Mary. *The Feminist Mistake: The Radical Impact of Feminism on Church and Culture*. Wheaton, IL: Crossway, 2005.

Katz, Jack. "The Social Psychology of Adam and Eve." *Theory and Society* 25 (1996) 545–82.

Kelley, H. "The Myth of Matriarchy: Symbols of Womanhood in Galician Regional Identity." *Anthropological Quarterly* 67 (1994) 71–80.

Kerber, Linda. "The Republican Mother: Women and the Enlightenment—an American Perspective." In *Toward an Intellectual History of Women: Essays by Linda K. Kerber*, 41–62. Chapel Hill: University of North Carolina Press, 1997.

King, J. Christopher. *Origen on the Song of Songs as the Spirit of Scripture: The Bridegroom's Perfect Marriage-Song*. Oxford Theology and Religion Monographs. Oxford: Oxford University Press, 2006.

Kirk, Geoffrey. *Without Precedent: Scripture, Tradition, and the Ordination of Women*. Eugene, OR: Wipf & Stock, 2016.

Kirschbaum, Charlotte von. *The Question of Woman: The Collected Writings of Charlotte von Kirschbaum*. Edited by Eleanor Jackson. Translated by John Shepherd. Grand Rapids: Eerdmans, 1996.

Kissil, Karni, and Maureen Davey. "Health Disparities in Procreation: Unequal Access to Assisted Reproductive Technologies." *Journal of Feminist Family Therapy* 24 (2012) 197–212.

Kluge, Friedrich. *An Etymological Dictionary of the German Language*. London: Bell, 1891.

Kraemer, Sebastian. "The Origins of Fatherhood: An Ancient Family Process." *Family Process* 30 (1991) 377–92.

Kraus, Cynthia. "Classifying Intersex in DSM-5: Critical Reflections on Gender Dysphoria." *Archives of Sexual Behavior* 44 (2015) 1147–63.

Kroonen, Guus. *Etymological Dictionary of Proto-Germanic*. Leiden Indo-European Etymological Dictionary Series 11. Leiden: Brill, 2013.

Kunze, Astrid. "The Gender Wage Gap in Developed Countries." In *The Oxford Handbook of Women and the Economy*, edited by Susan L. Averett et al., 369–94. Oxford University Press, 2018.

Lakey, Michael. *Image and Glory of God: 1 Corinthians 11:2–16 as a Case Study in Bible, Gender and Hermeneutics*. LNTS. New York: T&T Clark, 2010.

Ledgerwood, J. L. "Khmer Kinship: The Matriliny/Matriarchy Myth." *Journal of Anthropological Research* 51 (1995) 247–61.

Leithart, Peter. *Baptism: A Guide to Life from Death*. Bellingham, WA: Lexham, 2021.

———. *Deep Exegesis: The Mystery of Reading Scripture*. Waco: Baylor University Press, 2009.

Lerner, Gerda. *The Creation of Feminist Consciousness: From the Middle Ages to Eighteen-Seventy*. Women and History 2. New York: Oxford University Press, 1993.

———. *The Creation of Patriarchy*. New York: Oxford University Press, 1986.

Letham, Robert. "The Hermeneutics of Feminism." *Them* 17 (1992) 4–7.

Levi, Jennifer L. "Symposium: Radical Nemesis: Re-Envisioning Ivan Illich's Theories on Social Institutions Foreword." *Western New England Law Review* 34 (2012) 341–50.

Levitt, Heidi M., and Kimberly Ware. "Anything with Two Heads Is a Monster: Religious Leaders' Perspectives on Marital Equality and Domestic Violence." *Violence Against Women* 12 (2006) 1169–90.

Lewis, C. S. *The Four Loves*. London: Bles, 1960.

Lewis, Charlton T., and Charles Short. *A New Latin Dictionary: Founded on the Translation of Freund's Latin-German Lexicon*. Edited by E. A. Andrews. New York: American, 1907.

Lewis, Simon L., and Mark A. Maslin. "Defining the Anthropocene." *Nature* 519 (2015) 171–80.

Lillback, Peter A. *The Binding of God: Calvin's Role in the Development of Covenant Theology*. Texts and Studies in Reformation and Post-Reformation Thought. Grand Rapids: Baker Academic, 2001.

Liu, Tessie P. "*Le patrimoine magique*: Reassessing the Power of Women in Peasant Households in Nineteenth-Century France." *Gender & History* 6 (1994) 13–36.

Livingstone, David N. "Preadamites: The History of an Idea from Heresy to Orthodoxy." *SJT* 40 (1987) 41–66.

Lottin, Alain. "Vie et mort du couple: Difficultés conjugales et divorces dans le nord de la France aux 17e et 18e siècles." *Le XVIIe siècle* 102–3 (1974) 59–78.

Lubac, Henri de. *Corpus Mysticum: The Eucharist and the Church in the Middle Ages*. Edited by Susan Parsons and Laurence Paul Hemming. Translated by Gemma Simmonds. Notre Dame, IN: University of Notre Dame Press, 2006.

———. *Medieval Exegesis*. Translated by Mark Sebanc and E. M. Macierowski. Grand Rapids: Eerdmans, 1998.

———. *Scripture in the Tradition*. Translated by Peter Casarella. New York: Crossroad, 2000.

Luther, Martin. *Lectures on Galatians, 1535, Chapters 5–6; Lectures on Galatians, 1519, Chapters 1–6*. Edited by Jaroslav Pelikan and Walter A. Hansen. Vol. 27 of *Luther's Works*. Saint Louis: Concordia, 1964.

MacDowell, Douglas Maurice, et al. "Marriage Law: Greek." In *The Oxford Companion to Classical Civilization*, edited by Simon Hornblower et al. Oxford: Oxford University Press, 2014. Ebook.

MacIntyre, Alasdair. *Whose Justice? Which Rationality?* Notre Dame, IN: University of Notre Dame Press, 1988.

Marshall, Peter. *Heretics and Believers: A History of the English Reformation*. New Haven, CT: Yale University Press, 2017.

Martin, Douglas. "Phyllis Schlafly, 'First Lady' of a Political March to the Right, Dies at 92." *New York Times*, Sept. 5, 2016. https://www.nytimes.com/2016/09/06/obituaries/phyllis-schlafly-conservative-leader-and-foe-of-era-dies-at-92.html.

Matthews, Glenna. *"Just a Housewife": The Rise and Fall of Domesticity in America*. Oxford: Oxford University Press, 1989.

Maynard, Mary. "Beyond the 'Big Three': The Development of Feminist Theory into the 1990s." *Women's History Review* 4 (1995) 259–81.

McFarland, Ian A. *In Adam's Fall: A Meditation on the Christian Doctrine of Original Sin*. Challenges in Contemporary Theology. Malden, MA: Wiley-Blackwell, 2010.

McLanahan, Sarah, et al. "The Causal Effects of Father Absence." *Annual Review of Sociology* 39 (2013) 399–427.

McLeod, Frederick G. *Theodore of Mopsuestia*. The Early Church Fathers. London: Routledge, 2008.

Meconi, David Vincent. *The One Christ: St. Augustine's Theology of Deification*. Washington, DC: Catholic University of America Press, 2013.

Medick, Hans. "The Proto-Industrial Family Economy: The Structural Function of Household and Family During the Transition from Peasant Society to Industrial Capitalism." *Social History* 1 (1976) 291–315.

Melton, Gordon J., and Gary L. Ward. "A Survey of the Women's Ordination Issue." In *Women's Ordination: Official Statements from Religious Bodies and Ecumenical Organizations*, edited by Gordon J. Melton and Gary L. Ward, xiii–xxxv. Churches Speak on 6. Detroit: Gale Research, 1991.

Meslin, Michel. "Head: Symbolism and Ritual Use." Encyclopedia, Oct. 25, 2025. From *Encyclopedia of Religion*, translated by Kristine Anderson, 1987. https://www.encyclopedia.com/environment/encyclopedias-almanacs-transcripts-and-maps/head-symbolism-and-ritual-use.

Meyers, Carol L. "Was Ancient Israel a Patriarchal Society?" *JBL* 133 (2014) 8–27.

Milbank, John. *Theology and Social Theory: Beyond Secular Reason*. 2nd ed. Political Profiles. Malden, MA: Blackwell, 2006.

Mill, John Stuart. *The Subjection of Women*. New York: Appleton & Co., 1869.

Miller, Colin. "Ivan Illich, Catholic Theologian (Part I)." *ProEccl* 26 (2017) 81–110.

Miller, Eric C. "Phyllis Schlafly's 'Positive' Freedom: Liberty, Liberation, and the Equal Rights Amendment." *Rhetoric and Public Affairs* 18 (2015) 277–300.

Moberly, R. W. L. *The Bible, Theology, and Faith: A Study of Abraham and Jesus.* Cambridge Studies in Christian Doctrine 5. Cambridge: Cambridge University Press, 2000.

Mol, Jurrien. *Collective and Individual Responsibility: A Description of Corporate Personality in Ezekiel 18 and 20.* SSN 53. Leiden: Brill, 2009.

Monter, E. William. *The Rise of Female Kings in Europe, 1300–1800.* New Haven, CT: Yale University Press, 2012.

Mueller-Vollmer, Kurt, ed. *The Hermeneutics Reader: Texts of the German Tradition from the Enlightenment to the Present.* New York: Continuum, 1985.

Muller, Richard A. *After Calvin: Studies in the Development of a Theological Tradition.* Oxford Studies in Historical Theology. Oxford: Oxford University Press, 2003.

Murata, Sachiko. "Feminine Spirituality: The Lost Dimension in the Western Perception of Islam." *Forum Bosnae* 39 (2007) 218–31.

Murphy, Gannon. "Reformed *Theosis*?" *ThTo* 65 (2008) 191–212.

Murphy-O'Connor, Jerome. *Keys to First Corinthians: Revisiting the Major Issues.* New York: Oxford University Press, 2009.

Neale, J. E. "The Elizabethan Acts of Supremacy and Uniformity." *English Historical Review* 65 (1950) 304–22.

Neusner, Jacob, trans. *Genesis Rabbah: The Judaic Commentary to the Book of Genesis; A New American Translation.* 3 vols. BJS 104–6. Atlanta: Scholars, 1985.

Nienhuis, Nancy E., and Beverly Mayne Kienzle. *Saintly Women: Medieval Saints, Modern Women, and Intimate Partner Violence.* Routledge Studies in Medieval Religion and Culture. New York: Routledge, 2018.

Nietzsche, Friedrich W. *On the Genealogy of Morals.* Translated by Walter Arnold Kaufmann. New York: Modern Library, 1968.

Nussbaum, Martha C. *Frontiers of Justice: Disability, Nationality, Species Membership.* Tanner Lectures on Human Values. Cambridge, MA: Harvard University Press, 2006.

O'Brien, Conor. "Bede's Theology of Circumcision, Its Sources and Significance." *JTS* 67 (2016) 594–613.

O'Brien, Peter T. *The Letter to the Ephesians.* Pillar New Testament Commentary. Grand Rapids: Eerdmans, 1999.

O'Donovan, Oliver. "Transsexualism and Christian Marriage." *JRE* 11 (1983) 135–62.

O'Keefe, John J., and R. R. Reno. *Sanctified Vision: An Introduction to Early Christian Interpretation of the Bible.* Baltimore: Johns Hopkins University Press, 2005.

Olsen, V. Norskov. *The New Relatedness for Man and Woman in Christ: A Mirror of the Divine.* Loma Linda, CA: Loma Linda University Center for Christian Bioethics, 1993.

Oman, John. Introduction to *On Religion: Speeches to Its Cultured Despisers*, by Friedrich Schleiermacher, translated by John Oman, ix–lviii. London: Paternoster, 1893.

Onians, R. B. *The Origins of European Thought About the Body, the Mind, the Soul, the World, Time, and Fate.* Cambridge: Cambridge University Press, 1954.

Origen. *Homilies on Genesis.* Edited by Philip Schaff. Vol. 3 of *A Library of Fathers of the Holy Catholic Church.* Oxford: Parker, 1842.

———. *Homilies on Joshua.* Edited by Cynthia White. Translated by Barbara J. Bruce. FC 105. Washington, DC: Catholic University of America Press, 2002.

———. *Homilies on Judges*. Translated by Elizabeth Ann Dively Lauro. Washington, DC: Catholic University of America Press, 2010.

Osiek, Carolyn. "The Feminist and the Bible: Hermeneutical Alternatives." In *Feminist Perspectives on Biblical Scholarship*, edited by Adela Yarbro Collins, 93–105. Chico, CA: Scholars, 1985.

Palmquist, Stephen. "Immanuel Kant: A Christian Philosopher?" *Faith and Philosophy* 6 (1989) 65–75.

Parmentier, Martien. "Greek Patristic Foundations for a Theological Anthropology of Women in Their Distinctiveness as Human Beings." *ATR* 84 (2002) 561–65.

Pascal, Blaise. *"Pensées" and Other Writings*. Edited by Anthony Levi. Translated by Honor Levi. Oxford World's Classics. Oxford: Oxford University Press, 2008.

Peters, John Durham. "Bowels of Mercy." *Brigham Young University Studies* 38 (1999) 27–41.

Phillips, Paul, and Jessica Poulin. "Labour Force in Canada." *Canadian Encyclopedia*, Feb. 7, 2006; last edited Nov. 21, 2023. https://thecanadianencyclopedia.ca/en/article/labour-force.

Pius X. "Pastor Aeternus." Vatican, July 18, 1870. From *Acta Sanctae Sedis*, 6:40–47. https://www.vatican.va/content/pius-ix/en/documents/constitutio-dogmatica-pastor-aeternus-18-iulii-1870.html.

Plato. *Meno*. Translated by Benjamin Jowett. In *The Collected Dialogues of Plato*, edited by Edith Hamilton and Huntington Cairns, 353–84. Bollingen 71. Princeton: Princeton University Press, 1961.

Pokrifka, Junia. "Redeeming Women in the Grand Narrative of Scripture." In *Women in the Bible*, edited by Robert B. Kruschwitz, 11–22. Christian Reflection. Waco: Center for Christian Ethics at Baylor University, 2013.

Porter, Stanley, and Jason Robinson. *Hermeneutics: An Introduction to Interpretive Theory*. Grand Rapids: Eerdmans, 2011.

Poska, Allyson. "The Case for Agentic Gender Norms for Women in Early Modern Europe." *Gender & History* 30 (2018) 354–65.

Poythress, Vern S., and Wayne A. Grudem. *The Gender-Neutral Bible Controversy: Muting the Masculinity of God's Words*. Nashville: Broadman & Holman, 2000.

Raab, Kelly A. *When Women Become Priests: The Catholic Women's Ordination Debate*. New York: Columbia University Press, 2000.

Rad, Gerhard von. *Genesis: A Commentary*. Translated by John H. Marks. OTL. Louisville: Presbyterian, 1966.

Radner, Ephraim. "The Nuptial Figure." In *Hope Among the Fragments: The Broken Church and Its Engagement of Scripture*, 121–38. Grand Rapids: Brazos, 2004.

———. *Time and the Word: Figural Reading of the Christian Scriptures*. Grand Rapids: Eerdmans, 2016.

Radner, Ephraim, and George Sumner. *The Rule of Faith: Scripture, Canon, and Creed in a Critical Age*. Harrisburg, PA: Morehouse, 1998.

Ribar, David C. "Why Marriage Matters for Child Wellbeing." *Future of Children* 25 (2015) 11–27.

Ridderbos, Herman N. *Paul: An Outline of His Theology*. Grand Rapids: Eerdmans, 1975.

Rieff, Philip. *The Triumph of the Therapeutic: Uses of Faith After Freud*. New York: Harper & Row, 1966.

Roberts, Michelle Voss. *Body Parts: A Theological Anthropology*. Minneapolis: Fortress, 2017.

Robinson, H. Wheeler. *Corporate Personality in Ancient Israel*. Philadelphia: Fortress, 1964.

Rogers, Susan Carol. "Female Forms of Power and the Myth of Male Dominance: A Model of Female/Male Interaction in Peasant Society." *American Ethnologist* 2 (1975) 727–56.

———. "Once upon a Time . . . : Comments on the Myth of Female Dominance." *Anthropologica* 41 (1999) 155–60.

Rubin, Gayle. "The Traffic in Women: Notes on the 'Political Economy' of Sex." In *Toward an Anthropology of Women*, edited by Rayna R. Reiter, 157–210. New York: Monthly Review, 1975.

Ruddiman, William F. "The Anthropocene." *Annual Review of Earth and Planetary Sciences* 41 (2013) 45–68.

Ruether, Rosemary Radford. *Religion and Sexism: Images of Woman in the Jewish and Christian Traditions*. New York: Simon & Schuster, 1974.

———. *Sexism and God-Talk: Toward a Feminist Theology*. Boston: Beacon, 1983.

———. "Sexism and Misogyny in the Christian Tradition: Liberating Alternatives." *Buddhist-Christian Studies* 34 (2014) 83–94.

Russell, Letty M. *The Liberating Word: A Guide to Nonsexist Interpretation of the Bible*. Philadelphia: Westminster, 1976.

Sabean, David Warren. "Intensivierung der Arbeit und Alltagserfahrung auf dem Lande—ein Beispiel aus Württemberg." *Sozial-wissenschaftliche Informationen für Unterricht und Studium* 6 (1977) 148–52.

———. *Kinship in Neckarhausen: 1700–1870*. Cambridge Studies in Social and Cultural Anthropology. Cambridge: Cambridge University Press, 1997.

Saiving Goldstein, Valerie. "The Human Situation: A Feminine View." *Journal of Religion* 40 (1960) 100–112.

Saller, Richard P. *Patriarchy, Property, and Death in the Roman Family*. Cambridge Studies in Population, Economy, and Society in Past Time 25. New York: Cambridge University Press, 1994.

Sanday, Peggy Reeves. *Female Power and Male Dominance: On the Origins of Sexual Inequality*. Cambridge: Cambridge University Press, 1981.

Santoro, Giuseppe, et al. "The Anatomic Location of the Soul from the Heart, Through the Brain, to the Whole Body, and Beyond: A Journey Through Western History, Science, and Philosophy." *Neurosurgery* 65 (2009) 633–43.

Schaff, Philip. *The Creeds of Christendom: With a History and Critical Notes*. Grand Rapids: Baker, 1966.

———. *Mediaeval Christianity, A.D. 590–1073*. Vol. 4 of *History of the Christian Church*. New York: Scribner's Sons, 1886.

———, ed. *The Seven Ecumenical Councils*. Vol. 10 of *NPNF*[1]. Buffalo, NY: Christian Literature Co., 1889.

Schlafly, Phyllis. *The Power of the Positive Woman*. New York: Jove, 1977.

Schlegel, Alice. "Toward a Theory of Sexual Stratification." In *Sexual Stratification: A Cross-Cultural View*, edited by Alice Schlegel, 1–40. Columbia University Press, 1977.

Schleiermacher, Friedrich. *On Religion: Speeches to Its Cultured Despisers*. Translated by John Oman. London: Paternoster, 1893.

Schlier, Heinrich. "κεφαλή." *TDNT* 3:673–81.
Schoeps, Hans Joachim. "The Sacrifice of Isaac in Paul's Theology." *JBL* 65 (1946) 385–92.
Schottroff, Luise, et al. *Feminist Interpretation: The Bible in Women's Perspective*. Minneapolis: Fortress, 1995.
Schreiner, Thomas. *Covenant and God's Purpose for the World*. Wheaton, IL: Crossway, 2017.
———. "The Valuable Ministries of Women in the Context of Male Leadership: A Survey of Old and New Testament Examples and Teaching." In *Recovering Biblical Manhood and Womanhood: A Response to Evangelical Feminism*, edited by John Piper and Wayne Grudem, 273–93. Wheaton, IL: Crossway, 2021.
Schroer, Silvia, and Thomas Staubli. *Body Symbolism in the Bible*. Translated by Linda M. Maloney. Scripture. Collegeville, MN: Liturgical, 2001.
Schüssler Fiorenza, Elisabeth. *In Memory of Her: A Feminist Theological Reconstruction of Christian Origins*. New York: Crossroad, 1984.
Schweizer, Eduard. "σάρξ." *TDNT* 7:105–23.
Scott, Joan. "Gender: A Useful Category." *American Historical Review* 91 (1986) 1053–75.
Scruton, Roger. *Sexual Desire: A Philosophical Investigation*. New York: Continuum, 2006.
Segalen, Martine. *Historical Anthropology of the Family*. Translated by J. C. Whitehouse and Sarah Matthews. Themes in the Social Sciences. New York: Cambridge University Press, 1986.
———. *Love and Power in the Peasant Family*. Chicago: University of Chicago Press, 1983.
Shafi, Monika. "Caregiving, Work, and the Debate on 'Why Women Still Can't Have It All.'" *Women in German Yearbook* 30 (2014) 149–63.
———. "Discourses of Work: Uwe Timm's *Kopfjäger: Bericht aus dem Inneren des Landes*." In *Gegenwartsliteratur: Ein germanistisches Jahrbuch*, edited by Paul Michael Lützeler et al., 11:149–69. Tübingen: Stauffenberg, 2012.
Sklba, Richard. *The Teaching Function of the Pre-Exilic Israelite Priesthood*. Rome: Pontificium Universitatem S. Thomae de Urbe, 1965.
Slaughter, Anne-Marie. "Why Women Still Can't Have It All." *Atlantic*, July/Aug. 2012. https://www.theatlantic.com/magazine/archive/2012/07/why-women-still-cant-have-it-all/309020/.
Smith, C. U. M. "Cardiocentric Neurophysiology: The Persistence of a Delusion." *Journal of the History of the Neurosciences* 22 (2013) 6–13.
Smith, James K. A. *How (Not) to Be Secular: Reading Charles Taylor*. Grand Rapids: Eerdmans, 2014.
Smith, Mark S. "The Heart and Innards in Israelite Emotional Expressions: Notes from Anthropology and Psychobiology." *JBL* 117 (1998) 427–36.
Stasson, Anneke. "The Politicization of Family Life: How Headship Became Essential to Evangelical Identity in the Late Twentieth Century." *Religion and American Culture: A Journal of Interpretation* 24 (2014) 100–138. https://doi.org/10.1525/rac.2014.24.1.100.
Stephens, William. *The Family in Cross-Cultural Perspective*. New York: Holt, Rinehart and Winston, 1963.

Stockett, Miranda K. "On the Importance of Difference: Re-Envisioning Sex and Gender in Ancient Mesoamerica." *World Archaeology* 37 (2005) 566–78.

Strong, James, et al. *The Strongest Strong's Exhaustive Concordance of the Bible.* 21st Century ed. Grand Rapids: Zondervan, 2001.

Study Committee on Domestic Abuse and Sexual Assault. *Report of the Ad Interim Committee on Domestic Abuse and Sexual Assault to the Forty-Ninth General Assembly of the Presbyterian Church in America (2019–2022).* Presbyterian Church in America General Assembly, June 2022. https://pcaga.org/wp-content/uploads/2022/06/2301-AIC-on-Domestic-Abuse-Updated.pdf.

Sweeney, Conor, and Brian T. Trainor. *Politics of Conjugal Love: A Baptismal and Trinitarian Approach to Headship and Submission.* Eugene, OR, Pickwick: 2019.

Tannahil, Reay. *Sex in History.* New York: Stein & Day, 1980.

Taylor, Charles. Foreword in *The Rivers North of the Future: The Testament of Ivan Illich as Told to David Cayley,* by Ivan Illich and David Cayley, ix–xiv. Toronto: House of Anansi, 2005.

———. "The Politics of Recognition." In *Multiculturalism: Examining the Politics of Recognition,* edited by Amy Gutmann, 25–73. Princeton, NJ: Princeton University Press, 1994.

———. *A Secular Age.* Cambridge, MA: Belknap, 2007.

Theodore of Mopsuestia. *Commentary on the Gospel of John.* Edited by Joel C. Elowsky. Translated by Marco Conti. Ancient Christian Texts. Downers Grove, IL: IVP Academic, 2010.

———. *Pauluskommentare aus der griechischen Kirche.* Edited by Karl Staab. Münster: Aschendorff, 1984.

Thiselton, Anthony C. *Hermeneutics: An Introduction.* Grand Rapids: Eerdmans, 2009.

Thomas, Robert L., ed. *New American Standard Exhaustive Concordance of the Bible.* Nashville: Holman, 1981.

Thomas, Yan. "Vitae necisque potestas: Le père, la cité, la mort." In *Du châtiment dans la cité: Supplices corporels et peine de mort dans le monde antique,* 499–548. Rome: École française de Rome, 1984.

Tolbert, Mary Ann. "Defining the Problem: The Bible and Feminist Hermeneutics." *Semeia* 28 (1983) 113–26.

Torrance, James B. "Introductory Essay." In *The New Relatedness for Man and Woman in Christ: A Mirror of the Divine,* by V. Norskov Olsen, 13–23. Loma Linda, CA: Loma Linda University Center for Christian Bioethics, 1993.

Trible, Phyllis. *God and the Rhetoric of Sexuality.* OBT. Philadelphia: Fortress, 1978.

———. *Texts of Terror: Literary-Feminist Readings of Biblical Narratives.* OBT. Philadelphia: Fortress, 1984.

Trueman, Carl. *The Rise and Triumph of the Modern Self: Cultural Amnesia, Expressive Individualism, and the Road to Sexual Revolution.* Wheaton, IL: Crossway, 2020.

United Nations. *The Beijing Declaration and the Platform for Action: Fourth World Conference on Women, Beijing, China, 4–15 September 1995.* New York: Dept. of Public Information, United Nations, 1996.

———. "Gender Equality." United Nations, n.d. https://www.un.org/en/global-issues/gender-equality.

Utne Reader [Eric Utne]. "100 Visionaries Who Could Change Your Life." *Utne Reader* 67 (1995) 1.

Vadianus, Joachim. *A worke entytled of ye olde god [and] the newe: Of the olde faythe and the newe, of the olde doctryne and the newe, or orygynall begynnynge of idolatrye.* London: Byddell, 1534.
Van Asselt, Willem J. *The Federal Theology of Johannes Cocceius (1603–1669).* Translated by Raymond A. Blacketer. Studies in the History of Christian Thought 100. Leiden: Brill, 2001.
Van den Heuvel, Danielle. "Gender in the Streets of the Premodern City." *Journal of Urban History* 45 (2019) 693–710.
Vanhoozer, Kevin J. "Ascending the Mountain, Singing the Rock: Biblical Interpretation Earthed, Typed, and Transfigured." *Modern Theology* 28 (2012) 781–803.
Verrett, Brian A. *The Serpent in Samuel: A Messianic Motif.* Eugene, OR: Resource, 2020.
Wagner, Wolfgang, et al. "Male Dominance, Role Segregation, and Spouses' Interdependence in Conflict: A Cross-Cultural Study." *Journal of Cross-Cultural Psychology* 21 (1990) 48–70.
Walsh, Julie. "Jael's Story as Initial Fulfillment of Genesis 3:15." *Priscilla Papers* 33 (2019) 22–37.
Waltke, Bruce. "1 Corinthians 11:2–16: An Interpretation." *BSac* 135 (1978) 46–57.
Washburne, Marion F. "Masculine and Feminine Occupations." *North American Review* 179 (1904) 555–68.
Watson, Francis. "The Authority of the Voice: A Theological Reading of 1 Cor 11.2–16." *NTS* 46 (2000) 520–36.
Watts, Isaac. *Hymns and Spiritual Songs.* Sutton, MA: Goodridge, 1808.
Wenham, Gordon J. *Genesis 1–15.* WBC 1. Dallas: Word, 1987.
Wenkel, David H. "Noah as a New Adam in the Narrative Substructure of Romans 5:12–21." *Journal of Theological Interpretation* 14 (2020) 74–86.
Westerkamp, Marilyn J. *Women and Religion in Early America, 1600–1850: The Puritan and Evangelical Traditions.* Christianity and Society in the Modern World. New York: Routledge, 1999.
Westminster Assembly. *The Westminster Shorter Catechism: With Scripture Proofs.* Edited by G. I. Williamson. Edinburgh: Banner of Truth, 1994.
Wiesner-Hanks, Merry. "Forum Introduction: Reconsidering Patriarchy in Early Modern Europe and the Middle East." *Gender & History* 30 (2018) 320–30.
Wilcox, William Bradford. *Why Marriage Matters: Thirty Conclusions from the Social Sciences: A Report from Family Scholars.* New York: Institute for American Values, 2011.
Wilken, Robert L. "Exegesis and the History of Theology: Reflections on the Adam-Christ Typology in Cyril of Alexandria." *CH* 35 (1966) 139–56.
Williams, Rowland. "Bunsen's Biblical Researches." In *Essays and Reviews,* by Frederick Temple et al., 50–93. Cambridge Library Collection—Religion. Cambridge: Cambridge University Press, 2013.
Williams, Terry A. "Demystifying Male Dominance in STEM Subjects." *Women in Higher Education* 23 (2014) 9–19.
Wilson, Brittany E. "Pugnacious Precursors and the Bearer of Peace: Jael, Judith, and Mary in Luke 1:42." *CBQ* 68 (2006) 436–56.
Witherington, Ben, III. *Torah Old and New: Exegesis, Intertextuality, and Hermeneutics.* Minneapolis: Fortress, 2018.
Witt, William G. *Icons of Christ: A Biblical and Systematic Theology for Women's Ordination.* Waco: Baylor University Press, 2020.

Wolters, Al. "Head as Metaphor in Paul." *Koers* 76 (2011) 137–53.
Wright, Christopher J. H. *Deuteronomy*. NIBCOT. Peabody, MA: Hendrickson, 1996.
Wyclif, John. *Select English Works of John Wyclif*. Edited by Thomas Arnold. 3 vols. Oxford: Clarendon, 1869.
Young, Frances M. *Biblical Exegesis and the Formation of Christian Culture*. Cambridge: Cambridge University Press, 1997.
Zinn, Grover. "Hugh of St. Victor and the Ark of Noah: A New Look." *CH* 40 (1971) 261–72.
Zucker, Kenneth J. "Epidemiology of Gender Dysphoria and Transgender Identity." *Sexual Health* 14 (2017) 404–11.
———. "Sex/Gender Research and Meta-Analysis." *Archives of Sexual Behavior* 49 (2020) 365–66.

www.ingramcontent.com/pod-product-compliance
Lightning Source LLC
Chambersburg PA
CBHW070327230426
43663CB00011B/2243